'79

THE MOD REVIVAL
TIME FOR ACTION
ESSAYS FROM THE FRONTLINE
BY GARRY BUSHELL

First published in 2012 by Countdown Books Ltd
This edition © Red Planet Books Ltd 2019
Text © Garry Bushell 2012-19

This edition published November 2019

Email: info@redplanetzone.com

Printed in the UK. by DG3

A catalogue record for this book is available from the British Library

ISBN: 978 1 9127 3337 8

REDPLANETMUSICBOOKS.COM

TIME FOR ACTION

CONTENTS

MOD: THE PROLOGUE

FORTY years! When the Mod Revival broke cover in 1979, most of the British music press wrote it off as a forgettable fad destined to wither on the vine. Forty years on, Mods May Day 2019 sold out the Islington Assembly Hall. Secret Affair's Glory Boys 40th Anniversary Tour is playing to packed houses all over the UK and Budstock 60, celebrating Buddy Ascott's 60th birthday, lured 350 veteran Mods to London's 100 Club.

These venues might not be the Hollywood Bowl, or even Hammersmith Odeon, but it shows that New Mod meant much more than the cynical music press ever knew. Forty years on, the bands of '79 such as Secret Affair have played to Mod audiences as far away as Japan, Australia, Russia and California. Forty years on, Chris Pope is still churning out great new songs for Pope and for the Chords UK. Forty years on, I've just been contacted by George, a 15 year-old Mod, who is not only writing a school essay on the subject, but has also formed his own three-piece band and is writing original material. So much for that 'forgettable fad' tag.

Back in the heady summer of 1979, most rock writers wrote off the Mod Revival as a hype manufactured by the British film industry. They saw it as a bid to ensure that the movie of *Quadrophenia* movie did at least as well as the previous Who-inspired film *Tommy* four years before.

In fact, those with our ears closer to the ground had been aware of the burgeoning revival – I called it a renewal – for more than a year.

It was an organic development, a reaction against the curdling of the first wave of punk. Its actual roots could be traced to The Jam, and more specifically their *All Mod Cons* album, released in November 1978, but there were other parallel developments too.

Most of the Mod Revival bands and the teenagers that followed them, saw the film as marking the beginning of the end of their scene. It was the moment when the mass media would trample all over the fragile purity of it all and stomp on it as mercilessly as a rocker's daisy roots.

I started working for *Sounds* in the summer of 1978, hired alongside Dave McCullough as a punk sharpshooter to counter the cynicism of the more jaded staff writers in the office. I'd seen the Jam first, a couple of times as a fan in 1977; I'd seen the band who became the Purple Hearts that year too – supporting Generation X in Barking under the name (which they later denied) of Jack Plug & The Sockets, and I'd written about both in my fanzine. At *Sounds*, I interviewed Glasgow's The Jolt as early as August 1978; I knew the kids who became the Glory Boys when they were punks and skinheads. I wrote the first rock press reviews and features on the Chords, the Purple Hearts, Secret Affair, Long Tall Shorty and more besides. So I knew the Revival was always much more than a dull fad to hype a movie. The fact that we're still talking about it 40 years on confirms it.

I never classed myself as a Mod, although I did have a thing for Ben Sherman shirts and Harrington jackets; I was a disaffected punk who kept his eyes open. And there were clear echoes of original Mod in first wave art school punk. Even Generation X had taken their name from a cult classic book by Charles Hamblett and Jane Deverson published in 1964.

The articles in this book are a living history, written as the Mod Revival took shape. I haven't changed the opinions I expressed at the time, but I have expanded the pieces based on my contemporary notebooks and diaries.

WE HAD BETTER start at the beginning. Most people's view of original Mod was shaped by the tabloid press coverage of the time, all those banner headlines about 'Wild Ones' invading the nation's beaches. Inevitably, there's much more to the real story than teenage anarchy and Carnaby Street.

Original Mod was about aspiration, improving your life, not settling for the job your dad did. It started with a small group of North London teenagers, many Jewish, who created their own unique and exclusive style. Most of them were from humble, lower middle class origins and all of them were exhibitionists. These pioneers, kids like Wayne Kirven, Steve Sparks and John Simon, combined influences – principally American jazz, French new wave cinema and Italian cool – to cook up something we now see as quintessentially English.

In his 1959 novel *Absolute Beginners*, Colin MacInnes calls a young Jazz fan who dresses in sharp Italian clothes a 'Modernist' – probably the first time the name was used in print. The term derived from Modern Jazz, as played by Miles Davis and Charlie Mingus. French films, like Jean-Luc Godard's 1960 movie *A Bout De Souffle* starring Jean-Paul Belmondo and Jean Seberg, were also much admired.

Above all, there were the clothes; the schmutta. Stylish Italian waiters riding around Soho on scooters in their bum-freezer jackets were their inspiration; sparking off what John Simon calls "the cult of the male peacock." The Mod pioneers weren't as yet a group, but rather a sprinkling of highly individual stylists with a huge attention to detail. They wanted to stand out, so they sought out unusual clothes, such as the green buttoned down shirt that Miles Davies wore on the *Milestone* album. And they had suits made; smart, round-shouldered single-breasted whistles with two and a quarter inch lapels and slanted two inch flap pockets. The trousers were low-fitting with slanted frog-mouth pockets. They had to 'schlep' all over town to get the clothes right but the finished look was as eye-catching as it was unique.

In 1962, *Town* magazine ran an article about these style-crazy teenage trend-setters, with the sub-head: 'Young men who live for clothes and pleasure.' Among them was Wayne Kirven, then 17, and a 15-year-old Marc Feld who regarded himself as a young Beau Brummel and became better known by the stage name he adopted later: Marc Bolan (who was also claimed as an inspiration by the punk pioneers.)

So, naturally and organically the Mod style developed. Suits were constantly amended. Bell bottoms came in briefly. Fred Perry style sportswear was adopted – it was ideal for dancing in sweaty clubs – and soon after Levi Jeans which were pricey by the standards of the day. Italian haircuts became fashionable at the start of the Sixties, followed by the Perry Como cut, the college boy and then the French crew cut. Scooters began to be identified with the look around 1959; gangs of scooter-boys could be seen by 1960, and with them the first Parka coats. Hush Puppies and ski pants were a popular look for girls around this time.

These new Mods rebelled against the old grey world of poverty, austerity, rationing, and the class system designed to keep the young in their place. It was drab, man, it was a drag, and it was yesterday. With the right look and the right attitude, you could rise above it. In their book *On Fashion*, Shari Benstock and Suzanne Ferriss argue that Mod "mocked the class system that had gotten their fathers nowhere". The young Mods worshipped leisure and consumerism. Work was just something you had to do to pay for your clothes and the all-night clubs. Hundreds of chemist shops would be broken into for the uppers to keep them going.

IN HIS SUPERB and impeccably researched book, *Mods*, Richard Barnes pinpoints 1962 as the year Mod changed from being a scattering of individuals into a youth cult as such. After that, the look developed at an even faster pace. City gent suits complete with brollies caught on briefly, followed by the 'waisted' English suit, and, as the cult became increasingly street-level, so casual clothes like cycle shirts and cycle shoes came in. The Lonsdale sports shop in Beak Street became popular, as did back-combing the hair. This time also saw the emergence of the Ace Face Mod, the elite stylist who was a fashion leader, as opposed to the ticket, the younger mod who followed the trends. Mod was all about obsession. It was intense. You had to look dead right. You had to be neat and you had to be clean.

The Mod shirt of choice had a button-down collar. Initially they were American, but then Ben Sherman successfully marketed a cheaper home-grown version using tartans and candy stripes.

The music changed too. American Forces Radio introduced the first Mods to the underground sounds of black American music, the blues and then rhythm and blues, out of which grew the true Mod music, Sixties soul as pioneered by assembly-line car worker turned music magnate Berry Gordy and his glorious Tamla Motown label (not to mention Stax, Volt, and the other Atlantic labels Dial, Fame, and Music Enterprises.)

Gordy was an amazing character. In 1959, he only had a few hundred dollars to his name but he was a hustler and he employed a network of enthusiasts: Tamla's receptionist Janie Bradford doubled as a talent scout, singer Mable John drove Gordy around before he could afford a car, and the incredible William 'Smokey' Robinson knocked up 'answer' songs aping recent hits. The Miracles 'Shop Around' was their first million-seller in 1961, and the Marvelettes had their first Number One with 'Please Mr Postman' that same year. After that the success never stopped, with smash singles from the Supremes, the Temptations, Stevie Wonder and more. Motown was the Hit Factory, out-selling even The Beatles. It gave R&B a stylish pop sheen, making it easily accessible to a young British audience – unlike the harder, rawer and more raucous sounds of James Brown, whose funk was undiluted and uncompromising. (If Elvis made love to the microphone, James Brown fucked it to death – and back to life again. Brown's 1962 *Live At The Apollo* was the first million-selling R&B album and he inspired everything from disco to hip hop).

In England, a derivative R&B scene developed, spawning The Rolling Stones and The Pretty Things, but their scruffiness and lack of authenticity meant hardcore Mods scorned them.

The first band to score real credibility was The Who (formerly the High Numbers) from West London. They had their image contrived for them by leading ace face Pete Meaden (the man who defined Mod succinctly as "clean living under difficult circumstances" and who had managed them at the start).

But of course The Who were more than just a look; what made them special was their guitarist Pete Townshend whose lyrics combined Mod angst and the sense of the young as a class apart from straight society.

One-time Marxist Townshend had a knack of writing songs that mirrored the thinking of a typical Shepherd's Bush Mod. Dressed in Union Jack suits, Townshend smashed his guitar on stage and wrote anthems that perfectly captured teenage frustration, songs like 'I Can't Explain', 'Anyway Anyhow Anywhere' and best of all 1965s stuttering scorcher 'My Generation' with its barely concealed taboo-busting innuendo: "Why don't you all f-fade away?"

When pin-up Who singer Roger Daltrey raged: "I hope I die before I get old" a million teenagers appreciated the sentiment.

Other rock bands were formed by Mods or were associated with the mod look, principally The Kinks, The Yardbirds and The Small Faces, who were East End Mods, small and neat with a tendency to jump on any passing arty fad. But, even they weren't really accepted by the Mod purists. To the hardcore, there were only ever two components to genuine Mod music: American Soul, the blacker the better, and Jamaican Ska which was also to become the defining music of the skinheads.

The golden years of Mod were 1963-1965 with the scene developing at a frightening pace. This was the time of Carnaby Street, before commercialisation killed it, coffee bars, dances, amphetamines to keep you moving for whole weekends without sleep. London's Soho was Mecca for the Mods. The scene was thriving, with clubs like The Allnighter (at The Flamingo in Wardour Street) and La Discotheque. The Marquee, also then in Wardour Street, was a major venue for live R&B.

As well as revolutions in music and fashion, Mod sparked an explosion of creativity and social-climbing. Ronan O'Rahilly opened his Radio Caroline pirate station on Easter Sunday 1964, in memory of his granddad who had died during the IRA's Easter rising of 1916. Cathy McGowan made TV history presenting *Ready Steady Go!* – the first (maybe the only) pop TV show to move at teen pace and avoid being patronising.

Tom Wolfe spelt out the ethics of Mod best in his essay, *The Noonday Underground*: 'What is it with this kid? Here he is, 15 years old and he is better dressed than any man in the office. He has on a checked suit with a double-breasted waistcoat and a step-collar on it and the jacket coming in at the waist about like so, and then trousers that come down close here then flare out here, and a custom-made shirt that comes up like… SO at the neckband, little things very few people would even know about, least of all those poor straight noses in the office who never had a suit in their lives that wasn't off the peg. They have better accents, but he has…THE LIFE…and a secret place he goes at lunch time – a noonday underground. And nobody is even lapsing into the old pub system either, that business where you work your gourds off all day and then sink into the foaming ooze of it all. You can buy enough pills and other lovelies of the pharmacological arts to stay high for hours. In THE LIFE even the highs are different. The hell with bitter, watercress and old Lard-belly telling you it's TIME...'

As science teaches us, for every action there is an equal and opposite reaction. Mod didn't happen in a vacuum. The antithesis to this smart urban self-made elite were the Rockers, the tribe of leather-wearing "grease-balls" who hung on to leather and the Fifties, and thought the Mod look was for wimps. Girly boys. Mods thought the Rockers were coarse and out-of-date; thick yobs with no class. With more than a little help from the media, battle lines were drawn up, and after Fleet Street exaggerated a Clacton Easter Bank Holiday run-in out of all proportion ('Chaos In Clacton'), the genteel Southern seaside resorts of Margate, Southend, Hastings, Brighton and Bournemouth all saw genuine clashes between the two cults. On March 30, 1964, the *Daily Mirror* splashed with 'Wild Ones Invade Seaside – 90 Arrests', with the sub-heading: 'Police Chief sends SOS for reinforcements'. Disgusted of Royal Tunbridge Wells had a seizure.

In May that year, the Battle of Brighton Beach was illustrated with dramatic pictures of Rockers jumping off a seaside sun terrace to escape the Mod hoards. Nik Cohn wrote of 'ecstatic weekends – 72 hours without sleep and all you did was run around, catcall, swallow pills and put the boot in. For the first time in your life, the only time, you were under no limitations and nobody controlled you and you caught sight of Nirvana'.

Mostly the action was saved for ritualised Bank Holiday battling because the two groups tended to hail from different areas. Mods dominated the cities, especially London, the London suburbs, and the Home Counties. Rockers held the countryside and the Northern towns. Where the two groups crossed over aggro abounded. In the East End, Hackney's Victoria Park and Leyton Baths were notorious for Mods and Rockers' 'offs'.

LEYTON BATHS WERE regularly used as a music venue in the early Sixties. The centre's swimming pool would be covered by boards, creating an artificial dance floor. Acts including The Beatles, Rolling Stones, Small Faces and Marianne Faithful all played the venue. When the Stones played there in 1963, 3,000 fans packed in – with as many outside. But tensions developed between Mods and Rockers at the venue exploding in regular bloody battles. In the biography of Buttons, a notorious British Hells Angel leader (*Buttons, The Making of A President*), he recalls: "A system of segregation developed at the Leyton Baths between our rockers and the mods. We covered the front near the stage and the mods hung in the dark of the rear of the hall. There used to be a lot of close fighting, sometimes with knives and people would stumble out of the baths, cut and bleeding. I think this was possibly the main reason why the baths were eventually closed for gigs."

Buttons, who later became President of the Hells Angels' first London Chapter, also describes a fight between a fellow Rocker, named Ritchie, and a mod, saying: "He attacked Ritchie, who waited for the guy to lunge, let the knife slip by him and hammered the mod on the neck with a pick-axe handle. The squishing sound coupled with the skin splitting was a nice effect."

Trying to winkle out the reasons for the wildness, Agony Auntie Marje Proops interviewed a young mod girl Teresa (Terry) Gordon in the *Daily Mirror* of May 23, 1964. Patiently Terry explained: "We've got a different attitude to life. Mods enjoy life, they like to dance. Rockers don't dance. Mods like blues and blue beat rhythm music, and they go to clubs and dances. Rockers just listen to pop music. Rockers carry knives, Mods don't have weapons. You've got to be a Mod or a Rocker to mean anything."

But in between the two extremes there were several groups of unfortunates who just couldn't get it right. Terry talked about 'states' in the *Mirror* – the contemptuous Mod handle for kids who thought they were mods but were hopelessly out of touch with the real look and feel of modernism. Mockers were neither one thing nor the other. For example, they might wear a nylon version of a rocker's leather and top it off with a mod haircut. But at least the Mockers were consciously mixing up the two fashions. Another sub-group, the Mids, combined elements of the two opposing styles without sussing on that they looked about as cool as *The Towering Inferno*. Partly because of the violence, partly because the very essence of Mod was change – that constant search for the new, the ultimate look – Mod began to decline after '64, and by 1966 the movement was on the skids with increasing numbers of modernist youths becoming attracted into other areas, Pop Art, flares, Psychedelia and hallucinogenic drugs. They cross-fertilised with students, and the Hippy Underground with all its attendant follies blossomed. Tune in, turn on, cop out... what a con that turned out to be.

David Lazar, the mod-turned-avenging-columnist hero of Tony Parson's seminal novel *Limelight Blues*, twigs that the life-style is dying when his mates mock his immaculate mohair whistle as 'passé', start ear-wigging Dylan instead of Motown and dump their pills to puff on joints.

In real life, Ronnie Lane's realisation came when he chanced upon Rod 'The Mod' Stewart out on the West Coast of America – Rod started slating his perfectly pressed "gangster suit" while flamboyantly modelling a floral blouse from Miss Selfridges's.

There were two major reactions against this development – one in the North, the other in the South. By their own admission the Northern mods caught on to the cult later, but held on to it longer. In the North change was slower and different and the Northern scene was still flourishing long after trend-setting London townies were into acid or aggro. Mod DJs everywhere had always prided themselves in their ability to search out new artists and new labels, developing beyond the more mainstream strains of Stax and Tamla. Naturally, Northern DJs continued this trend, and their searching eventually evolved into the distinctive sound of Northern soul – fast, brassy, and often bootlegged. Based around speed-fuelled all-nighters in Wigan and surrounding areas like Cleethorpes and Manchester, Northern Soul developed in the early Seventies as a Mod off-spring with marked differences. The cult made such a fetish of obscurity that musical values arguably went by the board while for practical purposes suits, collars and ties were replaced by vests and baggy trousers – aesthetically unappealing, but all the better to dance in.

Aside from soul music, the other constant in the North's evolution were the staple diet of cross-country scooter runs. These clubs spanned the years from the Sixties to the late Seventies Renewal, and even though at times the clubs' memberships might have been down to five or six enthusiasts, the tradition wasn't allowed to die.

In the South, the Suits evolved; the hard Mods who grew into skinheads; and as we shall see revivalist late Seventies skins like Tom McCourt were among those who rallied to the Mod flag when their own cult became over-run with boneheads.

Of course, youth cults are at their healthiest when they are developing naturally. When the practitioners are looking back and trying to recapture a lost moment then they are inevitably more constrained and less creative. Yet I would argue that those artists with a true Mod soul, like Paul Weller, Mick Talbot, Billy Hassett and Dave Cairns have been able to use their influences to develop music that was original and inspiring; music that stands the test of time and that proves the Mod Revival was the Renewal I always said it was.

FRIARS AYLESBURY

AT THE MAXWELL HALL

SATURDAY JUNE 17th at 7.30 p.m.

Here comes the weekend

THE

JAM

+ THE JOLT

AC Sound & Vision

Tickets: 199p from Earth Records Aylesbury, Sun Music High Wycombe, Hairport Amersham, Free 'n' Easy Hemel Hempstead, F L Moore Bletchley Dunstable and Luton, Hi Vu Buckingham, or 199p at door on night if available (Enq. 84568/88948). Life membership 25p

BUT WE'RE ALRIGHT, WE'RE NICE AND WARM HERE, NO ONE TO HURT US EXCEPT OURSELVES

FRIARS AYLESBURY

AT THE MAXWELL HALL

SATURDAY JUNE 17th at 7.30 p.m.

Here comes the weekend

THE

JAM

+ THE JOLT

AC Sound & Vision

Tickets: 199p from Earth Records Aylesbury, Sun Music High Wycombe, Hairport Amersham, Free 'n' Easy Hemel Hempstead, F L Moore Bletchley Dunstable and Luton, Hi Vu Buckingham, or 199p at door on night if available (Enq. 84568/88948). Life membership 25p

BUT WE'RE ALRIGHT, WE'RE NICE AND WARM HERE, NO ONE TO HURT US EXCEPT OURSELVES

FRIARS AYLESBURY

AT THE MAXWELL HALL

SATURDAY JUNE 17th at 7.30 p.m.

Here comes the weekend

THE

JAM

+ THE JOLT

AC Sound & Vision

Tickets: 199p from Earth Records Aylesbury, Sun Music High Wycombe, Hairport Amersham, Free 'n' Easy Hemel Hempstead, F L Moore Bletchley Dunstable and Luton, Hi Vu Buckingham, or 199p at door on night if available (Enq. 84568/88948). Life membership 25p

BUT WE'RE ALRIGHT, WE'RE NICE AND WARM HERE, NO ONE TO HURT US EXCEPT OURSELVES

MAYBE TOMORROW

AUGUST - SEPTEMBER 1978

1978-1981: A GREAT TIME FOR GREAT BANDS, GREAT MUSIC AND EVEN GREATER MEMORIES

Lee Huggie Norbal – 78 Dalston mod

THE JOLT:
THE BIGGEST THING SINCE BERT WEEDON AND THE DROGGS

North Yorkshire. August 5, 1978

THE MOD REVIVAL

SO there I was, all innocent, standing peaceably by an idyllic boating pool in Saltburn-by-the-Sea, emptying a can of diesel oil over the ducks and helping myself to a baby's ice cream when...

Three hobbit-sized tartan lunatics run up, sweep me off me plates and start to swing me low, like a sweet chariot, over the cool clear water while mouthing threats in broad Glaswegian gobbledegook.

Naturally I couldn't tell you exactly what they said, without the aid of Bletchley Park decoders what Londoner could? But it was something along the lines of either I agreed to "gi'us a good wreett-up, Jimmy" or they'd dump me in the lake.

Naturally I capitulated quicker than Badoglio in '43.

Laugh? I almost bought meself a drink. The poor fools believed me. They didn't realise that when I got back to civilisation I'd reveal the full shocking truth about them.

Truth like: the brains behind The Jolt is manager Dougie Lockhart's three-year-old daughter Melanie, an avid Lurkers fan! (Gasp! - Ed)

Drummer Iain Shedden is heavily into birching and sleeps strapped to a giant pink teddy bear called Clarence! (Double gasp! - Ed)

Robbie Collins writes his songs by taking the chords to Small Faces numbers and playing them backwards! (What else is new? - Ed).

Only kidding, kiddoes (except for the bit about Iain); in reality The Jolt are a group that it's easier for the average Sassenach to admire than understand. They have tenacity, spirit, and above all the nifty knack of knocking out energetic, modern Rhythm & Blues with choons. They are undoubtedly the best thing to come out of Scotland since the road to Newcastle.

THE JOLT formed in September 76 while guitarist/songwriter Robbie and bassist Jim Doak were working as lowly clerks in the Civil Service and Iain was a journalist writing the pop page for his local rag. As the first Scottish punk band they attracted a lot of attention and built up powerful local support. But (always the 'but') their impetus was bollocksed up by a disillusioning encounter with "the London scene", accusations of betrayal and a duff first single.

Robbie who is short, stocky, surprisingly shy and soft-spoken, spells out the grim details.

"We only worked for about three months," he recalls. "We were getting quite a lot of gigs and a bit of interest so we just decided to chuck our jobs and go pro.

"The second real gig we played as the Jolt was the Crown Hotel in Wishaw - that's an industrial town about fifteen miles east of Glasgow, where me and Iain come from – Jim is from Shotts. There were only half a dozen people in the place and basically they were just slagging us off, saying 'We don't want this kind of thing in Scotland'. It was negative but they kept talking about us all week.

"The hotel manager could see we were causing a lot of interest so he brought us back. We had 20 consecutive gigs there, one every Saturday, and by the end we had won people over, we finished up with a great crowd."

It was a gradual thing. "When we'd first get there, there'd be half a dozen guys playing pool," says Iain. "We'd go on in the main hall, which was empty, and start playing and then you'd see these heads peeping round the door while we were on, and people saying, 'Have you seen this?'. The following week there'd be a few more..."

Jim: "Part of the whole thing was that it was different, it was getting in the papers. People thought, 'Ah an actual punk rock group, here, in this hotel, let's check it out, see what all the fuss is about...' Me and Iain learnt to play our instruments virtually from scratch, it was like a baptism of fire."

"There was a great sense of something happening in Scotland," says Rob. "We felt that anyway, and the gigs used to be really great. There was a spirit of being part of some sort of revolution and when we got to London (last September) it just didn't seem to be true anymore. That's when I wrote 'Everybody's The Same'..."

'Everybody's the same / nothing's changed / It's all the same / It's just been rearranged / Everybody's so cool / Scared of looking a fool / Don't make a stand / So faceless and bland / Your revolution was just an illusion / You've just become another institution.' ('Everybody's The Same')

"It applies to everybody," he says. "Even the audiences we got in London too, especially at the Marquee..."

Jim: "The people at the Marquee were supposed to be anti-establishment and against the rules. They've got a little scene of their own and they're very upset if someone tries to change it. They've just got a new set of rules. At the time we were really pissed off. The time we'd started playing was the time it was really getting off the ground in London. We arrived a year later and everything had changed."

Rob: "We used to be disillusioned about it, but I don't know, there were so many bands I suppose it just had to get diluted. Everybody started worrying about what was hip and what wasn't. Only a few groups seem to be sticking to their guns - like the Clash. Everything they say in sincere. Good for them. But I don't think there's a new wave scene anymore."

IT WAS A gamble for the Jolt to leave Scotland and all they achieved at the time was a cold shoulder from the press and ‹the scene›. They lost their Scottish following and found fellow Sweaty Socks almost inevitably accusing them of 'selling ooot...' sorry, out.

"People think you're trying to be a star automatically if you go to London," says Rob. "You used to get bands up there saying 'We'll never leave Glasgow, we've got guts; we don't need to go to London'."

Iain: "Really it's the other way about. It takes guts to go out on a limb, but some people turned their backs on us because we went."

Rob: "They thought we'd betrayed whatever it was they saw as happening up there, but they've now just drifted away anyway. What have they done? And we were expected to explain everything we did and do whereas at the start we were just getting up and playing out music..."

'I just want to have some fun/I don't want to hurt no one/but I can see that you think that›s a drag/ You won't ever let it be/You keep on and on at me/You think I should have some master-plan/I don/t want to sound callous/But maybe you're just feeling jealous/Or are you really such a fool as that?/I ain't gonna justify my actions by telling lies/You'll get no excuses from me.' ('No Excuses')

So why did you come down to the Big Smoke, folks?

"We came down to get work," answers Jim. "There's only a certain amount of gigs in Scotland and if you keep playing them you get stale."

Robbie: "We could have stayed in Scotland for an extra six months but it would have made no real difference. Plus we learned a bit living down in London..."

Like how insular the whole gigging/ligging rock press set-up can be.

Having a weak, under-produced first Polydor single 'You're Cold'/'All I Can Do' didn't help.

"The guy who produced it was under the delusion that it was still '76, and you could do things roughly and cheaply and it'd still work," explains Robbie, an edge of unmistakable frustration in his voice.

In reality it sounded little more than a demo tape. But now some ten months later and another failed single, a cover of the Small Faces classic 'Watcha Gonna Do About It' out of the way, the group have notched up an impressive eponymous debut album, The Jolt by The Jolt, and stand poised for a gruelling four months on the road. A tour which as the old cliché goes could possibly make or break them...

Their material is certainly in their favour. Robbie has a knack for writing powerful r&b songs which reveal his Sixties obsessions, but pack the punk punch too. Okay, some of the chord progressions and riffs sound a tad too familiar, but in the main songs like 'Radio Man' and 'Can't You Tell It's Over' are proper nuggets of catchiness (a technical term) made all the more poppy by Robbie's singing.

Yeah, this guy sings rather than merely emulates the gruff primal growls of artists like Jagger, England's very own white-washed James Brown, who the whole band admires.

Talking about their influences Robbie waxes lyrical about early English rhythm and blues – the great rock explosion before punk, where the awesome raw pain-wracked blues of urban black America – Bo Diddley, Ray Charles, Chuck Berry, Muddy Waters, Fats Domino – became transmuted into teen arrogance of the Stones, The Who, The Yardbirds, The Kinks, The Animals, The Pretty Things etc etc.

1962-64 spelt MOD, Radio Caroline, Cathy McGowan, Carnaby Street, and smart, spotty kids, in bum freezer jackets and chisel-toed red suede shoes perched on scooters easy riding out of Shepherds Bush, popping pills, chewing gum and speeding down to Margate for three day running battles without sleep on the sea-front.

It also spelt the most exciting burst of musical energy since rock 'n' roll – and until today's generation staged our own musical white riot.

Robbie takes his influences and moulds them into modern anthems, but like I said in my album review a fortnight ago, their real impact comes over live...

We were all pretty worried about the gig last Thursday, supporting the Motors at Saltburn (estimated population 21). The venue, the Philamore, is tucked away at the foot of a hill over-looking great strips of green fields and the North Sea. (Sea view, Jimmy...)

It was very scenic and all that, but cows and seagulls shit too much and rarely make paying customers.

We shouldn't have fretted. Out of cars and vans they came, from as far away as Middlesbrough and Redcar. A capacity crowd. A pretty straight-citizen looking capacity crowd, mind, the nearest thing to a punk was a guy in a Stranglers t-shirt, but an open-minded and receptive bunch.

The Jolt set starts with a daft snatch of Lord Rockingham XI's 'Hoots Mon (There's a Moose In The Hoose)' – och, aye - then the boys came on, Rob and Jim smartly be-suited with unblemished white plimsolls and finger-cutting trouser creases.

"We're the Jolt, this one's called 'Decoyed'," says Robbie. Wham bam, no niceties.

ON STAGE THE group are pure concentration. Jim and Robbie's mouths gape open as they devote all their attention to the business in hand. Jim looks and moves like The Clash's Mick Jones, loping back and forwards, hair sweated together. Rob doesn't move so much but he moves more than did in London last year – all the band were that over-awed by being under such critical gazes that they stayed rooted to the stage. Now they hang loose and have fun while staying as tourniquet tight. It makes a difference.

Tonight was good: twelve songs, and a well deserved encore. There's no mistaking the band's heartfelt aggression. When Robbie sings those DJ-baiting lines on 'Radio Man' he really means it: 'If London's burning Glasgow's razed / And guys like you stoke up the flames...'

That song was written when no punk group could even play in Glasgow. MOST of the Jolt songs have a temporal theme. The time Robbie and Jim wasted at Glasgow University before they dropped out, of an Arts and Science course respectively, that they'd started because they didn't know what else to do. The time that's been wasted through early Jolt experiences...

'Work hard if you want to get on / Don't look now five years have just gone / Work hard and you've got it made / You've got no choice you'll still be a slave / You'll get decoyed by the promises made' ('Decoyed').

'All the people that I once used to know / I feel the same but they just seem to get old / Just never had anything better to do / They drift along waiting for some dream to come true / Somebody's stolen my life away / Ain't gonna worry about a rainly day' ('I Can't Wait')

That's the new single, coupled with a live version of Bobby Troup's '(Get Your Kicks On) Route 66', featuring Jim on vocals; an unadulterated, unashamed r&b standard that immediately wins over the Saltburn crowd.

THERE ARE MESSAGES in many of the Jolt's songs but they don't see themselves primarily as a preachy band.

"We're not trying to build messages in every song," says Robbie. "There are points in some of them for people to take if they want. We just like everyone to have fun – that's what gigging's about."

Iain agrees. "We don't want to get bogged down in that sort of thing," he says. "A lot of the songs are more personal statements than general 'answers', personal things that could apply wider..."

Jim: "Because you're not just singular. The things that happen to you

TELEPHONE 01-387-0428/9

MUSIC MACHINE

CAMDEN HIGH ST. OPP. MORNINGTON CRESCENT TUBE. N.W.1

Wednesday 20th
TRADITION
plus Fusion
Admission £1.00

MondaY ¼ × TH
CHELSEA
Plus The Fall
Plus Snivellin' Shits
Admission £1.00

Thursday 21st
HI-TENSION
plus Abbraka
Advanced Tickets £2.00 From Box Office

£Tuesday 26th
THE JOLT
Plus Hollywood Killers
Admission £1.00

Wednesday 27th
SORE THROAT
plus The Vye
Admission £1.00

Friday 22nd
SANDY AND THE BACKLINE
Plus Showbiz Kids
Admission £2.00

Monday 16th October
THE PIRATES
Advance Tickets £2.00 From Box Office

Saturday 23rd
GONZALEZ
plus support
Admission £2.00

Mo: day 30th October
SLADE
Advance Tickets £2.50 From Box Office

LICENSED BARS – LIVE MUSIC – DANCING
8PM – 2 AM MONDAY TO SATURDAY

could be happening to somebody else."

People criticised you for not taking many chances on the album. Do you think that's valid?

Jim: "Show me any debut album which has ten songs which each cover a different style. Everybody's got a style."

Robbie: "Considering what our roots are what we've done is take out influences and move them on. Maybe it comes over sounding a bit safe, but I think that's to do with the production a lot. I'd like to do the second album a lot rougher, with a lot more guitar."

When the band started wearing the suits around Christmas time, cynics thought the Jolt were leaping on the Thamesbeat/Powerpop bandwagon. Fair comment?

"No," says Robbie. "We didn't start wearing suits until all of that had died away."

Jim: "Powerpop was the last thing on our minds cos anyone with brains could see it was going to be dead. The Press killed it before they'd given it time to grow. We're wearing these suits now out of a genuine affection for other groups who had that style."

The afore-mentioned Mod England legends.

Robbie: "We'd have done it earlier if we had the money to get gear like that cos it's really what we've always been about. Although we're obviously not going to wear these suits forever."

Jim: "Basically we're scruffy cunts, we just dress up occasionally."

This interview ain't spicey enough, I say accusingly, why not come clean about the glamour of the rock world, the drugs, the sex, the travelling?

"We've been to the Isle of Man," reveals Iain.

Did you get birched?

Iain: "I asked and asked but they wouldna do it til I'd done something wrong."

Jim: "He wears a rubber mask too."

Manager Dougie, (ex-shoe assistant, and Wishaw's answer to McLaren) injects: "That's what the song 'Chains' was written about," he lies. (It's actually about inhibitions)

Iain: "The best bit of being in the Jolt is when Dougie gets us all in the bath together."

And? And?

Iain: "He washes us..."

The dirty bastard. I bet he made you make records with failed train robbers too.

"No, we're waiting for the Kray twins to come out," laughs Jim.

"With Doug and Dinsdale's help we could take over Golders Green and declare UDI."

The Jolt live in a rented house in Golders Green when they're in London.

Dougie jokingly claims they have terrorist connection: "They've got the Red Army Faction's phone number in their book," he says.

Nein, nein, nein?

"We're urban guerrillas," claims Iain. "The Golders Green Popular Front."

Jim: "We were very upset when Guy died." (Timely gorilla reference, Jim's bananas).

Roadie Peter is not popular in Golders Green since he innocently walked into a kosher butcher's and asked for pork chops – fellow roadie Craig was behind this. And he was also behind the disgusting tale of why Jim shouts "Slobber it into me I'm bonkers" on the live version of 'Route 66', a tale so revolting that it defies description in a family newspaper. Tsk, as tasteless as a month-old haggis these boys. (But buy me a pint and I'll give you her name, no questions asked).

So how about some Jolt predictions on the future?

"We're going to become a mass youth phenomenon," claims Robbie.

"Aye," says Jim. "The biggest thing since Bert Weedon and the Droggs."

*The following month, I caught up with The Jolt again when they played London's Marquee club. Here are my notes: 'Episode 62 of our popular series on the life of simple, everyday Scottish folk in which our three Mod heroes led by Robert The Spruce are joined by additional guitarist Kevin Key (late of the Subs – not the UK Subs) and turn again to find the streets of London paved with appreciation...

In actual fact Kevin's addition could just provide the extra wallop to turn the Jolt from an energetic modern world mod combo into a popular energetic modern mod combo.

Tonight was KK's debut gig, although he played like he'd been there since the beginning, and the difference he made was telling. The sound was thicker, stronger, sharper, it forced grey out... Yeah I thought I was sounding like a Jolt commercial too, but they really are worth checking out.

The lazy-arse DJ never turned up so the group came on early and powered through 17 songs which included most of the album and four new numbers - three Collins compositions in the standard Jolt mould, powerful and convincing.

Plus a song from Kevin, 'All The Girls On the Street' (Ena and Elsie?)

which suggests he's going to be a creative catalyst rather than just another body on stage.

The crowd took the boys to their bosoms (Enough of that - Ed). Wild allegations that they were "better than the Jam" flew about, and a group of neo-Mods from Romford called the Purple Hearts asserted that "Mods were back, OK!"

To me, the set sounded fine, and apart from maybe a few pacing issues, there's no real let-up in the bombardment of high-tempo numbers, reservations were few and far between.

They encored with 'Again And Again' (again) and a version of 'Watcha Gonna Do About It' which underlined my contention that if success was ever measured in commitment these boys would be as huge as Nessie.

PURPLE HEARTS

In October 1978, I reviewed the Purple Hearts live supporting The Tickets at the Bridge House, Canning Town. The Corvettes were opened. The piece ran on 21st October, just call me Mystic Meg:

The Purple Hearts are Mods. They come from Romford, and believe in Pop as Art. They're also surprisingly tight and professional, hammering through a snappy seven numbers that conjured up references like The Who/Small Faces/Jam/Rich Kids. Simon Stebbing is an excellent guitarist and compounds the whole image by hurling his guitar Townshend-like at the floor. Mods are coming back, maybe the Purple Hearts will ride the wave.

NEWS OF THE WORLD
GOSSIP AND LETTERS...

The line up for the "Great British Music Festival" at
Wembley in November has been announced.

The Jam will headline the New Wave night on Wednesday
29th November. Other acts on the bill that night are
Generation X, **Slade**, **The Pirates** and **Patrik Fitzgerald**.
Compere for the evening is Capital Radio DJ Nicky Horne.
Thursday night will be headlined by Lindisfarne and John
Miles and the closing night is Saturday 2nd December
which will see David Essex headline with **The Rick Kids** and
The Real Thing amonst the support acts.

MARQUEE TRUCE: The Dispute between the Marquee
Club and the Musicians Union has been solved. The union
were on the brink of pulling out bands from teh club over
the management's refusal to agree terms of payment for
musicians.
But last week the union received a letter from the
Marquee management agreeing to the union's minimum
rate of £8.25 per musician.

marquee

90 Wardour St., W.1

01-437 6603

OPEN EVERY NIGHT FROM 7.00 pm to 11.00 pm
REDUCED ADMISSION FOR STUDENTS & MEMBERS

Thurs. 3rd, Fri 4th & Sat 5th August

THE ENID
Plus friends & Ian Fleming

Thur 10th & Fri 11th (Adm £1.50)

WILKO JOHNSON
SOLID SENDERS
The Young Ones & Ian Fleming

Sun 6th August (Adm £1.25)

RACING CARS
Plus friends & Mandy H

Mon 7th & Tue 8th August

STEVE HILLAGE
Plus guests & Jerry Floyd
Advance tickets to members £1.40
Non members at the door £1.60

Sat 12th August (Adm. 75p)

THE BUSINESS
Reaction & Ian Fleming

Wed 9th August (Adm £1)

NEW HEARTS
Plus guests & Jerry Floyd

Sun 13th & Mon 14th August

THE VIBRATORS
Plus guests & Jerry Floyd
Advance tickets to members £1.25
Non-members at the door £1.50

READING FESTIVAL
AUGUST BANK HOLIDAY WEEKEND

OPENING UP
IN FRONT OF OUR EYES
OCTOBER -NOVEMBER 1978

THOUGH WE WERE ALL BANDS WITH RECORD LABELS
AIMING FOR THE MAINSTREAM, I LOVED HOW THE MOD
REVIVAL WAS SO DETERMINEDLY NICHE WITH ITS OWN
IDENTITY AND D-I-Y ETHOS OF FANZINES AND CLUBS ETC.
A TROPE THAT ALLOWED IT TO PROLONG AND SPREAD FAR
AND WIDE GEOGRAPHICALLY.

Antony Meynell - Squire

THE JAM:
ALL
MOD
CONS

November 4, 1978

I F the single 'David Watts'/'A Bomb' was a hint that the widespread critical relegation of The Jam to "spent force" status was to say the least a trifle premature, 'Down In The Tube Station' was a whacking great nudge in the ribs pointer to the possible strengths of this, the band's third and most satisfyingly rounded album.

Normally the inclusion of three previously available tracks is enough to lop at least one star off of an album's rating but in this case the platter in question is so well-constructed and such a convincing statement of musical maturity, artistic triumph and compositional strength that nothing – nothing – detracts from its whole.

The Jam hit me from the start – a smartly be-suited unit of power, with that guitarist with his battered red Rickenbacker, the lean hungry looks and his bitterness and certainty. And non-conformity...

The first album, *In The City*, hit like a loco locomotive, the second, *This Is The Modern World*, came in for some stick (far too much, in my opinion) due mostly to a couple of weaker tracks and the undernourished production. Then came singles that were nothing special, the unhappy US tour and the revelation from Bruce Foxton back in September that they had scrapped songs lined up for this third album for being "too boring and samey".

It must have been that pressure and frustration that drove Weller to create the thing of beauty that is *All Mod Cons*.

From the Vespa on the inner sleeve to the backward guitar on 'In The Crowd', *All Mod Cons* looks back spiritually to the mid-Sixties while remaining firmly locked into Seventies power and concerns.

They just blast away twelve years of blind alley 'progression' and take up the mantle of Townshend / Lennon & McCartney for the modern world. Which I know is a bold claim to make, but it's one based on the way they marry drive and hate with sensitivity and pop sensibility. The Jam push back their musical confines while maintaining a bitter forcefulness.

They move effortlessly from the title track's crisp awareness of parasitical manipulation to Paul's tender acoustic love-song 'English Rose' (for Gill?).

Weller translates his thematic concerns into his finest lyrics to date. Gratuitous violence: 'A Bomb', 'Tube Station'. The stifling mass: 'In The Crowd' with its look-back to 'Away From the Numbers'. The controlled rage of 'Mr Clean' with its contempt for middle class smugness, the driving pop rock of 'Billy Hunt', Weller's Frankie Abbott...

To sum this up in 400 words is nonsense. I've left so much unsaid. This afternoon I am going to try and catch them at rehearsals. Tune back next week, same time, same paper, for the full story.

THE JAM

ALL MOD CO[NS]

New Album

APOCALYPSE TOUR 78

NOVEMBER

7th UNIVERSITY OF ST. ANDREWS - Fyfe
10th POLYTECHNIC - Sheffield
12th UNIVERSITY - Leeds
13th APOLLO - Manchester
14th ODEON - Birmingham
15th COVENTRY THEATRE - Coventry
17th CORN EXCHANGE - Cambridge
18th A.B.C Great Yarmouth
20th UNIVERSITY - Cardiff
21st THE DOME - Brighton
22nd UNIVERSITY - Canterbury
24th GUILDHALL - Portsmouth
28th COLSTON HALL - Bristol
29th WEMBLEY ARENA - London

THE JAM

33⅓

ALL MOD CONS

Featuring The New Single

DOWN IN THE TUBE STATION AT MIDNIGHT

THE JAM AND THE MOD REVIVAL

Finsbury Park, North London. November 1978

' I first felt a fist, and then a kick/I could now smell their breath.../They smelt of pubs, and Wormwood Scrubs/And too many right-wing meetings/My life swam around me/It took a look and drowned me in its own existence...' ('Down In The Tube Station At Midnight')

SO IN BETWEEN reviewing All Mod Cons the other weekend, and eating my Sunday dinner, I came across his news item in the *Mirror*.

It said starkly: 'When Mr Shelbourne went down, the gang took turns to kick him. They concentrated on his head and face, all standing around and taking turns. His nose, cheekbone and jaw were all shattered. All he can remember is a noise like a rushing train behind him.'

This is the modern world, all right, and what more pointed reminder that Paul Weller is confronting late Seventies reality could you 'wish' for?

You hear so much crap about The Jam – that they're 'revivalists', stuck in a Sixties rut etc. *All Mod Cons* takes these unfounded criticisms, scrunches them down into a ball as small as the idiot minds that repeat them, and kicks it straight into touch.

Not only is it the most impressive Jam album to date, it's also a dynamic unit of modern music.

This band may have their spiritual roots in Mod England of yore, but The Jam are 100 per cent part of today's scene. No bull. You've read the rave reviews, all you've got to do now is hear it to believe it...

IT'S not just the album's name that recalls that earlier, aspiring lower class youth culture with its stress on looking good, living fast and having fun. It's the Ska album and the Vespa outline on the inner sleeve, the Op Art target design on the label, the clothes the group wear. When I meet the band for the first time last Monday, Paul Weller turned up in a parka with US army stripes.

They're rehearsing at the Rainbow in Finsbury Park – a far cry from Woking pubs and fighting feedback down at the Roxy. Watching the band work through their volcanic 21-song warm up for the current tour rubbed in how far things have moved on from punk's original see-a-band/form-your-own ideals.

If truth be told, I'd been worried about meeting Weller. His press reputation as a "lousy interview", a moody loner prone to biting the head off any hapless hack who asked the wrong questions, had gone before him. Utterly wrongly. In the flesh, I found him friendly and easy to talk to; eager to be understood.

I ask about the violence he writes about, the mindless mob attack of 'Tube Station' with its *Clockwork Orange* reflection in the newspaper pages.

"I suppose you could point to all sorts of social problems, like housing and unemployment to explain away violence," Paul says. "I think it all boils down to over-population. Those songs are just trying to express how it feels. 'Tube Station' is a kind of love song in a way as well; it tries to show how it feels when you die without seeing the person you love again.

"The main thing is, I always try and write songs that I can relate to and that other people can relate to. It's not always me in the songs, I use characters."

Can music ever change things like random assault, make people think a bit more?

"Well most of the kids who buy our records probably aren't like that anyway. Like all Sham's lot – Gary Dickle, Binsy – they're all really great blokes. You probably won't ever get across to the people who do that sort of thing. I agree with Jimmy Pursey when he says that they're the kids you should be trying to play to, but it's just a fact that there are some people who you will never get across to because they are just vindictive bastards. They'll be the first ones to put on the SS uniforms and the leather jackboots.

"I mean, I can't understand kids who are National Front. People say it's because there aren't enough jobs or the houses are too close together but that still doesn't explain a lot of things. I can't see any kids my age or under wanting to do National Service, which is NF policy. The NF would ban rock music. It would just go out the window. So I don't know who's voting for them or why; maybe young kids who don't know the full facts, or older people who should know better if they lived through the '39-'45 war. I always think it's middle class people who vote for them."

The Jam dropped their Union Jack badges once because of the alleged "NF connotation" but have now re-instated them.

"If you drop the flag it shows you are succumbing to the BF," says Paul. Just because you're proud to be British doesn't mean you have to be racist and totally bloody-minded about everything."

He goes on: "The only politics I believe in is democracy. Music is not going to change anything. I mean everyone's doing their bit writing anti-violence and anti-racist songs, which is better than writing what a nice day it was on Tuesday, but most people who buy our records agree with that anyway."

THE JAM HIT a bad patch creatively a few months ago. A lot of songs they'd recorded for this their third album were scrapped as too dull or samey. Critics had started writing them off, so they were under a lot of pressure to deliver. The resulting album is stunning – twelve tracks including the instant classics 'Tube Station' and 'A Bomb In Wardour Street', the ballad, 'English Rose', the Kinks' cover 'David Watts', the tense and angry 'Mr Clean'. It's a gem.

"Everyone works better under pressure," Weller reckons. "It's like when there's a war on and we all stand together. Most of these songs were written since last August. Some we took the best of other numbers and joined them together. 'Billy Hunt' was practically re-written from scratch. 'To Be Someone' had a few different arrangements and was edited down. 'Tube Station', 'In The Crowd' and 'The Place I Love' were written in the week before we went into the studio."

He shrugs. "I'm prolific in three week bursts and then I have long dry periods."

'English Rose' isn't mentioned on the album sleeve, is that because you wrote as a personal song for Gill? (Gill Price, his long-term girlfriend)

"Nah, it was just written...well, I suppose it was. I wrote it in America and it was a sort of dual thing with Britain as well. I got homesick! It's really a surprise track. The lyrics aren't there either because in a way I'm embarrassed by it, really, because it's a feeble love song."

Is 'Place I Love' Woking?

"No, it's nowhere really, just a bit of subconscious poetry..." He looks up and smiles. "The first version of that was really obscene. It was disgusting, full of fucks and cunts and shits. The song is about trendies and it was meant to be written in a very childish manner."

Two of the new numbers, 'Billy Hunt' and 'To Be Someone' have comic themes. "A lot of our songs have humour in them," he says.

"But that probably doesn't come out because people take the lyrics at face value."

While the title track hits the music business right on the canister: 'All the time we're getting rich/You hang around to help me out/But when we're skint – Oh God forbid – you'll drop us like hot bricks/I'll tell you what/I got you sussed/You'll waste my time when my time comes.'

'Mr Clean' is one of the strongest new tracks.

"There's a lot of tension in it," Paul agrees. We describe it on stage as being against the bourgeoisie. Well, it's not really; it's about the sort of person who in public is morally upstanding when all he really wants to do is screw the secretary."

TIME FOR ACTION: THE MOD REVIVAL

Paul comes from a decidedly un-bourgeois background. The son of a builder and a cleaner, he was ambitious as a kid but not in a showbiz "I'd deep-fry my first born for a TV slot sense'. No, Weller's ambitions are for his songs, his craft.

The Jam formed in Surrey in 1972, and spent their early years gigging twice, maybe three times a week in Woking's Workingmen's clubs, which explains their tightness on stage. Bruce Foxton's bass style is busy and loping. Rick Buckler is a drum machine, maintaining a non-stop percussive pounding. They're a ferociously workman-like rhythm section. And okay, Weller's voice may not be the Mae West – someone compared him to "a foreman barking orders on the East India Docks". But his songs are irresistible.

Paul Weller eats and sleeps music. "I never got into glitter and glam rock and all that crap," he says, wrinkling his nose with distaste. "But I love Motown and bluebeat and Ska. Mod was a very personal thing to me. I loved the music and the clothes, the collective image of it. I had a scooter at the time."

He loved Colin MacInnes' book *Absolute Beginners* too.

I have to bring up the M word. What with the album title, and the start of filming on The Who's new *Quadrophenia* movie, along with the beginnings of a grassroots Mod revival it looks like we're in for a full scale revival.

"Yeah," he says. "I can see there's going to be a big Mod revival in the Summer, which will be really boring because it'll be all beach fights all over again, just like the punks and Teds last year."

What do you think of *Quadrophenia* anyway?

"I like the cover," he says. "A lot of the lyrics are too intelligent for what the story is meant to be about. I think Jimmy Pursey is going to do it better..."

The Jam – far more than a cheap imitation of the "maximum R&B" of The Who. The Jam are awash with sullen aggression, attitude and great tunes. They're probably the most important band in the country right now.

SEVENTIES

BOYS
FEBRUARY - APRIL 1979

NO ONE LOOKED LIKE SIXTIES MODS. IN 78-79 WE WERE ALL BUYING CLOTHES FROM SECOND HAND SHOPS, TRYING TO BE COOL WHILE WEARING DEAD MENS CLOTHES. THEY WOULD BE CALLED RETRO SHOPS NOW! NO ONE LOOKED COOL, ONLY MAYBE THE PURPLE HEARTS

Terry Rawlings - 79 Veteren & Author

THE JAM
IN THE
FRENCH
CITY

Paris. February 27, 1979

BEFORE the Great British Musical Festival, the fledgling new Mods had felt for the most part like isolated individuals. Now they knew other kids just like them felt the same way as they did, but they still had no idea how many of them there were.

The next event in the re-birth of the cult were The Jam's gigs in Paris and Reims. The three-day adventure may have been the worst thing to hit Anglo-French relations since Agincourt, but the trip was also a key moment as the scattered Jam fans realised they were part of something bigger, something that was magical, something growing.

The key players were Grant Fleming, Dave Lawrence, Billy Hassett and Alan from Hayes. But the English away contingent that week also included kids from Southend, Dagenham, Barking, Stratford, Deptford, Shepherds Bush and as far afield as Newcastle.

The merry mob assembled at London's Charing Cross station at 6.30am, setting off on the 7am for Dover. Grant Fleming, who wrote the trip up months later for Maximum Speed, recalled that their only toiletries were 10p disposable toothbrushes hastily purchased from the station bogs. So much for germ-free adolescents.

The mood was excited; the talk was of new bands, of cheap clothing emporiums, football, Jam trivia and less cerebrally Dave's backside. Mr Lawrence had brightened up the first leg of the journey by dropping his strides to reveal the two eyes he'd had tattooed on his buttocks. Nice. Many more would get 'shit-faced' in a different way over the following days.

They caught the hovercraft over, and then the Boulogne-Paris train, which soon degenerated into playful beer fights. Grant notes: "Batty from our mob then appeared with a fire extinguisher but was persuaded to put it back unused before we all got nicked."

The bad behaviour continued unabashed at Paris when the over-excited parka-clad youths "offered out" a group of French rockabillies and old habits kicked in - a couple of reprobates (who we can now name safely as Norman and Waitsy) ordered a couple of burgers, demolished them, and did the offski without paying for

MOD PILGRAMAGE

GO TO FRANCE TO SEE

THE JAM

IN PARIS AND REIMS

MEET AT CHARING X 0610 Monday 26 Feb
DEPART CHARING X 0700 Monday 26 Feb
Travel by Hovercraft and Train arriving in PARIS at 1420 Monday

Go to gig at LE STADIUM, PARIS Monday 26 Feb

DEPART PARIS 0902 or 1106 Tuesday 27
ARRIVE REIMS 1032 or 1241 Tuesday 27

Go to gig at CINEMA OPERA, REIMS at 2 Tuesday 27 Feb

DEPART REIMS 0618 or 0708 or 0958 or 1128 Wednesday 28 Feb
ARRIVE PARIS 0803 or 0840 or 1131 or 1400 Wednesday 28 Feb
Then change Stations to connect any of following trains:

DEPART PARIS 0920 or 1010 or 1420 Wednesday 28 Feb
ARRIVE CHARING 1340 or 1540 or 1940 Wednesday 28 Feb
X

FARE: LONDON-PARIS RETURN £18-50 (Tickets must be bought by 23 Feb
British Rail stations everywhere)

PARIS-REIMS RETURN £10-40 (To be bought in Paris)
£28-90

PASSPORTS NOT NEEDED. TAKE A PHOTO WITH YOU AND GET A IDENTITY CARD
(VALID 60 HRS)

PARKAS ESSENTIAL FOR DOSSING, TAKE UNION JACKS FOR SUPPORT.

them.

In the city there's a thousand things these kids want to say to you and most of them seemed to involve the words "French minge."

Naturally all of the away firm jumped the Metro ("much easier than the London Oxo cube"). A proper Fagin's gang, they were.

They located the venue – a sports hall in the south of the city – and passed some time with a spot of light shop-lifting. The local beer was selling for 30p a litre so by 7pm they were completely pie-eyed. Al, who'd missed the 7am train, then turned up late armed with 'blues' to lift the mood.

The arrival of a mob from Shepherds Bush meant that Mod numbers had swollen, to everyone's surprise, to around fifty strong. Quite a sight to greet the French crowd of punks, posers and students who'd now filled the venue.

Grant recalls: "Some French bird was giving out speed for freemans, which was much welcome and quickly gobbled. The Jam hit the stage to be confronted by a singing swaying mob waving Union Jacks – they must have thought the Sham Army were in. There were a few minor scuffles between us and the French, them of course coming off worse, and after the gig we went backstage for a drink and a chat. The group thanked us for coming."

They ended up in the Rose Bon Bon Disco, most commandeering the dance floor as the DJ obliged with a string of Tamla classics and Who and Stones songs. While the rest, hit by post-speed come-down, sat in a corner for four hours wrestling with remorse and paranoia.

Kicked out at 4am, most of the contingent slept rough in the Metro. Grant and four others tried gate-crashing a French hotel but were chased out by a geezer with a loaded gun. Too risky.

The next morning, some flaked away back to Blighty leaving a smaller 'firm' to carry on for day two, catching the 10am train to Reims for more of the same – drinking, shop-lifting, insulting shop keepers, chatting up the mademoiselles. The show went well, although Grant recalls: "The local wankers tried to antagonise us and were rewarded with a few clouts to the head..."

After the gig, The Jam joined them in a local bar for drinks, Paul Weller staying until the early hours. Mercifully he missed the after-show. Standards of behaviour, already poor, would rapidly degenerate.

The hotel suffered badly in an orgy of drunken shagging, fighting and fire extinguisher antics (courtesy Grant). A window was smashed, a cistern was pulled off the wall (Smash the cistern!) and a fresh turd was delivered as room service.

Two van loads of gendarmes swiftly turned up and calmed them all down, promising to return in the morning. Natch, the shrewder Mods beat a retreat first thing catching the 6.30am train to Paree. The rest were caught on the hop and made to pay £40 for the window. They probably got off lightly.

THE LITTLE ROOSTERS

The Bridge House. March 3, 1979

'I am the little red rooster / Too lazy to crow for a day...'
ONCE Garrie Lammin wanted a runnin' riot, now all he wants is...to be the Rolling Stones.

Garrie (real name, Gary) used to play scorching lead guitar with no-holds-barred, East London boot-boy punk outfit, Cock Sparrer. When they split he got a job customising cars. "And I could have stuck it," Gal says. "Except this geezer working there kept playing Stones tapes and I kept thinking - 'that should be me'..."

Out went the crop, in came the Ronnie Wood mullet. Lammin quit his job, formed a new band, locked them away in rehearsals and finally unveiled them at the Bridge last week.

Only the Tardis could take you back in time quicker.

Like most of us in our early twenties, Garrie got his teenage rocks off with good time rock 'n' roll bands like The Faces, Small and otherwise, which is precisely the mood The Roosters aim to reproduce.

The aim is pretty true, a quick glance at my less-than-sober scribbling (sozzled short-hand, inebriated inking, pissed penmanship, drunken doodles and other refugees from Whicker Island) reveals hosts of Faces, Small Faces and Stones comparisons.

The other Roosters are John Hunt bass, Graeme Potter drums and Gary Eves on keyboards, and they're tight as Ebenezer Scrooge at a pay-bar. But it's Garrie Lammin on lead and vocals who really makes the connections - this guy fronts bands like Red Rum used to win the National. With conviction and charisma. He's a rock natural if ever I saw one.

There are nine Lammin/Potter originals in tonight's set, and just the sort of mix you'd expect. Mid-tempo mid-Sixties R&B numbers like 'Am I Talking To Myself' rub shoulders with a full frontal real-good-time belters like 'Madame You Amuse' and the slower, more soulful 'Girl I Got A Lot To Loose'.

They also throw in the lighthearted bluesy 'Roostering With Intent', a strong potential single in 'Don't Break My Heart' and there's even reggae influence evident in 'Don't Wanna Take No More' with its rather fine lead break. Plus an encore of Chuck Berry's 'Little Queenie' to boot.

Defects? John Hunt's backing vocals in places, Gary Eve's keyboards in places, but in fairness it was his first gig ever and they've got plenty of time to smooth over the rough edges. In the meantime if you remember Steve and the Boys, and Mick and the boys in their pre-punk prime with affection you could do a lot worse than check out the Roosters.

Aww, hey man, rock 'n' rollers, don'cha just luv 'em?

THE PURPLE HEARTS: PARKAS & THE RUMOUR OF A MOD REVIVAL

East London. March 10, 1979

' I wonder why we've got so much to prove/I wonder why we carry on like we do...' ('Millions Like Us)

A TATTY roneoed handbill lays inky side up in the mush, screaming out its message to all and sundry. 'Purple Hearts', it proclaims, 'The Sound Of The Eighties!'

THE MOD REVIVAL

Underneath, in semi-punk lettering, a roar of 'Youth Explosion' hovers over the heads of Mods on the march, a Sixties snapshot embellished by a Roy Lichenstein pistol-in-fist design, the words 'Pop Art' and the details of a forthcoming gig at the Moonlight Club in West Hampstead.

Another advert for another group...well, yes and no, because something is happening here and I'm not quite sure what exactly is going to come of it...

Last month I wandered in to the Bridge House and I thought I'd stepped through some groovy kind of time warp – scores of kids were mulling about in parkas sporting Jam badges, Who badges, union jack patches, short neat haircuts, collars and ties. By Fred and Perry! Is this the modern world?

Talk of a 'Mod revival' has been in the air for a while now and you might well cringe at the prospect of another business manufactured fad, but the truth is, like the skinhead rebirth of late '77/'78, the current resurgence of aspects of Sixties Modernism is coming from the bottom up. Open your eyes, it's everywhere. Count the scooters at the south coast resorts; tot up the growing number of Mods at gigs from spotty kids to 'reformed' skinheads, even the old Chicken Run at Upton Park (created by Sixties Mod football hooligans) has been re-established.

Naturally, like ex-skins, ex-Mods can already be heard bemoaning their latter day equivalent's alleged superficiality. But these new Mods have got new bands too. In the wake of Paul Weller's open affection for the period, scores of bands who in many and varied ways feel a degree of affiliation with the look/soul/feel of Mod have emerged: The Jolt from Glasgow, The Teenbeats from Hastings, The Indicators and The Fixations from London, The Ricky Tics from Nottingham, The Purple Hearts from Romford , innumerable groups calling themselves The Scooters...

By the sacred gusset of Cathy McGowan, something exciting this way comes...

At the moment it's healthy, from the streets if you like, but it won't stay like that. Wide-boys and fly-boys will latch on to it, and Mod paraphernalia will start retailing at ridiculous prices. Sociologists will latch on to it, too, and serious/dreary think-pieces will appear in newspaper colour supplements. Like everything else it will be taken away from the people who created it and turned against them. Worst of all the music press will probably react with catch-all Power Pop style overkill, drowning the groups' individuality in cheap and easy sensationalism. The Purple Hearts realise this.

"We wanna get this straight right now about Mod revival and all this shit..." the speaker is Hearts vocalist Robert Manton. Rob is excitable and right now he's excited. "Obviously we think of ourselves as Mods, and that's like a state of mind, but it don't mean we gotta sleep in our mohair suits, we don't wanna be tied down by an image, we'd rather be thought of as a group for teenagers, for anybody..."

Point taken, Rob, but how, why, and wherefore the Mod bit?

"When I was at school, I was in to Mod - just the image of it," he says. "I didn't know much about it, but I liked the look. When punk came along we were all in to that – I went out and bought 'Anarchy' the day it came out, blah, blah, blah. Early '77 we saw The Jam and we formed a punk band, and after the first gig we said 'Well, we want to be like The Jam and all wear suits, 'cept we couldn't afford it...'

"Personally i got pissed off with punk by the middle of '77, I went down the Vortex and, I dunno, the sense of community, everybody together having a laugh...that had all gone. I just drifted out. By early '78 I weren't calling myself a punk anymore, but for a time it was a real split personality thing."

Guitarist Simon Stebbing takes up the story. "Yeah, so last year we thought let's be what we've always wanted to be and be a Mod band, so we became The Purple Hearts in May '78. But let's face it the only thing that stopped us before hand was the fact we couldn't play our instruments..."

All true. The first time I saw them was at the Barking campus of the North East London Poly in June 1977 when my old mate, part-time Rock Against Racism promoter Mel Biggs did his good Samaritan bit and let this week-old mid teen punk band tag on the bottom of the Buzzcocks bill opening up for The Fall and The Verbals. Only then they were called The Sockets (aka Jack Plug and The Sockets) and they were, umm, basic. Spirited but basic. None of them could play – they'd only picked up their instruments two weeks before the show. But this didn't stop them playing original numbers, including a mini rock-opera-in-a-song called 'Reg.' Not too surprisingly, The Sockets (sometimes also known as Robbie Hatchet & The Sockets) unplugged themselves after about a dozen so-so gigs (including once at The Roxy and an appearance on a float in the Romford Carnival – presumably for an easy get-away).

Times change. They became Purple Hearts – the name taken from Dexamyl, an anti-depressant containing amphetamine that was popular with sixties Mods – in May 1978. I saw them at the Bridge last October and was well impressed by the band's tightness and developing ability.

POP ART

"Obviously we think of ourselves as mods, and that's like a state of mind, but it don't mean we gotta sleep in our mohair suits, we don't wanna be tied down by an image, we'd rather be thought of as a group for teenagers, for anybody."

THE PURPLE HEARTS, regarded by many as the best, hail from Romfor Essex.

Purpl Hear

Bassist Jeff (year, just Jeff) describes epic single-to-be, 'Jimmy', thus:
"It's a Pop - Art - Teen - Confusion - Anthem!"

P · H
ACTION TESTED

PEPSI

DÉCO

arnaby St.

screaming
its message to all
sundry. Purple
earts' it proclaims,
The Sound Of The
Eighties'

ICI

PURPLE HEARTS AT : BARKIN
F.C. APR 29TH
MOONLIGHT CLUB M
MUSIC MACHINE

ey cover three oldies — The Monkees'
pin' Stone', David Bowie And The
r Third's 'Can't Help Thinking About
and wicked Wilson Pickett's
wrenching 'If You Need Me.' But it's the
t originals that make up the bulk of their
et that leave no doubts as to what

Pop Art

"The Purple Hearts are the ga
Newton's Third Law and Einstei
the toilet seat!"

They had a set of rough-edged tunes, anchored to unsurprising Jam, Who, Small Faces reference points. Since then gigs have come slowly but steadily; tonight's appearance supporting the Tickets being just average but indicative of their strengths.

Onstage, Manton holds the attention, standing all cocky in his silly plastic shades and bellowing in to the microphone with rough conviction. Jeff Shadbolt (aka Just Jeff) on bass, Gary Sparks, drums, and Si Stebbing on lead make for a competent together unit. And though they throw in covers such as 'I'm Not Your Steppin' Stone' and 'Can't Help Thinking About Me' (a David Bowie & The Lower Third oldie) they don't play 'Sixties' music. There are 60s influences but the feel and overall sound is definitely a serious, Seventies post punk t'ing.

Their own songs have songs have character and something to say. In particular 'Jimmy' about the paucity of sheep-like fashion following with riff redolent of 'A-Bomb', 'Beat That' about marrying too young, and the up-tempo teen confusion anthem, 'Frustration':

'I'm going round in circles / Just a thinking of this mess / My mind goes in to spirals / I don't know I'll have to guess / I get Frustration! / I wear it like a suit / But the jacket fits too tightly / And there's lead inside my boots'

Although in reality when it comes to their career they're anything but confused.

"I don't think we're good enough to make records yet," motormouth Manton confesses. "We want more experience - we're pretty young, y'know." (All of them are under 19).

"The next big thing really is to get in and make a demo," says Gary Sparks who replaced original drummer Nick Lake last year. "That's as far ahead as we're thinking, and that's for gigs rather than record companies."

'Everybody's living in their private hell / That's a sinking feeling we know so well...'

In conversation their one recurring concern is youth - as in state of mind.

"You get teenagers who act as if they're middle aged," says Rob, getting excited again. "And they aspire to everything their parents aspire to. They see a kid pissed singing 'Wild Youth' on a Saturday night they'll say, ''ook at that prat!' But you've got to enjoy yourself when you're young.

"The Purple Hearts stand for youth, though on the other hand some of the things teenagers do are pretty sick. Youth is just split up into gangs all fighting each other and it's all fucking stupid, y'know? But see the potential is there for Mod to be really good - for there to be more Mods than any other youth culture and for all them to be together."

'Millions like us, oh yes, there's millions like us/With tunnel vision, making indecisions...'

Simon agrees. "Yeah, as long as they learn from the past rather than just copy everything, and make the same mistakes," he says, sagely.

"Society is geared towards conformity and not having fun," Rob continues. "Just do your job and that's it. And youth is being is being shit on, kids come out of school and you're working twice as hard for half as much money...."

Something they know about as they're all still doing dead end day jobs, which, despite exotic claims of male prostitution and vibrator manufacturing, turn out to be messenger, carpenter, car-sprayer and warehouse hand.

I would have thought many of the above complaints were about CLASS rather than age, but Simon tells me: "We stand for rebellion, but it's not political. We're not into politics."

OK, last question Rob, what do you mean by "The Purple Hearts stand for Pop As Art"? (As quoted in my live review in October).

"Well our art is pop, and our pop is art," he says. "We fill the gap between art and life."

Jeff snorts. "I bet you didn't think of that," he says, accusingly. "Where did you get that from?"

Rob smiles. "Look," he says. "If you don't know, he won't know." He turns to me, and implores: "Listen just put it down - we fill the gap between art and life."

But Jeff is on a piss-taking roll. "He's got it twice," he laughs. "He don't want it three times...come on lads, all together now..."

Jeff, Simon and Gary shout out in unison: "WE FILL THE GAP BETWEEN ART AND LIFE."

Hey boys, I say, you said that without moving your Vespas.

*FOOTNOTE: the Hearts always deny that they ever called themselves 'Jack Plug & The Sockets' – but I would swear on a stack of bibles that's what one of them told me in 1977, so either that was a wind-up or a brief flirtation that they (rightly) decided to ditch on the grounds that it was too daft.

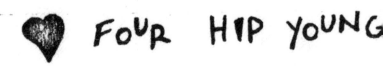 FOUR HIP YOUNG

TH

Purple

AT TH
4ᵀ

POP
ᵃˢ
ART

ENFIELD
TOWN
STATION

IF YOU
BE
AT LEAST

MEN E.T.C. E.T.C.

HOP POLES - ENFIELD
FEB - 79

LANCASTER
ROAD →

THE
HOP
POLES

ER ST.   BAKER ST.

CIVIC
CENTRE

BE

GOT TO
·UARE
E FAIR

THERE

THE CHORDS

Kings Arms. April 7, 1979

AWLREADY AWLREADY, the letter we printed recently from the Romford punks was probably the most sensible statement to-date about the rapidity sprouting Mod Revival. It's happening, right, but it's happening in fun, It's a laugh, and everyone knows it'll all get gumbyised when 'Quadrophenia' comes out and the Biz and The Sun catch on anyway.

So what us rock journalists are after are the groups who aren't just afting riding 10 day media miracles, the ones with the musical muscle to ensure survival when the fad fades into Anne Murray mania or whatever else catches idel paper appreciation.

Groups like The Chords. I'm hee tonight on a tip-off from one of Southend's leading mods who whispered hot nothings into me shell-likes to the effect that The Chords were 'better than the Purple Hearts', and with all due respect to that rapidly developing Romford combo, he was right, (and I just saying that cos they come from South East London either).

The Chords are Bert Scott (drums) Billy H (vocals/rhythm guitar), Chris Pope (lead guitar and Martin Mason (bass/vocals): a powered piece who've been together since March '77 when they started out on Tamla standards and who've matured through line-up changes into a surprisingly tight and competent modern Mod music machine, their own songs rubbing shoulders with choice golden oldies in a 13 song set.

Can't tell you much about presentation as the band were hid from sight behind a sea of parka-packing modsters but sound was well impressive - despite a dodgy vocals-too-low sound mix - combining crashing power chords drive in a Jolt/Jam vein with a convincing grasp of melody. Pop with guts ma babes, and well structered stuff boot.

Of their own songs 'Somethings Missing', 'Maybe Tomorrow' and ' I Don't Wanna Know' made the strongest impact on first hearing but the real test came with covers - 'Knock On Wood', 'She Said She Said', 'Tell Me' and 'Circles' - which they handled with admirable aplomb' a full-driving encore version of the Small Faces 'Hey Girl' being particularly excellent.

What's left to be said? I'm not gonna jump on any bandwagon and sprout lengthy after-dinner speeches about the Mod Movement. No, what's important is that as well as/despite the trappings. The Chords are a fine promising and entertaining young band and you'd be doing yourself a favour to see them soon.

PRESENT

THE CHORDS + THE PURPLE HEARTS

SUPPORTED BY

BACK TO ZERO

AT 'THE CAMBRIDGE' NORTH CIRCULAR RD, EDMONTON N.18
[JUNCTION WITH THE A.10, GT. CAMBRIDGE ROAD]

THURSDAY 26TH APRIL 7.00 p.m

TICKETS £1.00

THE CHORDS: FOUR CHORD WONDERS

'MAYBE TOMORROW, MAYBE SOMEDAY'

Edmonton. April 28, 1979

THE MOD REVIVAL

I SUPPOSE it's because of how wonky punk went that I've been holding back on Mod. I'm wary of that too-much-too-soon curse. But it's difficult not to get excited at gigs like this. Things haven't moved so fast since the early days of London punk and the atmosphere feels just that dizzy again now; there's a buzz of genuine anticipation at shows, I'm discovering good new groups all the time, watching the whole thing grow.

It's probably impossible not to get caught up in the sense of urgency, fun and expectation oozing from every smartly clad Mod orifice. These teenage tickets believe in themselves totally. And while Mods should be aware of the big punk mistakes and the inevitable bad influences that will be brought to bear on their fledgling movement, they shouldn't be robbed of their optimism, no matter how naive it might seem to the 'hardened veterans'.

Something good will come of the Mod renewal; just how much good no one can tell yet, but it's largely up to what the participants do.

'Will come'? What am I waffling about? Something good has come already and right up there in the vanguard are The Chords, a young, powerful South East London four piece who Paul Weller saw and snapped up as support for the Jam's Rainbow gig on May 10, who are supporting The Undertones on the tail-end of their current tour, who look set to sign with Jimmy Pursey's label and get a single out in the summertime when the weather is fine and you can shoot right up and touch the sky….And, and, and, this is their eleventh gig ever…

That's right. Eleven gigs in six weeks, and one of them was the Green Man Plumstead, which I'm not sure even counts. Eleven gigs and fame already? "It's all happening too soon," drummer Brett Scott confides. "Much too fast, but it's all down to whether you can cope with it. I think we can."

It's the old dilemma —you need time to develop but you crave attention. I think The Chords have got their heads screwed on. I think they'll cope. I think they'll survive the hype.

TONIGHT'S gig has been fixed up by the Maximum Speed mod-zine at the Cambridge Hotel pub in Edmonton, North London, and 300-odd Mods have packed the place out. It's still completely a street movement, but there are already five times as many as there were five weeks ago…

Back To Zero are supporting The Purple Hearts and The Chords who toss up to see who will top the bill — it's that free and easy. The Chords provide the double-headed coin.

Missing Back To Zero in the tireless pursuit of getting a together interview man (incorporating an ongoing drinking as much 'Forsyte Saga' as possible situation) we stumble back into the hall for the eminently enjoyable Purple Hearts set — they get better all the time —and listen to Mods making cruel jokes about Billy Idol's coiffure, the Gen X man having materialized at the back of the hall to check out the scene (baby).

Hoisting up a huge Union Jack (with absolutely no fascist connotations whatsoever), The Chords hit the stage and power-drive into a Goliath-like rendition of the Small Faces' 1966 hit 'Hey Girl'. The crowd readily punches the air in time to the 'Hey! Hey! It's All Right' chorus chant and get into their odd mutant-pogo twisting dance style.

Then KER-RASH come the power-chords as the band launch into 'Don't Go Back' the first of their own numbers…when disaster strikes and lead guitarist Chris Pope (no relation) cuts his fingers painfully.

Gritting his teeth — what a trooper, huh kids? — Pope soldiers on for a shortened set, which is more than enough to give an adequate account of the band's scope and ability.

Two guitars, bass, and drums come together to make music as tight and muscular as a circus strongman with Scrooge-like tendencies. The numbers are fast and furious but retain a strong sense of melody — like Chris says it's a meeting ground for punk attack and pop sensibility.

Similarities with the early Jam have already been bandied about and the Woking Wonders are the obvious frame of reference for newcomers but The Chords' songs aren't one dimensional and already you can see their music developing; contrast an early number like 'Dream Dolls' with more recent composition 'Maybe Tomorrow' for example and you can hear how their grasp of pop structures is growing — they're writing better songs all the time.

Their own numbers mingle with a strong set of cover songs. At a normal gig, they play Eddie Floyd's 'Knock On Wood', the Beatles' 'She Said, She Said', and Sam & Dave's 'Hold On I'm Coming', exuding confidence. Anything they lack in skill is made up for by their energy and enthusiasm. Diminutive vocalist Billy H (Hassett) really looks the part — he looks like he means it — and there's no musical weak leak. Tonight they hammer through a snappy nine numbers, and an encore. Of course.

I COULD hardly believe that it was their third gig ever when I saw them at the Kings Head in Deptford last month, but they assure me it was. So I'm eager for history. The Chords' story begins at St Thomas The Apostle, a Catholic school in Peckham, south London where fourth form school friends Billy (from Deptford) and bassist Martin Mason (from Bermondsey) acquire their respective guitar and bass and start jamming together. They formed a three piece in December '77 and practiced on Stones and Who numbers. Chris Pope (from Catford) joined the following month, bringing a host of Tamla covers into their rehearsal repertoire. This is their first ever gigging band, except for Brett (from Orpington, Kent) (Ha — Street Ed) who'd banged out the old jungle riddums with punky no-hopers Meat.

Brett joined on January 15 this year and, after a month of rehearsing, The Chords materialized. Like The Purple Hearts they are both wary and glad of the Mod renewal.

"It is a good thing," Billy says empathetically. "And all the bands are different which is great. At the moment I think there's room for all of us."

Martin suggests that the new Mod movement is coincidental to the band's arrival, but "it has provided us with an audience."

Chris: "Though at the same time we know there's a danger of being pigeon-holed as 'Just a mod band' except we think we're capable of playing well enough and producing singles good enough to last when Mod dies down.

Otherwise we won't deserve to survive."

Many people in the know agree, which is why the agencies are fighting over the band at the moment. As yet though, they remain unaffected by all the attention in a viable 'nice blokes, light-hearted badinage-permeating conversation' type of scenario (Eh? — Ongoing Ed).

And they're still firmly ensconced in unglamorous occupations. Chris, 18, is doing A-levels, old man Brett, 20, is at Roedean, sorry is a store-man in Bromley, Billy, 19, was a draughtsman 'till last week, and Martin, also 19, is on year one of a Law degree.

"We're obviously influenced by punk," says Chris. "We all still like the Clash for example, but we're playing what we want to play."

"Most of the mod bands are punky," Billy says.

More and more Mods drift round the table adding their two pennies worth till acting manager Tony Newman wanders up and throws in a casual "We've been offered another gig — tomorrow night at the Rock Garden. What d'ya reckon?"

"Yeah, I don't mind," Chris smiles.

What's he gonna with his first million, I wonder?

"Buy a parka!" he replies.

What else can a poor boy do? Well, for that money, buy a park, probably. I might even get meself a Zoot suit. With side vents five inches long.

NEWS OF THE WORLD GOSSIP AND LETTERS...

BE THERE OR BE SQUARE: Over 400 mods cammed into Canning Town's Bridge House last Monday for the start of the pub's regular Monday Mod nights. Already it appears hosts of agents and journalists are treating the Bridge as the new Mod Mecca. Meanwhile amongst the crowd were such nouveau mods as Little Roosters' Gary Lammin replete with Who badge and Italian suit. Seems the Roosters have at last found a movement they can identify with "And there won't be no trouble with mods" claimed ex-Cock Sparrer. "Cos we'll be too worried bout keeping our clothes clean to fight." Asked about West Ham's dire performance lat Saturday a spokesman for the Bridge replied something entirely unprintable...

STOP STIRRING - THE MODS ARE ALL RIGHT

I WAS very annoyed by last weeks mods article. I am a MOD and proud of it. I am a mod because I love the music and the clothes, not because I like fighting Rockers, damaging shops and injuring innocent holiday makers. To describe the possibility at Mods versus Rockers battles as a "whole lot of excitment on a few Smith Coast beaches" is totally irresponsible.
Unfortunately words like "fun" and "revenge" have been used by other papers and if much more like this is said the situation will worsen. I don't want to end up in hospital because I happen to like Motown, so please when you write about Mods in future just stick to the music and the clothes, after all that's what it's all about - **TONY Sydenham.**

BEGIN APRIL WITH
THE Purple Hearts

6 TH
TOPALEX
ALEXANDRA ROAD, SOUTHEND.

7 TH   SUPPORTING "THE PRESS"
MOONLIGHT
WEST END LANE, WEST HAMPSTEAD
(WEST HAMP TUBE)

8 TH   SUPPORTING "LEW LEWIS"
MARQUEE
WARDOUR ST, LONDON WI
(TOTTENHAM CT RD)
TUBE

10 TH   SUPPORTING "LEW LEWIS"
NASHVILLE
CROMWELL RD, WEST KENSINGTON
(WEST KENSINGTON)
TUBE

WITH CHUMMY

AS A TEENAGER I FELL IN LOVE WITH THE FASHION AS WELL AS THE LIFESTYLE BUT IT WAS ICONIC BANDS LIKE SECRET AFFAIR THAT WERE THE DRIVING FORCE BEHIND THIS CULTURE AND EVEN NOW 40 YEARS ON, THE ENERGY AND PASSION IS STILL THERE.

Tracey Wilmot

THE JAM / STRANGE TOWN / NEW SINGL

THE CHORDS

AT THE

GREEN MAN

PLUMSTEAD HIGH ST.

FRI 8TH & SAT 9TH

SEPT.

DURING THE MOD REVIVAL LONDON WAS SUCH AN EXCITING TIME & PLACE TO BE GROWING UP. I SPENT FAR TOO MANY EVENINGS AT THE BRIDGE HOUSE OR THE WELLINGTON WATCHING THE PURPLE HEARTS, THE CHORDS & OTHERS WHEN I SHOULD HAVE BEEN DOING HOMEWORK. BUT I WOULDN'T CHANGE A THING

Toni Fox - 78 Mod

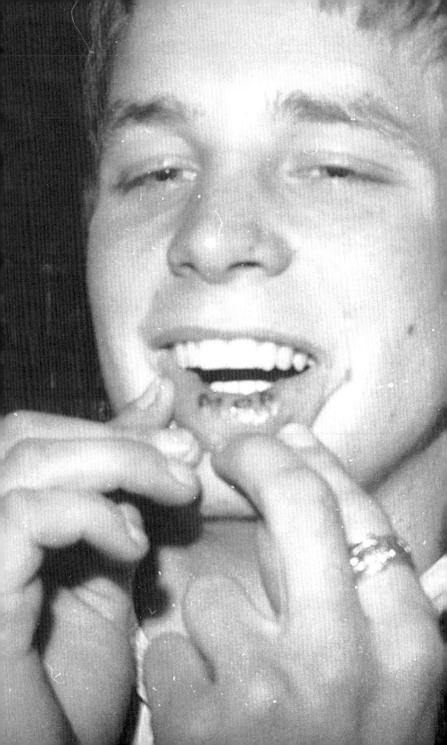

SO COOL

MAY 1979

TIME FOR ACTION?
YEAH IT WAS!

Hoxton Tom McCourt

THE NATION DECIDES

General Election Special May 1979

The UK General Election was held on May 3rd 1979. Ahead of polling day, I was tasked to put together a guide to how various pop and rock herberts intended to vote. As Mods were included, I thought you'd want to see it.

The piece was headlined 'The Nation Decides' – 'a report compiled by Garry 'Trotsky' Bushell, our man in the Tooting Popular Front with the four and a half swing to Lager.'

THE WORLD of politics was shocked to its foundations today following the unveiling of the results of a top secret poll commissioned by Sounds amongst rock musicians. The poll indicated that a staggering 57 per cent of rock 'n' rollers, and an incredible 92.4 per cent of punk rockers will be voting Labour this Thursday.

"Already they're calling the Sounds poll the one that lost Callaghan the election," ashen-faced editor Alan Lewis told a stunned press conference in Covent Garden's exclusive White Lion pub this morning, before revealing the full extent of left-wing infiltration of the modern music scene, evidenced by quotes like:

Joe Strummer, the Clash: "I'll be voting as far to the left as possible. I don't believe in conservatism or Fascism, the Tories are the National Front in suits."

Graeme Douglas, Eddie & The Hot Rods: "I'm voting Labour. Anyone who votes Conservative needs their bloody head examining.

I think I'd become a political assassin if that woman gets in. Actually I saw Jim Callaghan speak at Wandsworth the other day, it was a great gig."

Phil Lynott, Thin Lizzy: "I cannot accept the Conservative Party because of Margaret Thatcher, even though with my new found affluence I might be better off. I'll vote Labour."

Frankie Miller: "Labour. It's the only party for working people. I can never understand anybody in life wanting to give power to a Tory politician."

IN response, the Tories have the support of Lulu, Ken Dodd, Vince Hill, Lynsey 'Rock Bottom' De Paul (who's flown back to Britain just to vote), and the Bee Gees. Maurice Gibb told the national press, "I hope and pray the Tories win and I hope all our fans will vote for them. At the moment with the tax situation as it is, although we are top of the pops we just can't afford to appear over here."

To which Graeme Potter of the slightly less well-known Little Roosters replied "I'm voting Labour to keep the Bee Gees out."

'MONEY IN My Pocket' is the central concern of tax exile Rod Stewart and fellow Tory Dave Greenfield of the Stranglers who said: "No way would I vote Labour. I'm voting Tory because I'm for free enterprise."

Although his other Strangling buddies aren't convinced: Jet Black is voting for the Ecology Party as "the atomic policy of this country is sheer lunacy." Hugh Cornwell announced: "I'm not voting for anybody they're all idiots." And JJ Burnel demonstrated his penetrating grasp of all things political by informing us that it was a secret ballot.

Amazing huh kids, and we always thought they were Trots…

MOST PUNK bands are more uniform in their voting intentions. The Ruts are voting Labour, as are Generation X and the Leyton Buzzards. Mick Mekon was convinced the Mekons and the Gang Of Four are too, explaining "It's quite obviously a wasted vote to vote for anybody else. You've got to vote Labour to stop Thatcher getting in, it's plain and simple."

Maggie comes in for a lot of stick all round, Nicky Tesco describing her as "evil" with the Dark's Phil Manning commenting "It's very obvious that Thatcher is playing a very dangerous, game mopping up votes from people who aren't extreme enough for the Front."

Richard Jobson of the Skids helpfully replied "Don't ask me; ask the Banshees." We tried but they were unobtainable, as were Ian Dury and Paul Weller.

Stiff Little Finger Jake Burns can't vote, but "I'd vote for the Labour party here — you can only vote against people back home. How can anyone vote for Thatcher when she's quoted in the Express today as wanting to bring back hanging for example?"

Surprisingly Doug of the revolutionary socialist punk band Crisis isn't voting at all: "Cos I live in a Tory stronghold so it's not worth it, but if you've got a Socialist Unity or Socialist Workers Party candidate in your area I'd urge people to vote for them or any left-wing candidate."

THE LABOUR vote is even more solid among the bands with large skinhead followings. Jimmy Pursey is voting Labour but also forming his own party "The Hersham Liberation Movement, which would fight for independence for Hersham so outsiders would need passports to get in, and we'd build a cathedral so we could call it a city."

Mensi of the Angelic Upstarts commented: "I'll be voting Labour because if Maggie Thatcher gets in I can't afford to emigrate." A spokesman for the UK Subs said: "If Charlie gets up in time he'll vote Labour. Pete and Paul are socialists and Nick Garrett says fuck off." Nice.

ON THE Mod front, the Chords echo the Labour battle cry, Billy H explaining "We're voting Labour 'cos we're fun loving and love drinking. Maggie Thatcher has no appeal."

Only one of the Purple Hearts is old enough to vote, guitarist Simon Stebbing who indicated he'd be keeping Steve Harley company on the Liberal bandwagon.

Gary Lammin of the Little Roosters commented "Rock 'n' roll is more important than politics but Labour is more important than the Conservatives, and seeing as I've got trouble with me back I'll be voting Labour."

THE FRINGE parties made a last minute burst with Mickey Geggus of the Cockney Rejects voting for the Repatriate Big Chins And Perms Party (which is believed not to be a direct reference to John McGready of the Tickets). Mr McGready himself got even sillier claiming to support Trevor Brooking, apparently standing for the West Ham United Party. And while we're on the subject of silly people, John Otway threw in a last minute Tory vote, saying "I don't like Margaret Thatcher, but the Tories support small businesses and I'm a small business."

Unable to confirm or deny the Village People's transatlantic support for the Liberal Party we move on to the definitive quote of the election from that lovely old lunatic Viv Stanshall, who said: "I'll vote for anybody who's got a silly name. Last time I voted for the Law And Discipline Party who's candidate was Mr A. Stern."

THE MOD REVIVAL

Perhaps Lord Sutch revealed himself to be rock's most on the ball politician when, asked by a journalist why he hadn't explained his policies, the man replied "Don't be a cunt, if I told you everyone would know."

* Despite the best efforts of the pop world, the nation fell dramatically to Mrs. Thatcher's Conservatives. Maggie ousted Labour's Jim Callaghan and was returned with a 43-seat majority after receiving 13,697,923 votes.

THE JAM TODAY

Sheffield. May 4, 1979

"It's just Pop music and that's why I like it. It's all about hooks and guitar riffs. That's what the New Wave is all about..." – Paul Weller

IT'S the first night of The Jam's latest UK tour, and we're relaxing before the show in the hotel bar: me, Weller, the thirsty Foxton, nice-guy Rick Buckler and a few others. Out of habit I ask for the set-list, even though I know all their songs backwards, and Paul takes the trouble to write it out for me in my notebook.

I read it back approvingly. Let's see, there's 'Modern World', 'Strange Town', 'Place I Love', 'London Girl', 'Angels With Dirty Faces', 'Complete Control'....do what?

"Just testing," the allegedly 'intense/moody' Weller laughs, adding a curt "We know you're gonna review it from the bar anyway. All you journalists are the bleedin' same."

Bloody cheek. I'm still thinking about calling my brief when after the show, Foxton ups the ante. "We knew you were at the gig," he says. "Because we saw your chin hanging down over the balcony like a net curtain..."

Now this is not the first reference to my alleged "double chin" that I will endure this trip from the little rat-faced bastard, nor sadly the last. Foxton (aka the face that launched a thousand horror films) has spent most of the coach ride and pre-gig imbibing muttering such pleasantries as "Fat chops!", and "Whatever you do don't mention the chin."

Bruce reckons I have more chins than a Hong Kong phone directory, and that my favourite tipple is double chin and tonic.

Some might suggest that this disgraceful tirade indicates a deep degree of self-loathing on the part of the Muppet-brained bass player. I'll merely let slip that the Sheffield University security men didn't have a clue who the fox Bruce was and refused to let him back-stage from the bar before the show, leaving him hanging about panicking like a slightly pissed plum...Karma, baby.

The Jam are good tonight. They're hot, in fact. So hot you can see the sweat dripping from Paul's fingers as he smashes and slashes at his Rickenbacker. They've got it all, this band: passion, a look and a unique sound. The Jam deal in terrific high energy songs with hooks and intelligence; his tunes and his words are worth hearing...

Off-stage, Paul Weller lives and breathes music. He sees what the band do as "pop music – that's all new wave is, Today's Pop Music for Today's Kids."

Meeting the coach at Staples Corner, I sit at the back with the sharp-dressed son of Surrey and his girlfriend Gill. I'm surprised to find that he doesn't share my glee at this morning news of that nice Mrs. Thatcher's election (Note to readers: kids, this is satire).

"How could a working class person vote Conservative?" he asks with genuine astonishment.

Eh, didn't Weller tell the NME he was voting Tory? Well, yeah, but that was "a private joke to wind up the Clash," he says.

"Thatcher made me laugh when she said she was a self-made woman," he fumes. "Of course she was - she had mummy and daddy's self-made money behind her." (In fairness, Maggie's Dad Alf Roberts was a greengrocer, not exactly a Rothschild).

"Try telling the girl behind the counter at Woolworth's she can be prime minister. 'Sorry dear, no qualifications. Can I interest you in a new car or an electric toaster?'"

It crosses my mind that the girl behind the counter at Woolies could always go to night school and get some qualifications if she were that bothered, and what the hell is wrong with toasters anyway? But Paul has already moved on to the subject of self-styled rock 'n' roll messiahs – he remains as distrustful of musicians with more good causes than good songs as he is of the notion that giving someone a guitar automatically gives them insight into current affairs and world politics...

JAM PACT

SPRING TOUR 1979

OFFICIAL BOOKLET

Coventry, 1978
Pic: Denis O'Regan

Tour Dates

4th May, 1979	SHEFFIELD	University
5th	SHEFFIELD	University
6th	NEWCASTLE	City Hall
8th	SALFORD	University
10th	LONDON	Rainbow
11th	LONDON	Rainbow
12th	LOUGHBOROUGH	Auditorium
14th	EXETER	University
15th	LIVERPOOL	University
16th	LIVERPOOL	University
18th	GLASGOW	Strathclyde University
19th	GLASGOW	Strathclyde University
21st	BRISTOL	Coulston Hall
22nd	BIRMINGHAM	Odeon
24th	PORTSMOUTH	Guildhall

THE MOD REVIVAL

The son of a builder and a cleaner, he was born in Sheerwater, near Woking in Surrey and grew up as John William Weller, acquiring the Paul along the way as a tribute to McCartney. At school (Sheerwater County Secondary) he was a Beatles obsessive.

But being out in the sticks, he never went to concerts. The first time he ever stepped foot in the Marquee was when the Jam played there. He's never seen the Who, and doesn't like anything they've done for years. But boy his eyes light up when the subject gets round to Motown, Stax, Otis Redding, Wilson Pickett, the Monkees, and sixties beat group, the Creation. There's a lot of solid Mod in Paul's record collection.

What's it like to be the daddy of a movement? I ask.

"Don't blame me," he laughs, but secretly he's chuffed, openly enthusing about the Chords, the one Mod band he's seen so far. He shows a lot of interest in what's happening at the grass roots and pumps me for info.

"The spirit seems good at the moment," he says."But I don't think the unity will last. Same as punk, once the record companies get involved and they're all competing then no-one will speak to one another.

"The general consensus is that it will be dead by August. I'll still be wearing me mohair suit in ten years time."

Paul Weller spends most of his money now on clothes, records and booze – just like he's always done.

THE New Mods' admiration for The Jam continues unabated, which is why about thirty faces from the East End (and Lou from the Elephant) have trekked up here to Yorkshire, where the M1 is cobbled, to see them play tonight. The plan is to pull local girls or sleep rough in cars, but many of them end up sneaking past the night porter into our hotel and blagging empty rooms.

It's quite fitting that this new movement has coincided with the Jam's rise from the doldrums of last summer to new artistic peaks.

'All Mod Cons', the Jam's last album, came out in November. I thought it was remarkable then and it's continued to grow in my affections ever since. In retrospect it was the album of 1978, no contest. 'Strange Town' /'Butterfly Collector' – the double-barrelled last single – hit the same creative high and was the band's biggest seller since 'In The City'.

"'Butterfly Collector' was about an actual person," Weller confides (suggestions on a postcard please). "Whereas 'Strange Town' is more of a flow of ideas, it's a free form poem, and it combines a lot of ideas. Like there's the UFO theme, and there are lines like 'You're betrayed by your accent and manners'. I used to think class war was a myth but you find whatever you do, the way you talk and the way you are marks you out."

It's going to be difficult to follow 'All Mod Cons', I suggest.

"Yeah, which is why we're not going to try," he parries. "We hope to get an album out by the Winter. I think it'll be a lot simpler than 'All Mod Cons' and that's all I can say. I've got a few ideas for songs but we haven't had a chance to write on the road."

The Jam have been on the road for longer than tarmac, following November's mega UK tour with Germany and France in February and March, and the States and Canada last month.

"America was great," Paul enthuses. "Especially LA where we got really excited and the audience smashed up the seats and threw them on stage. It was a real electric feel and the kids were great. People were coming five or six hundred miles to see us. Great!"

They had just eight days off before they were off on sixteen British dates. They haven't even had time to rehearse for tonight...

Battling through the complexities of Sheffield Uni and local accents ("Eee, trouble at t'gig") we eventually locate the venue. Hammersmith Odeon it ain't.

"Jesus, the stage is bigger than the hall," Paul notes. Bruce channels the spirit of Python to declare: "Eee, it's like a shoebox in t'middle of t'road."

Still, it holds 1500 people, we're assured, so, sound checks done we head to the hotel to watch Mork from Ork cavort and sink a few Forsyte Sagas. The early evening rapidly degenerates. Bruce throws ham rolls at me, I throw ham rolls back. Rick throws ham rolls at my snapper side-kick Virginia Turbett. (Odd, bands normally offer her sausage).

Then Bruce brings up the chin again, I challenge him to come clean about his dubious sex life.

"Pass me another bum, this one's got a crack in it," announces Paul, in keeping with his entirely serious sage-like image, which puts an end to it all.

Weller is actually nervous about the show, and throws up. Although he might just have been looking at Bruce for too long...

Paul's dad, the band's manager John is a revelation. He's grafted all of his life and is a proper Londoner. He's a portly fella with a mess of silver hair and a voice like Mike Reid – the Cockney comic not the DJ. Nice bloke too.

WE head back to the gig in good spirit. I hang out with the London boys while the band get changed and listen to Paul's personally compiled warm-up tape of classics: 'Long Shot Kick De Bucket', 'Reggae In My Jeggae'...heaven. This kills a bit of time before the three of them catapult on stage and Weller hollers: "This is the modern world!" – pronounced "wowld". And we're off.

I'm up in t'balcony overlooking the front of the audience who go seriously barmy from the first power chord. And I'm torn between the triangle on stage and the crazy crushed crowd below me, a hot and squelching human sea pushed and shoved wildly to the left and right.

Inevitably the stage wins out. Paul stands be-suited legs apart, slightly stooped over his creamy Rickenbacker. He looks like an angry stork. Bruce slugs away on his black bass, his face getting redder like he's about to spontaneously combust; while Rick's dead centre in a shirt and tie beating away seemingly oblivious to the heat: the three forces merging in a mighty geometric explosion of perfect punk/pop/modern r'n'r...call them what you will, I think they're sensational, the next great roll of the rock anthem dice. Intelligent. Musical. Looking backwards and forward at the same time, like Janus. This ain't Pop, it's Super Pop. And from where I'm standing there's not an ounce of Kryptonite in sight.

FOR fifteen blistering numbers the crowd dance, pogo, crush each other, faint and punch fists and fingers at the stage. Some of the London Mods stumble out exhausted muttering "not as tight as Paris" and "the audience is wrong" but no-one else is complaining.

'Mr Clean' is an early high, powerful and accusatory, losing none of its intensity on stage. When Paul sings the chorus, the audience nearly drown him out: 'Cos I hate you and I hate your wife/And if I get a chance I'LL FUCK UP YOUR LIFE, Mr Clean!' Is that seen?

'Butterfly Collector' is a brave live choice, handled exquisitely, with Weller standing alone in the spotlight for the verses with the audience slowly clapping in time. Then there's 'Away From The Numbers', 'Strange Town', 'A-Bomb', 'Tube Station' – fistfuls of modern classics.

The NME's Ian Penman recently accused The Jam of "writing singles for a mythical juke-box" – as if the very act of penning songs people might enjoy is a crime against artistic integrity.

Well, I've got news for you, pal: there's nothing mythical about the juke-boxes you'll find the Jam on these days.

THE distant echo of far-away voices playing far-away games...

Penman and his ilk wind me up like the proverbial clockwork orange. Who would have thought that a rock 'n' roll music for fun and against privilege would have spawned the self-indulgent, insular mind games that occupy today's music writers and 'genuine new wave musicians' – the cold and uninvitingly pompous twats with all the answers in formulas we're not smart enough to understand.

Smug, self-satisfied condescending snobs look down on you, your tastes, the bands you like, the records you buy... They think they're better than you, but they never soil their hands, never make a stand on anything tangible. They never do anything worth doing in their entire miserable existence.

Yet despite them, laughing at them, the late seventies revel in glorious popular music, and carving their name in big bold letters at the very top of the tree are the Jam, with battered penknives, Johnson and Johnson blazers and a dazzling array of musical wares.

The Jam: marrying refreshing rock insights and bitter-sweet sensitivity.

The Jam: music for the modern world from a band who've learned to live by hate and pain.

The Jam are NOW!

And of course no-one lets them get away without encores. 'Heatwave', 'Standards', 'Bricks & Mortar', 'The Batman Theme', 'David Watts' with the audience bellowing "be loik" and mouthing "Watts" but thinking Weller, Foxton, Buckler. Well maybe not Foxton.

Then the lights go up and they snake out slowly into the cold night until everyone's gone, even the band, except for me, sitting in the bar with my set-list, patiently waiting for 'Angels With Dirty Faces' and 'Complete Control'...

PS. Mr Paul Weller is 21 on May 25.

Historical footnote: the first time I saw The Jam was on April 17th, 1977, at the Roundhouse, opening for the Stranglers. A month later I caught them again at the Rainbow in Finsbury Park, supporting The Clash (9th May), with the Buzzcocks, Subway Sect and the Prefects. This was exactly how my review of their gig that night appeared in my zine, Napalm:

Everyone is standing for the Clash. Down the front they haven't got a choice – they've ripped up all the seats! It's been one of those nights.

The Jam get better every time I see them. They grab the crowd from the minute they come on stage. They're as tight as a Vulcan death grip, and they're sharp and different too. They've got songs, hooks, energy and Paul Weller is playing a Rickenbacker as smart and red as any Joe Strummer lyric.

CITY HALL
Northumberland Road, Newcastle upon Tyne 1

Sunday, 6th May, 1979, at 7.30 p.m.

MEL BUSH

presents

THE JAM

AREA £3.00   SEAT   N 31

Booking Agents City Hall Box Office
Northumberland Road, Newcastle upon Tyne (Tel 20007)
This Portion to be retained.

SMITH PRINT GROUP

Their best tunes are the single 'In The City', 'Away From The Numbers' and 'Art School', two of which are mini-anthems. Weller wants to say, he wants to tell us, about "the young idea..." he doesn't say what it is but I'm happy to settle for what the Jam do deliver: energy, harmonies and suits.

My only moan is they also trample old soul songs to death, but give 'em time. Their set is young and so are they.

SECRET AFFAIR & THE CHORDS

Bridgehouse, Canning Town. May 5, 1979

Monday night is Mod night at the Bridge, tonight's 400 plus audience made sure of that. Teenagers from as far away as Brighton and Southend pack through the doors to rub shoulders with the Purple Hearts who are right in front of the stage to see The Chords.

They could be construed as 'rivals', except thankfully no-one thinks like that; there's still a sense of unity, and urgency, in this rapidly growing scene. It's still fun...

The Chords are winners. They're fighting to be heard and the hunger burns in their eyes, specially tonight up against a sound quality sabotaged by the man on the mixing desk who had sodded off to look for a bass amp for headliners Secret Affair (Secret Affair apologized later). It left the South London band struggling, with the vocals drowned out, but still they re-convinced me that they're heading places.

Like The Purple Hearts, The Chords will be hailed as spokesmen by 'the Mod on the street', whereas Secret Affair will, I predict, be the first of the new Mod bands to cross over to wider markets.

They're four-strong, all veterans of less distinguished outfits: Ian Paine (vocals, trumpet) and Dave Cairns (guitar) are ex-New Hearts,

BRIDGE HOUSE 23 BARKING ROAD CANNING TOWN, E.16

Thurs. 12th	**REBEL** First single out now on Bridge House Records. First 100 people get a **FREE** copy	
Fri. 13th	**WARM JETS** plus PROTEX	40p
Sat. 14th	**JACKIE LYNTON'S**	50p
Sun. 15th	**H.D. BAND** Latest album out now	50p
Mod's Monday	**R.D.B.** plus RARE BREED	50p
	SECRET AFFAIR	40p
Tues. 17th	plus **THE CHORDS**	50p
Wed. 18th	**KENNY** They're back but better. more hit numbers	50p
	THE TICKETS plus DARREN'S DEAD FLOWERS	50p
		40p

Denis Smith (bass) is ex-Advertising, and Seb Shelton (drums) is a former Young Buck playing his first gig with the band tonight. The original line-up made their first public appearance supporting The Jam at Reading University last November.

Less one dimensional, less obviously post-punk, and much poppier and soulful than their contemporaries, they're tourniquet tight and confidently work through a 14 strong set including two choice Tamla covers: Smokey Robinson & The Miracles' 'Going To A Go Go' (from 1965, fact lovers) and a magnifique rendition of the Temptation's hit 'Get Ready' (actually written by Smokey).

Ian is a powerful, self-assured vocalist, punching his fist into the air to emphasize the songs' concerns: 'These days of change are here to stay', 'We're the glory boys, so scared of getting old, 'This is my world today'. 'It's time for a little more style'.

Concerns put over in a remarkably varied set, power packed with hook-laden potential singles and a strong Sixties feel that never sounds dated. 'Time For Change', 'Let Your Heart Dance' (introduced with an emphatic "Jungle rhythms — YEAH"), 'Time For A New Dance', these songs are as vital and absurdly catchy as the titles suggest. Competent, commercial, convincingly exciting…aw, this new energy, c'est si bon!

Secret Affair will not be playing in pubs for long. I'd wager me dad's lambretta badge on it.

IF ANYTHING IT WAS A MOVEMENT AND
MORE TO DO WITH THE PEOPLE THAN
THE BANDS... A REVIVAL OF THE FASHION
AND THE CULTURE. I THINK IT WAS A BIT
MORE PEOPLE POWERED THAN BAND
POWERED.

Ian Page

SPEED THRILLS: MAXIMUM SPEED

North London. Interview May 1979

T hose of us not bedogged by blind prejudice and who actually go to gigs without cotton wool in our ears have found much casual delight in the latest 'street' movement, the current and still expanding Mod Renewal.

Not only because of some superb music, smashing fashions, and general low level of violence and moronic gormlessness, but also because of the whole ampthetamine-rush of excitement surrounding the movement's growth from humble dives in East and North London to current festival status. And the magazine that has provided the most stimulating and thorough coverage of the whole kit and kaboodle has been the very first modzine Maximum Speed from the barren reachs of North London.

The men responsible are Clive Reams (21, a trainee manager in William Hills) Goffa Gladding (21, a civil servant - a Mod in the MoD) and Kim Gault who's also 21 and on the dole. This industrious trio also manage Mod band Back To Zero and promote gigs, so virtually all their spare time is devoted to Mod.

THE MOD REVIVAL

They had the idea for the 'zine back in January when BTZ were moaning about getting no publicity, though funnily enough the first issue - which was rush-written mostly by Clive - featured only the Chords, The Purple Hearts and Fixations. They printed and sold 45 copies of it for a mere 'four shillings.' Already they're getting offered fivers for first editions.

Since then the mag has become fortnightly and its print orders have risen steadily to 1,000 for issue five. Up to now Speed has covered most of the major new Mod bands, all the Mod events in South East England, as well as featuring lotsa stuff about scooter rallies, Sixties soul and many a live review, always with a high standard of writing (albeit with a cotton wool approach to criticism), a pinch of panache and a genuine affectin for the movement.

The current issue (5) is the best to date featuring interviewss with Paul Weller, Billy H and Speedball and lots more besides. "We handle everything, all the writing and financing," Clive says. "In fact all the losses we make on gigs we cover from the magazine."

"And we love it," Goffa enthuses. "Putting on gigs can be a hassle but the mag is sheer enjoyment."

How d'you reckon Mod is going to go?

Clive: "Well Secret Affair are gonna be massive and the whole thing is still growing like mad obviously."

Goffa: "A lot of people at the moment would like to see it stay as it is."

Clive: "Obviously we'd like to see it grow but a lot of people are getting disillusioned already...and you get these people who think all there is to it is chucking on a parka...But it's got to be massive by August Bank Holiday. Youth movements always grow when there's no football. And then it'll get another boost when Quadrophenia comes out."

So there'll be trouble down at Southend then?

Clive: "I think so. There'll be some trouble with Mods and rockers. But in general it's been pretty peaceable, Mods and skins get on really well. Look at the Bridge House. People are really into the music and the fashion. One think I do wanna say though and although Goffa and me disagree whether Mod would have happened without Punk all of us agree that it would have happened without Quadrophenia..."

Maximum Speed is available from 40, Sidlaw House, Portland Avenue, Stamford Hill, London N16. Send blank postal orders for 20p and a large SAE.

NEWS OF THE WORLD
___ ___
GOSSIP AND LETTERS...

It's a hard life in the Mod Army: **Basildon Mods Sta-Prest**
are finding being part of the Mod Revival ain't all instant
acclaim after all.

Booked for a gig at a pub in Hornchurch (known mostly
for its strippers) by the landlady, they were interrupted
after four numbers by the landlord, oblivious to the
presene of some twenty merry mos, who claimed that no
one in the pub wanted to hear this sort of music. Obviously
a democrat he conducted a straw poll of pub regulars and
when the result wasn't the overwhelming 'Get Em Off' he'd
anticipated he approached the band with a gruff "Well,
can't you play 'Johnny B Good!?"

DAYS OF CHANGE

JUNE - JULY 1979

NEVER MIND '79 & QUADROPHENIA...
'78 CHANGED EVERYTHING, THE JAM
AT THE GREAT BRITISH MUSIC FESTIVAL
AT WEMBLEY (& AT READING FESTIVAL),
THE WHO EXHIBITION AT THE ICA &
GIGS IN BRIGHTON BY THE TEENBEATS &
FORGOTTEN LOCAL HEROES, CHICANE!

Ian Bryden - South Coast Mod '78

SECRET AFFAIR: MODS WITHOUT PARKAS

June 9, 1979

LEGS astride, but immaculately trousered, Ian Page punches the air and sings. Yeah, sings. No need to shout when you've got a nifty, nasal whine of a voice as confident and full-throated as this skinny, well-tailored eighteen-year-old.

Page sounds like a reincarnation of minor sixties star Jess Roden, but dresses much better. And his belief in his band and his message burns like the Olympic flame…

The band is Secret Affair, the message is Mod and the medium is a set packed to bursting point with heart-felt, sing-along anthems. Page's lyrics are steeped in ambition, bravado and enough self-belief to overcome the pain of rejection.

THE MOD REVIVAL

'See us roaming these London streets / Feel those last year stares look down on old fashioned feet / Cos we're the Glory Boys — so scared of getting old / Yeah, we're the Glory Boys — we may look cold, but our hearts are gold...'

There are four Glory Boys on stage tonight, but vocalist Page in his sharp two tone teenage blue whistle is the visual mainspring. He's dancing Jack Flash, pills almost audibly rattling round his tin-ribs as he lives through the twelve numbers and then feeds off of the encores this modest but appreciative Watford crowd demand.

This band get encores as naturally as hot Saturday nights grouse and grizzle into grim Sunday mornings, and you don't need to be Bamber Gasgoigne to work out the whys and wherefores of that particular truth.

Like the Specials, Secret Affair are a dance band rooted in sixties music but whereas the Specials are firmly grounded in Bluebeat, the Affair take their base from the glorious early sixties sound of soul, the big wheels of Tamla Motown, the greatest pop catalogue ever written and, like Ska, the original soundtrack to the glorious 1960s Mod subculture. It's music you can dance to which still has a bit of what music experts call bollocks, a slice of aggression served with melody and a bucket-load of commitment.

Contrary to their plans, and almost against their will, Secret Affair find themselves as leading lights in the current Mod Renewal; but they're also much more than that, much broader musically, and many miles from any post-punk connotations. The noted mod fanzine Maximum Speed called them a 'new wave soul band' which I reckon hits the nail bang on.

They will also be the first band to transcend the movement.

I say this firstly because as well as being as tight as a duck's arse in a tracting universe, they also write songs possessed of that sort of instantly memorable irrepressible hook-line that can cause acute embarrassment on the morning after the gig before when you find yourself singing them out loud on the 9.05am Kidbrook to Charing Cross choo-choo.

SO far, in under five gigging months Secret Affair have built up a solidly loyal street following. They regularly pack out the Marquee and have generated a buzz, spelt BUZZZZZZZZ, so loud round the West End agencies and A&R departments that it all but deafens innocent bystanders and causes great distress to footloose and fancy free flea-bitten mongrels for miles around.

How big is this buzz? Imagine a battalion of Brobdingnag bees confined in a giant up-turned jam-jar and then magnify it twenty times. This band is hot.

Yet six months ago most 'informed commentators' would have confined Ian Page and guitarist Dave Cairns to the elephant's graveyard of failed music biz hopefuls, and daubed the word 'Hubris' on their tomb.

The two young men who craft Secret Affair's songs were formerly the backbone of the New Hearts, all round flopperoonies who floundered in the power-pop plague and played their last ever gig at Reading Festival last year. They'd signed to CBS in '77 and finally got out of the contract last month (the retainers stopped four months ago, they've lived on savings and intermittent gig income ever since).

The pressures, false promises, phoney friendship and the frustrating hollowness they experienced at the hands of the Biz have made them cynical and bitter.

"So," explains Ian. "When we decided to form Secret Affair, we put an advert in the music press small ads: 'Drummer and Bassist' wanted —must have a grudge against the business.'"

This attracted Dennis Smith, formerly of Advertising, on bass and Chris Bennett on drums. They spent the second half of last year writing their set and played their debut gig at the Jam's secret Reading University do at the beginning of this year. But the band weren't entirely happy with Bennett and finally managed to lure Seb Shelton away from the Young Bucks in April to replace him.

Both Dave and Ian are extremely articulate, Ian firing words out like an out of control Gatling gun. Before the gig, in the dressing room with the Purple Hearts, he's completely unmanageable, playing the Coronation Street theme on his trumpet and living out strange delusions of grandeur: "I am a Hamburger", "I am a dressing room" und so weiter. You are unhinged, pal.

"It's worth playing with Secret Affair just to watch Ian going through his tantrums," opines Purple Hearts singer Rob Manton.

True enough, but it's not exactly the best environment for in-depth interviews. So I drag the Hamburger and Dave Cairns out to the car park where in true British barbecue tradition we shelter from the teaming rain in a quiet Volvo backseat and-get down to business...

"WE CHOSE the name, Secret Affair" Ian explains, "because we all had a real no-bullshit attitude to what we were going to do. We weren't going to let anybody get their hooks in to us, y'know? It was the old cliché, if it works or if it falls to pieces we've done it our way. We've done exactly what we've wanted to do with no compromises — we don't need them bastards. If anybody was interested they're quite welcome to come along but then they'd be in on the secret."

Terry Draper for Engin-Ear Productions Ltd presents **MODS** Every Monday night 8.30 pm—3 am
MONDAY JULY 16th
SECRET AFFAIR
+ BACK TO ZERO + THE LITTLE ROOSTERS
+ D.J. Jerry Floyd
Licensed Bars and Food till 3 am
All bookings via Will Sproule of Ronnie Scott Directions, 01-439 7791
Admission £1.50

East End Mods, many of them ex-skinheads, started getting in on the secret early on. "We really didn't know Mod was going on," Ian is at pains to explain. "Our original idea was to have this group of kids called Glory Boys, a new kind of kid walking up and down Wardour Street taking the place over.

"And what they were, was kids with suss - they knew about the inside of the music business which made them cynics, but it was because they knew so much that they could be optimistic. That's why they could, change things.

"The original idea was that we'd go out and do so well live that we'd build up a really big following, so we literally had to be signed up — like the Banshees. But the Mod thing crept up on us...

"It's funny 'cos the New Hearts had always been very strictly a sixties based band, the clothes as well. I used to wear a red suit — that was a big mod thing — Dave used to wear ties and button-downs, all the band used to wear striped blazers but we never used to say we were Mod because we weren't conscious of that.

"Us and the Jam were the only two bands at the time who looked smart and interestingly enough when we first toured with them in '77 the papers called it 'The March Of the Mods'.

"When our second single came out one reviewer said 'This lot sound as if they could be riding Vespas and wearing parkas!'."

Yeah, but you were never that good were you? I say, playing devil's advocate. That's why so many people are now asking how come this ropey old power-pop outfit has spawned a band like you.

Not for one moment does Dave Cairns look like he might chin me for my cheek. Instead he simply acknowledges the point and says: "It was lack of musicianship in a lot of ways. The ideas we had were like high energy and very sixties but there was no dance beat. Nobody could dance to the New Hearts — it was bad musicianship in the rhythm section. That's why we've got these guys in.

"Our lyrics have changed too — it's just the way we've grown up over the last two years, but a lot of the ideas are the same; the frustrations are still the same."

"Except now we've got more suss," says an animated Ian – 'suss' is one of his favourite words. "We won't get fooled again."

How do you feel about this 'new wave soul' tag you've been given?

"It's okay in terms of old soul," Ian replies. "See if there was a formula to what we do, it would be, like, you listen to any old Tamla Motown track and if you take out the bass and drums and the feel of the bass-and drums, then add an angry powerful guitar and lyrics that apply to today instead of a silly love song then that is us, that is our sound.

"The bass and drums provide the dance, the guitar provides the energy and the lyrics provide the thought."

Dave goes on: "A guy from Maximum Speed said on London Weekend telly, what's happening isn't just a mod revival, the kids are starting to dress smart and get into music that isn't disco but is danceable — that's what we're about. I hate the Mod tag, I can see it all going sour as the press and the promoters move in, but the thing that will stay alive is that the kids are into dressing up and dancing."

Ian: "We hate the interpretation everyone else puts on mod. Yes we are mod but that's completely different from calling something else punk or heavy rock. Mod is a way of thinking, whatever the year, whatever the situation, whatever the music. It's a different approach to what else is happening at the time. That's what mod did then, that's what we're doing now. We're mods without parkas."

Got it, and thank you for the headline.

HISTORY lesson time. The New Hearts developed out of the pair's earlier college band, Splitz Kidz, who had met at Loughton College in Essex. They were seventeen when they got signed by CBS – two months after their first gig. Kids caught up in a manufactured hype. They were young, naive and understandably pissed off when Powerpop was shot-down by the music press and turned on by the punks. Joe Strummer dismissed the Powerpop bands in 'White Man In Hammersmith Palais': 'You've got Burton suits, ha, you think it's funny, turning rebellion into money...'

The New Hearts never 'got' the politics. They'd seen themselves as being in the mould of the Hot Rods and Dr. Feelgood. Their two singles, '(Just Another) Teenage Anthem' and 'Plain Jane' failed to bother the charts.

Walthamstow-born Cairns, now 20, is the son of an Epping Forest GP who learned the guitar after seeing The Who play Charlton Athletic's ground The Valley (Floyd Road) in 1976.

He was sixteen when he formed the New Hearts with Ian Page (real name Paine), who'd grown up listening to his older brother's Motown collection.

"It wasn't a very good band," Ian acknowledges. "But I did learn a lot of things during the New Hearts period. What we were doing was learning the craft of the three-minute pop song."

Their bitterness about the backlash that helped crush their first band translates in the lyrics of 'Time For Action'; a song written entirely by Dave, including the controversial line 'We hate the punk elite.'

"That refers to the tinsel-and-tat merchants," Ian Page explains. "The mob that made punk just another record industry movement and killed the spirit dead.

"The best thing about punk to me was the message – the idea of breaking away from the industry, but of course for all the anti-establishment talk they didn't actually do it. The Clash signed to CBS, the same as we did."

Is Mod just a handy bandwagon for you?

Ian: "We never refer to ourselves as Mod."

Dave: "What a lot of people are missing is the smartness. People seem to think that being Mod means wearing a parka with a Who sticker, over an old 'Target' t-shirt and looking scruffy. THAT ISN'T MOD. Mod was fashion and the Who came fucking years later. Fashion!"

Ian: "And that isn't 'sheep-like', it's the opposite. It's people shouting out for themselves and trying to make themselves as individual as possible — you get a basic idea of what Mod looks like and the whole idea is to look as different from the rest as possible within that framework..."

Dave: "And our kids care about their clothes. If you come to our gigs, the kids are all in smart suits and the only ones who turn up in parkas have got scooters outside. Our kids are into fashion. They go out every week looking for clothes and they're into go-go not pogo and that is what we're about."

Another potential headline.

When the East End Glory Boys latched on to Secret Affair they invited Page down to the Barge Aground in Barking. "I was blown away by it," he recalls. "The place was a sea of suits, and parkas, and good haircuts. It wasn't how I'd envisaged the Glory Boy look. I'd seen it more as spiv-like: suits, black shirts, white ties. But these kids were Glory Boys, they were sharp and they were sussed. And the look they'd chosen for themselves was Mod."

Most of them were working class ex-punks and ex-skinheads who had become disillusioned with the movements they had been part of.

Secret Affair flourished on the East London Mod circuit, playing venues like the Bridge House in Canning Town. They weren't the only band on the block, but they were the only ones you could dance to – Page's manifesto being to "take the disco out of dance music." And it's working. Their following is growing; the industry that kicked them out is now sniffing around them like a bloodhound on the trail of a killer in Winalot pants.

And if the message still hasn't sunk in, chew on some lyrics:

'Because these days of change will stay, remain / And the need for change don't need a new wave...' (Days Of Change)

'This is my world today / My world you're livin' in everyday / And this is my world today / And I couldn't have it any other way in my world' (My World)

And best of all: 'Standing in the shadows, where the in-crowd meet / We're all dressed up for the evening / We hate the punk elite / So take me to your leader / Because it's time you realised / That this is the time / This is the time for action / Time to be seen...' (Time For Action)

Speaking personally, I'm rather fond of the punk elite, but I won't disagree that this is indeed the time for action, and in the words of another SA song, the time for a new dance.

Watch them deliver it.

Watch out boys, your secret life's no secret any more.

PURPLE HEARTS

Watford. June 1979

Where was the engine driver when the boiler burst? The last great live music explosion has splintered into various teenage wastelands of late, and while scribblers hunt down half-cocked Holy Grails of their own, punk goes underground and Mod, the latest kids' movement, gets "the treatment" ((c) MFC) from the leeches and the mass media surgeons eager to corrupt and expose.

And I don't wanna hear no hippy boring me shitless, and I don't wanna go down the disco, and I don't wanna read about "anti-rock". No I don't wanna...

Down at the roots the beat goes on, and as Costello almost sang I would rather hang around there than anywhere else today...

The Purple Hearts are a good late Seventies rock band - too slow to be punk - and getting better every time I feast me peeps on them. A youth club band with good songs? A band with potential for sure.

The Hearts songs have a maturity now that augers well for the future of their particular brand of dance music: 'Frustration', 'Beat That' and 'Jimmy' are tried and trusted showcases for the group's basic strengths: Manton's cocky stage presence and powerful Essex vocals and Simon Stebbing's proficient guitar work.

'Millions Like Us' is the latest number in the set, inspried or at least set off by 'Questions and Answers: 'Millions like us, oh yes there's millions like us, with tunnel vision, making indecisions'. A raunchy, chugging rabble-rousing anthem with a mighty riff that gets under your skin like a tattooist's needle.

This bands are 100 times more relevant and exciting than 1,000 Robert Rentals. My only lingering question about the Purple Hearts is will they have to start making the pills again to tie in with the fashion?

More to the point will they have to bring back the Vietnam War? I can't tell you. I've got tunnel vision from making indecisions.

MONDAY MONDAY

The Bridge House. Canning Town. June 1979

I'm not exactly sure when Mod actually began again, but the first geezer I knew to consciously call himself a Mod was Grant Fleming and Grant would hang about the Bridge House in his parka in the spring of '78 with everyone taking the piss out of him because of it.

Of course skins were big then but a few months later I saw the Purple Hearts and just got to thinking how Mod could easily come back HUGE (Sounds 21/10/78) when a lot of the older Bridge House punters started talking about it too.

By February, when the Bridge put the Purple Hearts on you couldn't move for the parkas and Jam paraphenalia that marked the original '79 Mod wave. At the same time Mods were springing up in parts of North London, South London and on the South coast. But it was the Bridge that provided the first focal point for the movement when it began its regular Mod nights in April this year.

"It was by accident really," Terry Murphy, the Bridge's burly guv'nor explains. "Secret Affair turned up all suits and ties and looking tidy to play me their tape and I realised they were a Mod band, a good Mod band, and so I just wrote up 'Mod Night' on the posters."

And thus started Mod Monday, which has brought the Bridge a crowd of around 400 a week ever since, and a new problem - scores of underage mini-Mods who have to be turned away every week.

Although the pub has long put punk bands on (Sham, the Damned, the Cockney Rejects) they seem to have taken to Mod with much more ease and enthusiasm. It wasn't long before every Mod band of any repute had played there.

THE MOD REVIVAL

With mounting local and media interest it was only a matter of time until the idea of documenting Mod nights with a live album became a reality. 'Mod May Day '79' is released in two weeks.

Terry Murphy, a genial retired boxer, took over tenancy of the olde worlde flavoured pub in 1975 and immediately revived it as a live music venue. Aside from the odd big name secret gig (Marriott, Gallagher, Sham etc) much of the music was provided by heavy rock and boogie bands like Remus Down Boulevard, Crawler and Gerry McAvoy Jam. Unfashionable but lucrative.

When the pub began its reord label last year with the 'Week At The Bridge' album it was the boogie bands who featured. And that album steadily sold 3,000 copies (with 2,000 just being snapped up by Ariola Germany) so the label tentatively branded out into the singles market and are currently looking for a distribution deal.

Slowly through '78 to the present the pub has succumbed to demands from younger clientele and now you're just as likely to come across the Corvettes or Secret Affair as you are RDB.

If you go, that is, because for some reason a lot of people who don't go think of the Bridge as a violent pub.

But as Terry's son Glen, an amateur middle-weight boxer who handles the day to day running of the pub puts it: "It's not 1935 anymore. Okay it had a bad name before the war with the seamen coming in, but now you never get trouble. It's just a good atmosphere."

Maybe when Newham Council finally open the promised Canning Town tube station the pub will start getting the press attention it deserves.

VARIOUS ARTISTS: A TONIC FOR THE SUITS

Mods May Day '79 Bridge House BHLP. July 7, 1979

IT'S easy to hate an enemy you've never met. One reason the music press is so down on Mod is that they know sod-all about it. To them it's just a bunch of daft kids playing back-to-the-Sixties games.

I mean how many people have you heard slag off Mod and then, when pressed, admit "I haven't actually seen any of the bands, but I hate revivals"?

The real point is, what's going on isn't so much a revival as a renewal. It's not about trying to recreate a semi-mythical Mod past, rather, it's about taking the best of those former glories as a basis to build something new on.

Tonics, Sta Prest and the like are smart, of course, but this new Mod thing is more than just fashion. The music is generally of a high standard, but it's more than just that too. Mod is a feeling, a whole mood. A youth explosion. A teenage creation. It wasn't the brainstorm of some industry whizz kid, like Power-Pop was meant to be. Mod really did begin in places like the Bridge House, and it really was started by kids - some ex-skins, some ex-punks, some Sham fans, some Jam fans - creating a movement for themselves, by themselves. And having FUN.

This album recorded at the Bridge last May Day is a gem because it actually conveys the spirit and the atmosphere of those sweaty, beer-stained early gigs.

But let's not kid ourselves, not all the bands involved in Mod are God's gift to music. Like a lot of punk bands many of them have only got a couple of decent choons to their name, which is where the beauty of the compilation album comes in. It allows you to be selective.

And the Bridge have put together an essential purchase, all the more remarkable because most of the more noted bands aren't included. For example, standard bearers the Purple Hearts, the Chords and Back To Zero were all playing the Music Machine on the night this album was recorded.

The Merton Parka did play but asked to withdraw their tracks after signing with Beggars Banquet; as did the Specials who have been widely adopted by Mods and Skins because they're one of the best live acts around; a band who, as discussed above, are building tomorrow on the skankin' sounds of yesteryear.

So what we get are fifteen numbers from five bands: Secret Affair, Beggar, Small Hours, the Mods and Squire, of whom Secret Affair are by far and away the best. Here they are represented with a couple of class SA-formula dance tracks in 'Time For Action' and 'Let Your Heart Dance' (both possessed of instantly memorable choruses, driving soul feel and rocky guitar bite) and the more daring 'I'm Not Free (But I'm Cheap)' with its nifty guitar/ trumpet interplay.

This is not to belittle the other bands, however; all of them deliver enticing dance numbers, all with their own individual goodies - particularly Beggar's punchy 'Broadway Show', and the Small Hours' closing 'End Of the Night' with its seductive keyboard motif.

And although they all are obviously different, the album is jam-packed with exciting, toe-tapping, catchy serenades often with an irresistible early soul feel.

It's a shame the record doesn't come with video tape because if I remember rightly a lot of people really were dancing the night away.

The good-time, live music feel is re-inforced by the cheering, chatting and snatches of records played between the bands (all the songs appearing to be on the Bridge House label, funnily enough), making it like a page in a musical diary - a snapshot moment captured for posterity.

Maybe it will become a pop historian's treasure trove or maybe this time next year it won't mean anything at all. It doesn't really matter. What does matter is that this is a hugely enjoyable album, essential for voyeurs and pretty neat just to bung on between getting in from work and going up the Wellington for a knees-up, a bevvy and a ding-dong. This is the modern world...

WESTWAY PRESENT
MOD-DAY JUNE 79·HASTINGS
PURPLE HEARTS
FIXATIONS
TEEN BEATS
SCOOTERS
& CHICANE
+ DISCO D.J. JERRY FLOYD
HASTINGS PIER
SAT. 9TH JUNE
DOORS OPEN 5·PM LIC. BAR·FOOD
TKTS. £1·75 ADV. £2 DOOR ~ PIER BOX OFF. ~ DISC JOCKEY ~ STYLUS
PPROVED DRESS - MOHAIRS, MINISKIRTS, PARKAS

THE LITTLE ROOSTERS

East London. July 1979

G ARY Lammin's Little Roosters weren't really a Mod band, but they were on the Mod circuit. Their sixties influence was primarily the Rolling Stones and they are most famous now for having Alison Moyet as a backing singer.

The band was originally formed by various members of Cock Sparrer, and had a following known as the Riverside Characters. Their most famous fan was Joe Strummer who fell for their earthy blend of bar-room rock'n'roll when he caught them playing the Hope & Anchor.

Gary recalls "It was a mental night, the Hope was packed to such an extent that people were having to pass their drinks and money over each others' heads from the stage to the bar and vice-versa to the bar to the stage in order to get served. You literally could not move even if you wanted to. Girls were fainting. Blokes were getting edgy. By 8.45pm If you wanted to get in you couldn't. By 9.pm If you wanted to get out you couldn't, and the buzz that had been gently simmering for about 6 months now was about to explode like a million shining particles of bursting energy..."

When The Little Roosters finally came on stage they were dressed in a style that prompted the left-wing French newspaper beloved by Rhoda Dakar, Liberation, to describe them as "Circus Clowns on Acid." Which wasn't altogether unfair – they were no Pete Meadens. On the piano was Gary Eve "The Teddy Boy Mod Of Basildon" who schizophrenically sported a Ted's quiff and a Two Tone Tonic three piece whistle... Lammin came on stage brazenly smoking a Camberwell carrot. "Anyone hot?" he asked. "YEAH!" the audience replied. "Then may I suggest you have a bite on this," he smiled. "This will cool you down." And he handed the joint to the throng. It was one of those nights.

The gig was sensational, the Roosters at their best. Afterwards Strummer came backstage and offered to produce their album. It was a rock dream, the stuff of fantasy.

* It's almost as if Gary Lammin is jinxed. The bloke lives rock'n'roll but just can't break out of the pub rock ghetto. Cock Sparrer turned down Malcolm McLaren's offer of management and split just before the second wave of punk lit up the charts. D'oh. Then the Little Roosters turned into a commercial turkey. The album they made with Joe came out and was swiftly withdrawn – Lammin blames "music biz shenanigans." While Alison quit before they'd had the chance to convince her to take over lead vocals entirely, and they got thrown off the March of the Mods tour for, irony of ironies, being too individualistic...

Sparrer later reformed without him and play to large audiences all over the world to this day. Gary's new band, The Bermondsey Joyriders, strut away down at the Johnny Thunders end of rock; they perform with elderly White Panther John Sinclair and they're terrific. But so far, sadly, their talents remain unrecognised by what's left of the UK music industry.

MERTON PARKAS: YOU NEED WHEELS

Lambeth. July 1979

THE Merton Parkas surfaced at the Wellington in Waterloo. They were a cheerful band with a very poppy sing-along pub rock set including many a cover version. They were swiftly snapped up by Beggars Banquet who attempted to launch them as 'the' mod band, completely destroying their credibility in the process.

The record company press office attracted the interest of The Sun newspaper which devoted almost a page to the Parkas and the Specials in their 29th June issue with the Parkas getting the lion's share of copy under cringe-worthy headlines like 'FAB! THE MODS ARE BACK! PARKAS LEAD A SIXTIES REVIVAL!'

To the average London or Essex Mod it was outrageous that these Johnny-come-latelys who were a good laugh live but nothing special could be rocketed into such a commanding position, leap-frogging over bands who had been around longer and had better songs.

PARKAS PATCH OFFER!!

ONLY 50p + s.a.e.

MERTON PARKAS LOGO BADGE 25p + SAE

SEND TO: BEGGARS BANQUET,8 HOGARTH RD, LONDON SW5

NAME ....

ADDRESS ....

....

....

I ENCLOSE AN S.A.E. AND CHEQUE/P.O.

PAYABLE TO BEGGARS BANQUET RECORDS LTD.

☐ 50p FOR THE PARKAS SEW-ON PATCH

☐ 25p FOR THE MERTON PARKAS BADGE

PLEASE ALLOW 28 DAYS FOR DELIVERY

Chasing their ace, Beggars rush-released the boys' first single, which unfortunately was also to be the first single by a new Mod band. At least the punks had 'New Rose'. The Merton Parkas brought out 'You Need Wheels', which could kindly be described as a rather thin power-pop plod. Hardly the flyer that the new movement needed.

Buddy Ascott of The Chords said: "I don't blame the Merton Parkas, I blame the people who bought it. I mean, 'You Need Wheels'...was that really our 'Anarchy In The UK'?"

An anti Merton Parkas campaign called KAMP – Kill All Merton Parkas – sprang up with the Glory Boys issuing a piss-take mock-up of the single with the 'Wheels' cover suitably desecrated. A West Ham supporter known as Mid-Kent was widely suspected to be the instigator. The spoof single was a hoot. The band's name was replaced by 'Bay City Rollers', their faces by Pursey, Rod Stewart and Beano characters and the title became 'You Need Your Brains Tested If You Like Merton Parkas'. The single inside was titled 'We Need Songs' by ShowModdyModdy, which was devastatingly accurate, the Parkas being the plastic equivalents for Mod of those camp and corny teeny-bop Teds. Leading Mods sneered that the Parkas were just Butlins Redcoats - an insult to show Reds if you ask me.

'You Need Wheels' was a one-hit wonder, peaking at Number 40, although keyboardist Mick Talbot was to find fame, and credibility, later in Paul Weller's Style Council. The song was the first sign that Mod was reaching its first crossroads.

But were they unfairly targeted? The band themselves were likeable enough. Mick and his brother Danny had been playing working man's clubs together for four years, with a different guitarist. Two years ago that band split and the two Talbots with drummer Simon Smith and a forgotten bassist formed the Sneakers, a doomed power pop outfit.

They changed their name to the Merton Parkas – in honour of the leafy south west London borough of their birth - last November, bringing in bassist Neill Hurrell who worked in the boys' wear department of a chain store. Mick recalls "I went in, tapped him on the shoulder and said, 'Excuse me, can I have a blazer and a bass player, please?"

To Beggars Banquet, they were a god-send; a token Mod signing who could play well live and didn't take themselves too seriously. 'You Need Wheels' was chosen as being the band's "most commercial" song. They admit the production was "rushed" and insist that it isn't their best number.

Their influences are variously "old soul, Tamla, Atlantic, Stax and the blues" (Mick), "the Small Faces, the Monkees and the early Who" (Simon), and jazz musoes "Django Reinhardt and Stephane Grappelli" (Danny). Mick thinks Mod is more accessible than punk, "it's easier to be a Mod," he says. "It's more respectable."

But in their case, less successful... 'Wheels' peaked in the charts at Number 40. Danny told the NME: "We're not trying to innovate. We're just entertainers, that's all. I think that Chuck Berry is probably the best rock 'n' roll songwriter, and what does he sing about? Cars, girls and school."

But that was the 50s, Dan. Maybe that's all our generation have got to sing about, but Mssrs. Weller, Strummer, Pursey and Costello would beg to differ.

* THE Merton Parkas may have been one hit wonders, but they were also the first of the Mod Revival bands to release an album, Face In The Crowd. It didn't bother the charts. They disbanded in 1980, but Mick Talbot went on to find a creditable degree of success – seven top ten hits - and acclaim in Paul Weller's post-Jam band the Style Council, which also featured Dee C Lee (Diane Catherine Sealey, later Weller's wife for ten years) on vocals. The Style Council are best described as a living Pop Art experiment, and less flatteringly as a retro-obsessed mess. The Council disbanded in 1990. Best moment: Our Favourite Shop. Worst: A Gospel.

NEWS OF THE WORLD
GOSSIP AND LETTERS...

SECRET AFFAIR have signed a deal with Arista for exclusive marketing and distribution of their own label, I-Spy Records. The leading Mod band release their first single via the deal, 'Time For Action'/'Solo Strut', on August 17.

The group comprises Ian Page (lead vocals, trumpet), Dave Cairns (guitar, backing vocals); Dennis Smith (bass, backing vocals) and Seb Shelton (drums) and were formed by Page and Cairns formerly of the New Hearts, nine months ago in London's East End. Ian Page, who co-produced the single with Cairns, commented: "Despite many offers from other record companies, we signed with Arista because they were the only company to let us have our own label."

A film titled Stepping Out, featuring **Secret Affair** and documenting the current Mod scene, will go on release in October as support to the science fiction blockbuster Alien. Meanwhile, the group undertake their 'March Of The Mods' tour with **Purple Hearts** and possibly **Back To Zero**, commencing at Scarborough Penthouse August 10 and continuing at Birmingham Barbareilas 16, Manchester Factory 17,' Cheltenham Witcombe Lodge 16, Swansea Circles 20, Plymouth Clones 21, Newport Stowaway 22, Bristol Trinity Leisure Centre 23, West Runton Pavilion 24, London Lyceum 26, Canvey Island Paddocks 27, Sheffield Limit Club 28, Barnsley Civic Hall 29, Leeds Fforde Green Hotel 30, Newcastle Mayfair 31 and Liverpool Eric's September 1.

The Fixations play Hastings Pier Pavillion on June 9 with

TIME FOR ACTION

Purple Hearts and **Back to Zero** and London Windsor Castle
June 11.

SLIT UP A TREAT: Consider the sorry fate of Essex Mod
band the Little Roosters. After six months solid giggin all
round London and the Home Counties, the boys landed
a major break as third on the bill for this months March
Of The Mod's tour, and hence the chance of national
recognition. So the working members of the band Gary
Eves (keyboards) and John Hunt (bass) quit their jobs
andthe band cancelled a month's gigs only to be told less
than a week before the tour that they'd been given the
elbow in favour of **Back To Zero**.
And even then it was a journalist that told them, and not
theeir co-headliner **Secret Affair** and the **Purple Hearts**,
the people who'd taken the fateful decision.
Even though they take their inspiration from a different
rock period than most Mod bands (Small Faces, Faces,
Stones) the Roosters have built up a reputation in the
movement with solid hard work, debuting the Bridge
House in February and then progressing through all the
major venues.
"That's what hurts most," drummer Graeme Potter
sighs, "not being dropped but not even being told about
it. We've lost everything. And Secret Affair are forever
going on about Mod unity. I'll tell you what," his bitterness
exploding into anger, "Ian Page (of Secret Affair) has
turned out to be the Maggie Thatcher of rock. He's acting
like a Tory. When you're workers it's all stick together
brothers, but when you're the mill owner you shit on the
workers. He makes me sick."

HIGH WYCOMBE
ROCK DIARY
NAG'S HEAD   THURSDAY 19th JULY
LONDON RD   TOP MOD BAND
              MERTON PARKAS
THURSDAY 26th JULY + PANTHER 45
BLUES LOFT REUNION
PAUL JONES   TOM McGUINNESS
HUGHIE FLINT   SHAKEY VICK
DAVE KELLY ETC!!
THURSDAY 2nd AUGUST WORLD DEBUT.
        JIMMY NORTON EXPLOSION!!
Featuring:-DANNY KURSTOW STEVE NEW
GLEN MATLOCK, BUSBY (SUTS)
THURSDAY 9th AUG. - PHIL RAMBOW
AFTER THIS DATE THE MAIN ROCK
NIGHT AT THE NAG'S MOVES BACK
TO WEDNESDAY/S ON A REGULAR BASIS.

Understandably they're bitter but The Roosters are workers and their answer now is to plunge back into the hard gigging that's got them where they are today. With a single 'Going Round' in the pipeline with a major company, it shouldn't take too long for them to overcome these present setbacks and prove themselves to be an important part of the Mod Renewal.

IT HAD TO HAPPEN: say Hi to Britain's first female Mod band, **The Modettes**. They play West Hampstead's Moonlight Club on July 13.

THE MERTON PARKAS who last week signed to Beggars Banquet, will be rush-releasing their first single this week. Called 'You Need Wheels' it will come in a picture bag with a limited edition free **Merton Parka** sew-on patch.

AFTER FOLLOWING THE PURPLE HEARTS FOR A
WHILE I MET BILLY HASSETT AT THE PMOONLIGHT
CLUB. HE TOLD ME HIS BAND THE CHORDS WERE
PLAYING THEIR FIRST GIG AT THE KINGS HEAD,
DEPTFORD. MYSELF, JEFF SHADBOLT, GARY
CROWLEY & BETHNAL BOB WENT ALONG.
THAT WAS THE NIGHT THE MOD REVIVAL TRULY
STARTED. THE FIRST TIME MODS FROM DIFFERENT
PARTS OF LONDON CAME TOGETHER IN ONE
SMALL ROOM.

Tony Lordan - 78 Mod & Musician

THE WHO WERE MY GATEWAY DRUG INTO MOD AND I'M STILL AN ADDICT

Buddy Ascott - Chords

MILLIONS LIKE US

AUGUST 1979

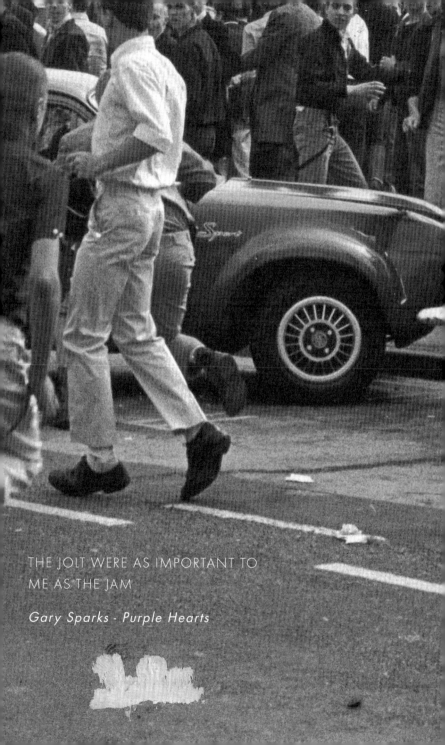

THE JOLT WERE AS IMPORTANT TO
ME AS THE JAM

Gary Sparks - Purple Hearts

WHO'S WHO

August, 1979

I n early August 1979, I asked the three Maximum Speed boys, Kim Gaunt, Goffa Gladding and Clive Reams – generally referred to affectionately as clowns, baboons or gibbons - to write a piece about who was up-and-coming in New Mod.

They name-checked BACK TO ZERO as the band generally regarded to be 'the next big one' after the Hearts/Chords/Affair/Merton Parkas.

BTZ had formed in the Enfield/Southgate areas of North London at the beginning of the year. MS described their sound as "catchy, melodic and yet moody." They'd built up a loyal following and had signed to Chris Parry's Fiction label. Their first single was to be 'Back To Back'/'New Side Of Heaven', both written by guitarist Sam Burnett.

The lads damned SQUIRE with faint praise, saying that they don't have a following and sound "lightweight," but added that they're respected for "being very melodic", were linked with Twist 'n' Shout Records and had a single 'B.A.B.Y.' out imminently.

They also mentioned BEGGAR, a band originally from South Wales who had re-located to Leyton, East London. Beggar's raw Merseybeat style of R&B had been showcased on the Bridgehouse 'Mods May Day' lp. Their stand-out song was 'Broadway Show'.

Plus The FIXATIONS, Holloway-based Mods who had been playing since the end '78. Although tight and professional, the boys allow that the band "have been criticized for lack of variation in style."

The TEENBEATS from Hastings, "currently the hip Mod band", respected for their energetic, exciting pop. Their cover of 'I Can't Control Myself' is now out on Safari Records. But Safari no interest from Top Of The Pops…

And The KILLERMETERS - the lads praised their "excellent" Psycho Records single 'Why Should it Happen To Me'.

Asked about the bigger bands, the three wise monkeys choose their words carefully. They were sitting on the fence for the MERTON PARKAS whose appearance in the Sun and "somewhat wimpy" single, 'You Need Wheels' had seen them dismissed by hardcore Mods as "cabaret-playing bandwagon-jumpers."

THE CHORDS, they said had "wasted a couple of months being protégées" of Jimmy Pursey, who they refer to accurately as "the Hersham Horror". But insisted that the boys were "back on track" with Polydor, adding "Vinyl success guaranteed."

Former covers band THE MODS are described as "The most improved band on the scene." The Mods supported the Undertones at Cambridge, and had begun to headline in their own right.

They described the PURPLE HEARTS as the "first Mods to get any music press coverage (by some twat name of Bushell)" and added that their first single 'Millions Like Us' and the March Of The Mods tour would "consolidate their position in Division One."

Finally they saw SECRET AFFAIR as future world dominators, with massive chart potential and "electric stage presence." The ones most likely to succeed, they concurred. Their debut single 'Time For Action' / 'Soho Strut' was out soon.

Bizarrely, they made no mention of Long Tall Shorty, the pioneering Mod band who ploughed their own furrow. More understandably they also over-looked Gary Lammin's strolling bones clones the Little Roosters.

THE LOW NUMBERS

London. August 4, 1979

'Away from the numbers, that's where I wanna be / Away from the numbers, is where I am free...'

FUNNY thing numbers. There are certain areas where you want them to be high – your IQ, your bank account, and in the case of Russ Meyer, the chest measurements of the women in your 'satirical' films.

But in other cases, such as round dodgers and visiting teams' goals, Halfins, we prefer those numbers to be low.

The original High Numbers went on to become The Who and notch up chart success the world over; will the Low Numbers follow suit or just f-f-f-fade away?

The band seems to be attracting some stellar fans.

"Pursey was sitting on the side of the stage grinning like a Cheshire cat, and Strummer was standing there tapping his feet and saying 'Amazing', and all these kids were pogoing like mad..."

Dave McCullough dissolves into a red-faced babble of barely intelligible Irish brogue on the subject of the excellence of the Low Numbers's performance supporting the Clash at their Notre Dame gig the other Friday while I'd been happily holidaying.

"Oi tell yus," the blarney-stone kissing one enthused. "They were even better than Thursday..." And on Thursday they'd apparently hit with all the power of a Sweeney swoop on a bank mob.

THE MOD REVIVAL

I first encountered the Low Numbers when a callow youth thrust their tape into my hands in the privacy of my own living room. Unusual you might think until you tumble that the youth in question was my own brother who happened to be working with Numbers guitarist/vocalist Phil Payne at the time.

I was excessively sceptical - as you would be if you knew my brother's musical tastes and realised the value young Tel puts on the likes of John Revolting and the Third Degrees. But I gave the tape a listen and was duly well and truly pleasantly surprised.

For it revealed a band possessed of a broad, beefy sound, thick and dirty, a hefty hybrid of such under-rated heroes as the Lurkers and the Members at full blast, with a nice line in raucous vocalising which earned them a tag of "the definitive Oi Oi band" from the laughing boys in the Sounds office.

E'er impetuous, gentle reader, I made a date to compare tape sound with live delivery at the Wellington in the wilds of Waterloo; a gig which was pretty promising if not as stunningly impressive as the Clash support slots.

Live, the Low Numbers exhibit the same forceful guitar work as on tape, plus drumming as heavy and solid as Meatloaf's stools, meaty bass work, and bellowed, heartfelt vocals. Together, it sounds as stocky as Mr Payne himself.

Surprisingly McCullough was equally blown away and a brief, vicious fist fight on the Long Acre cobbles ensued for the honour of singing their praises in print. Naturally, given my 117 viewings of the Dirty Dozen and as master of the ancient oriental art of the origami, I won. Now read on...

A FEW chats established that the band were the sort of likeable blokes you'd be happy to meet in any decent boozer, so just to prove it I did. And thus we assembled for a brief rabbit in the salloon bar of Covent Garden's prestigious White Lion where details were established as Forsytes were demolished...

The first issue was the connotations of their moniker...

"Yeah, but we thought of that name before the Mod thing came along," bassist Bob Martin explains.

"We were pissing about in a pub," elucidates drummer Derek Isabel. "And trying to think of a name. I said why not call ourselves the High Numbers. Bob pissed himself laughing and said 'No, how about the Low Numbers?'."

Phil Payne takes up the story. "We started getting known as a Mod band after we supported the Purple Hearts in Southend back in February," he explains. "And to be honest it's easier to get gigs if you are a Mod band than a punk band these days. But we don't want to be labelled. We're in-betweenies, although it's true that punk audiences like us more than Mod audiences do. Let's face it, if it wasn't for Sham, the Clash and the Sex Pistols we wouldn't be here now."

Me neither. The Low Numbers' story begins with two 17-year-old ex-school mates, Bob and Phil catching Eater at the Hope & Anchor early in 1977 and deciding they just HAD to form a band. The fact that they couldn't play was not seen as particularly problematic.

Their first drummer was a "loony black guy" who ended up nicking the drum kit, selling it and absconding. He was replaced by Del, an old soccer pal who they met in a pub and conned into buying himself a kit - even though he'd never played before either.

Months of learning and intensive practice later and they had two songs – the entirely reasonable 'We Hate Tony Blackburn' and 'NCP' (inspired by the National Car Park where Bob worked), which they showcased in a pub in their home manor of Camden Town by pretending to be a pop band. To the delight of the assembled shell-shocked grannies and traumatised bar staff they were promptly ejected.

The next few months were taken up with gate-crashing gigs, half-inching gear, and more name changes than British Leyland. They were The End, The Injections, who you might have seen at Roxy, Camden Action, and the Two Tones.

This learning process was important for them. They tightened up their sound and shaped up their identity, as they moved from the silly songs above to the numbers which made it on to that first demo tape which they recorded in February this year.

Numbers like Phil's 'Have A Go Hero' and 'Nine All Out', which are both based on real life experiences. 'Hero' is a dig at Camden cops who, Phil claims, regularly terrorise his local, one night beating up his brother really badly. Another song, 'Running' stems from an unseemly flight they had to make from a Camden curry emporium after the three of them realised that they were totally boracic lint (Skint – Translator Ed).

'Poor Freddie, had to go back/'E'd lost 'is overcoat/He found the police there waiting/They found him with some dope/And now he's sitting in a cell down in Tottenham Court Road station/He's been there twice before/He's got nicked, nicked, nicked/And 'We don't want you back anymore.'

Could happen to anyone.

Other folk were struck by the band's potential - notably James Timothy Pursey (put it down to similar tastes). "I tell you people slag 'im down," Phil says forcefully. "But Jimmy is the only geezer who gives a shit. We went to him with our cassette player, he played the tape, loved it and goes 'Yeah I'll have you in the studio'. It was that quick."

Bob takes up the story. "Then we never heard nothing for ages, and we gave up hope a bit until Jimmy saw us walking along Grosvenor Street and shouted 'OI, YOU! I lost ya number. I want you round the studio tomorrow.'"

They went and the result was the single 'Keep In Touch'/'Nine All Out' released this month as a JP Production via Warners. The studio sound loses none of their elephantine power though it is smoother and more sophisticated - a gap they hope to bridge with the eventual addition of a second guitarist.

'Keep In Touch' is very Jammy, though another newer song 'Kings Cross Squat' is more Ruts inclined - a healthy diversity.

The latest instalment of the Low Numbers story has been their rise from dismal dives to 'prestige' supports like the Clash and Sham last Saturday. This indicates that their days as postman, carpenter and photographic printer could well be numbered, so with that in mind I wondered if there was anything they wanted to bring up. Y'know, girls, glamour, money, philosophy, drugs...

"Yeah," says the laudably altruistic Bob. "Give Ten Pole Tudor a mention. Y'know he jammed with us at the Notre Dame Hall? Well I see him as the saviour of England. Honestly. If I was his manager I'd promote him as that."

Now ain't that nice?

MOD AT THE CROSSROADS

August 11, 1979

A ugust 1979. Just six happy, hectic months on from the birth of New Mod as a bona fide, recognized movement and everything has changed.

No-one is sneering anymore, which is a good thing, but the nature of Mod has already morphed so much that many of the pioneers and hardcore devotees are starting to question whether their 'thing' is over…

Consider the evidence. Six months on and Mod fills the West End clubs…The first official Mod single 'You Need Wheels' by the Merton Parkas is the pits (they need songs!) and has undeservedly charted…All of the major Mod bands now have singles in the pipeline…Aussie film director Lyndall Hobbs has brought in posers for her forthcoming 'mod documentary' (Steppin' Out)…David Essex records a single called 'M.O.D.' to the delight of ugly, jealous, chinless has-beens everywhere… Power-flop pop phonies and session men start donning Parkas… The price of clothes sky-rockets…there are little kids at Merton Parkas gigs who have never even heard of the Purple Hearts… and ahead of us, looming like the iceberg before the tilting bow of the Titanic, is Quadrophenia, the movie that is absolutely cast-iron guaranteed to spawn tens of thousands of trend-surfing Quad-Mods…

The Mod Renewal is at a crossroads, oh my brothers and only friends. Its short existence looks set to be engulfed by all things plastic and industry and cynical. If nothing else, its essence – its purity if you like - is threatened.

UNLIKE some one-week-stand slags we could all mention, Sounds has always, I think wisely, resisted the temptation to indulge in Flower-Flop style sensationalism about New Mod. But now with a monsoon of masturbatory mass media about to cascade into our lives, the time is right to examine the State Of Play, and talk to knowledgeable faces, respected within the movement, about the way things are going.

Whatever anyone else says the roots of New Mod were in the Jam and a handful of sharp-looking kids who were Jam fanatics in '77. Disillusioned with punk's downhill slide, after a confused, 'split-personality' period, these discerning teenage tickets gradually began to dress and think of themselves as Mods. People like Grant Fleming, Alan (Norman) Suchley, Large Al from Hayes, and Purple Heart Rob Manton.

In places like Canning Town's Bridge House and on the terraces of Upton Park in the spring of '78, parka-clad Grant stuck out like a sore thumb in the middle of another movement of disillusioned ex-punks, the skinheads. But by the Autumn and Winter many other Jam fans as well as a lot of the older East End and Essex skinheads were talking about 'going Mod'.

Simultaneously and in parallel, but unaware of each other, people like Billy Hassett in Deptford, Brian Betteridge (of Back To Zero) and the Maximum Speed boys in North London also began dressing and thinking of themselves as Mod.

The first clue had been at the Great British Music Festival in the December of that year. But the diverse groups didn't really get together until the Jam's February gigs in Paris for which Grant Fleming had printed leaflets himself under the grand title of 'The Mod Pilgrimage.'

The response took Grant completely by surprise. Around FIFTY self-styled Mods turned up.

"Everything grew out of Paris," Grant explains. "That's when we realized something big was happening. After that, the Purple Hearts gigs brought everyone together and it was like a party atmosphere wherever we went. Then Billy Hassett, who we'd met in Paris, said why don't we come and see his group, the Chords…

"It was just our own little movement then, a movement of about 100-150 kids with Mod as a way of life."

What exactly did that mean, I ask?

"Well Mod is a way of thinking, an attitude," he says. "It's fun-loving and smart. We were kids who wanted a laugh. We were into drinking, dancing, girls, going to gigs and taking pride in ourselves. That was what Mod meant to us. We had aspiration too. We wanted to do better than our parents had done."

So Mod defined itself in opposition to "mug punters" and the scruffiness and political clichés of much punk.

The new London Mod scene began in earnest this February. It was built around bands who'd been in existence since at least last year, like the Purple Hearts from Romford, Essex, the Chords from Deptford in South East London and Back To Zero from North London. Behind them came a range of other bands – not so much 'lesser' but less well known. While isolated groups like the Teenbeats from Hastings testified to the existence of 'foreign' non-urban pockets of Mod culture.

At the same time, on the London fringes of Essex, Ian Page and Dave Cairns, driven by bitterness and resentment towards the Business after their experience as the loser group the New Hearts, had formed a 'new wave soul band' called the Secret Affair whose followers were to be known as Glory Boys.

East End Mods were quick to, pick up on them and before long the polished, danceable but still gutsy combo were rightly being hailed as the leading New Mod band.

In these early days, there was some flirtation between the Southern Mods and the Northern equivalents in the scooter clubs. But the two groups soon found they had little in common. The Northern Mods with their wide flares and penchant for Stranglers stick-ons were sneered at by the Southerners who put music and fashion first (though some of the Northerners have come round of late). In general the two worlds were and are quite separate.

WHEN I first put pen to paper properly about Mod in February, I was pessimistic about its chances of avoiding media/business overkill. But I had reckoned without the burned fingers many Johnny Come Lately record companies had received from their over-enthusiasm about punk's money-spinning potential. In fact, the onslaught of signing has only just started.

This stand-off period allowed Mod three or four months of healthy development as a pure street movement incubating in the fertile gor-blimey soil of the Bridge House and the Wellington at Waterloo.

Absurdly criticized by non-participants for mere revivalism or alternatively for not accurately reproducing sixties archetypes (you can't win), the movement's relevance has rested on its ability to take the best of the past to build something of its own.

THE MOD REVIVAL

New Mod has begun to create a youth movement with vitality, direction and above all marvelous music. And in evidence m'lud, I'd nominate songs such as 'Millions Like Us' by the Purple Hearts and Secret Affair's rabble-rousing 'Time For Action'.

Okay, Mod has never approached the sense of threat and purpose which came with the Pistols and the Clash, but in the dismal Spring of '79 when punk as a meaningful movement was on its last legs (and before we saw the first heartening sparks of New Punk) Mod — along with those glorious Ska bands the Specials and Madness — was like a breath of fresh air to a tired circuit.

This period was well documented by ace mod zine Maximum Speed and the perhaps less sparkling but raw and heart-felt live Bridge House compilation album.

GROWTH has been steady and unforced but it brought problems. More and more groups sprang up of varying degrees of competence (none of them challenging the Secret Affair-Chords-Purple Hearts triumvirate) while the West End clubs started opening their doors to Mod, and Mod ranks were swelled by kids who thought there was nothing more to the movement than bunging on a parka.

There had been some silly press coverage but the worst came in June with the Sun going overboard about South London band the Merton Parkas — a good band hyped out of all proportion, who signed to Beggars Banquet and put out the first Mod single 'You Need Wheels' which was disgracefully derivative, dreary, underwhelming and ordinary. The song sounds like bad pub rock, which is a real shame as the first should have been as vital and worthwhile as 'New Rose' or 'Anarchy'.

This development split the Mod camp with the birth of the daft Kill All Merton Parkas Campaign (a much more vicious version of a previous short-lived and unfounded anti-Chords campaign) but the future ain't all gloom and despondency. On the contrary, as I write the major Mod bands are on the verge of releasing singles that on the strength of live performance promise to be excellent; this will be the 'proof in plastic' we've been waiting for.

Secret Affair have signed a deal with Arista for their own I-Spy label and release 'Time For Action'/'Soho Strut' this month. The Chords have signed with Polydor and release 'Now It's Gone'/'Don't Go Back' soon. While the Purple Hearts and Back To Zero have one-off deals with Fiction to release the mighty 'Millions Like Us' and 'Back To Back' respectively.

At the same time the Affair and the Hearts begin a national tour (the March Of The Mods) this month hopefully with Back To Zero while the Chords headline a UK tour next month with Long Tall Shorty.

So what with the Quadrophenia film being brought forward to mid-August, the movement now faces its biggest boost to date, unbridled press coverage, commercial interest and the first real test of its cohesion and worth.

Last Monday, I go down the Bridge for Secret Affair — the absolute business band. Despite everything, the feeling among punters for the movement is running as high as ever. The Glory Boys are there, looking sharp. And the atmosphere is all there too as Secret Affair prove once more that the excessive praise heaped on them is justified.

A lot of big Mod faces are there in the audience so I use the occasion to suss out public opinion, and find two distinct schools of thought. A lot of the pioneers think Mod as they conceived it is on its last legs, but there are perhaps just as many who look forward to the imminent explosion and think the scene is healthier than it ever was.

Cockney Grant Fleming fires the first salvo on behalf of the pessimistic party. "Mod ain't very interesting at all now," he says. "I know it was inevitable that it'd become commercialized so I can't really moan but I just don't feel aligned to it now.

"It caught on too quick. The NME piece, London Weekend Television, the Music Machine and all this Merton Parkas stuff in the Sun they were all nails in the coffin. It's all guest lists and posers now. Don't get me wrong, The Jam are still good and they'll always be there, and Secret Affair will be the next really big band — and I'm hoping they don't go Sham style cos Ian's a bit like Jimmy Pursey and I'm worried he'll alienate people who ain't Mod with his mouth. But Mod will be massive, sure and probably better but I feel as aligned to it now as I do to punk.

"Our crowd is still the same, we're Mods, but we're distinct. We don't feel part of the mass movement."

The same despondency was echoed by Tom 'Hoxton' McCourt and Bob Baisden from Dagenham, two suedeheads (yep another revival!).

"I got into the music ages ago," says Bob. "And I thought Mod was smart, and skins were too much trouble. But the little kids have jumped on the bandwagon now and all these middle class kids have appeared from nowhere. We were down at Vespas when they made that film and Lyndall Hobbs brought people we didn't know with her to interview. Y'know, like some of the old punks, they looked the business but when you go up to 'em it's all 'Buy us a gin and tonic Nigel'. Fakes."

Tom McCourt agrees. "Vespas is a joke," he says. "Steve Strange and that lot get in there...I'll tell ya, Mod used to be personal, now it's just a fashion."

Bob: "When I first changed from skinhead I bought a really tasty suit for two quid. Now the same suit would cost £20. It's gone exactly the same as punk only it didn't last so long. It's got too commercial too quick."

OTHERS don't share their pessimism however. Like Goffa Gladding from Maximum Speed who argues: "Okay if it'd been allowed to develop and the Sun etc had left it alone it'd be a lot healthier. And it is annoying when you meet kids who've only heard of the Parkas. But things are still happening. There's this tour which can't be a bad thing and we're still selling over 500 copies of Maximum Speed north of Watford. It's starting to take off outside London now and that keeps me optimistic. We've had such a good time up till now, I think it can only get better."

Dave Laurence is equally positive. Dave's another ex-Dagenham skinhead, now a leading Glory Boy with 'MOD' tattooed inside his lower lip.

"Mod is going great," he says. "It's getting loads of publicity and loads of people joining and that's what we want —a mass Mod movement. I'd encourage young kids to join in. Okay it does get out of hand with a lot of posers wearing parkas in boiling hot weather, but on the other hand musically the bands are getting better all the time. And once Quadrophenia comes out there'll be so many people wanting to be part of it."

What about the middle class posers, I ask?

"Class don't matter," Dave insists. "Mod ain't about class conflict, it's a way of thinking, and the more people who think Mod the better."

Secret Affair's Ian Page agrees with Dave's analysis whole-heartedly, adding: "How can you question a movement that is thousands of people strong? Mod is growing fast and healthily and all that proves to me is that the Biz is always wrong and the kids are right. And as long as we're getting put down, the harder we'll fight, the longer we'll stay. Things are going great. The fashion side's really working well now. We've formed our own label so we can sign other bands and hopefully start financing Maximum Speed. All the bands are playing different music. I tell you, the scene is healthier than ever."

TWO SIDES to every story. Take your pick. Whatever your point of view, one thing's for certain. For every Mod who drops out today, another twenty kids will join in tomorrow. Quadrophenia will keep the movement going over the Winter and after that it'll be up to the bands to deliver the goods. To put up or shut up.

"Yeah it will be up to us," Billy H of the Chords agrees. "Up to us to keep the scene healthy, for us and the Purple Hearts, Back To Zero and Secret Affair to stick together and not fall apart. Of course, there's competition, but we are together now. We talk, we keep in touch and discuss plans. We all know what happened to punk when the bands signed up, so it's up to us to learn the lessons and avoid the pitfalls. We're all friends, I can't see it happening. I believe we can stick together."

It's an optimistic hope, a worthwhile hope. And as the best bands begin to receive the popular acclaim they deserve we shall see just how much they can stick together.

For my part, despite what we read elsewhere my one ambition as regards Mod is to see the movement grow and the best bands successful. And now as the Press Officers and Biz types move in I'm quite happy to leave future scribbling to the free-dinner merchants.

If it goes no further, New Mod has created a vital vanguard of bands and given a lot of people including me a bloody good time for six months. Isn't that enough?

THE
TEENBEATS

Dublin Castle, Camden, August 1979.

The Teenbeats are a five-piece band from Hastings who specialise in pure pop, as catchy as a dose on the road but considerably more charming.

Granted song titles,such as 'Time For Change' and 'Strength Of The Nation' indicate a certain lack of imagination. Even their name has been done before.

In fairness though, they have the energy and appeal of fifty comedy sketch milkmen and their cover of The Troggs' 'I Can't Control Myself' always goes down well with live crowds - even with UK Subs fans, they supported Charlie Harper's boys in Sussex recently.

They have the bottle to do a ballad on stage too, called 'The Letter'. And their stand-out song is 'Wasting My Time' which sticks in the brain like an ice-pick.

The Teenbeats are Huggy Leaver (vocals), Eddie Mays (bass), Ken Copsey and Paul Thompson (guitars) and Dave Blackman (drums). Huggy started life as a punk in a band called The Plastics, but says he saw the Mod light last year. He put the band together in January this year and they debuted live in April. Their most remarkable gig to date was the infamous Hastings Mod festival, where, according to the estimable rogues at Maximum Speed they "really brought the pier down."

They started a residency at the Wellington in Waterloo last month, and continue to impress. BTZ's Brian Betteridge rates them as "the top Mod band not from London other than the Killermeters", which is probably a compliment.

*Sadly, the Teenbeats never fulfilled their promise. They were snapped up by Safari Records but their first single, 'I Can't Control Myself' was nobbled by a wimpy production job, and the follow-up 'Strength Of The Nation' was equally flat. Even Maximum Speed, who loved the band, were disappointed, writing: I'm absolutely flummoxed as to why such a great band can bring out such a lousy single. The zine also likened the single to "third rate punk".

According to the song's lyrics the strength of the nation was youth, but the nation's youth had the sense not to buy it. The Teenbeats never captured their live sound in the studio and broke up in 1981. Even sadder Dave Blackman passed away in 2009. Five of their songs can be heard on the mid-80s compilation Uppers On The South Downs - the two singles, plus 'Teenage Beat', 'I'll Never Win' and 'If I'm Gone Tomorrow.'

I can't control myself

C/W I'LL NEVER WIN"
OUT NOW ON SAFARI RECORDS   SAFE *17

<u>TOUR DATES</u>

FRIDAY 17th. AUGUST MUSIC MACHINE   CAMDEN

SATURDAY 18th. AUGUST GLBAL VILLAGE CHARING CROSS

MONDAY 20th. AUGUST GLOBAL VILLAGE   CHARING CROSS

THURSDAY 23rd. AUGUST   WHITE HART   ACTON

SATURDAY 25th. AUGUST MARQUEE **

SATURDAY 31st. AUGUST DOUBLE SIX BASILDON ESSEX

SATURDAY 1st./8th. SEPTEMBER GREYHOUND FULHAM PALACE ROAD

Bookings & Further Infomation : Pinball Artists Bond Street House, 14, Clifford St.,
    LONDON, W.1. 2JD.   01/499/2933.

YOUR SIDE OF HEAVEN

August 25, 1979.

The 17-date March Of The Mods tour featured Secret Affair, the Purple Hearts and Back To Zero; with the Hearts and the Affair alternating the headline slot. It kicked off on August 10th at the Penthouse, Scarborough and ended on September 1st at Eric's in Liverpool. I caught up for the third date, which was at Torquay Town Hall…

Here are my doodles from the night:

THE WORD is out, we're gonna shake and shout and if all you gotta do is pout and spout pious, groundless platitudes about Mod being "Big Biz hype" then you get out, of this page now and go flout your prejudices elsewhere.

Ahh, you can scream and holler you're blue in the boat but the only way to convince people is by delivering the goods and that's exactly what this the March Of The Mods is doing. It's cool, clear blast of fresh air featuring three of the best bands within the Renewal's sharp-dressed confines.

Three bands taking their music out of the Smoke to a skeptical, if clearly intrigued England at large. Tonight some 500 of the curious turn up at the Town Hall, several decked out in token 'Mod' outfits.

And I get the same sort of tingle that you get when you take your first girlfriend home to mum for the first time. Are they gonna hit it off or start throw the dinner plates at each other like deranged Greek waiters?

THE MOD REVIVAL

No sweat, sweets, only the dead or the hopelessly hip (ha) could resist the sheer dance attack of the Affair...but I'm leaping events. Back To Zero are the support band and hence perpetually kick things off while the co-headliners juggle their running orders. Sadly, tonight, BTZ's set is sabotaged by an outrageously tinny sound mix reducing their clean, individual style to a too-much-of-a-muchness, indistinguishable grey mess. A shame, because this band is surely worthy of further attention.

Their own numbers, penned by Barney Rubble lookalike guitarist-Sam Burnett, include an alarming number of gems, rightly, categorized by the Maximum Speed trio as 'catchy, melodic yet moody.' So infectious, energized pop like the vigorous soon-come single 'Your Side Of Heaven' and its harder sibling 'Back To Back' get the feet tapping before their best number, the slower but immaculate 'Modern Boys' warms the cockles of your heart.

Their cover of the Dave Clark 5's 'Glad All Over' was dullsville and pointless however but a fine version of Chris Kenner's 'Land Of A Thousand Dances' – the song that gave Wilson Pickett his biggest na na-na-na-na hit back in '66 - more than compensated, and earned them an encore they just about deserved.

Give these boys a decent sound mix and they're magic (more details next week).

Secret Affair came next and I doubt if there's much more I can say about them. They are simply the best, the most mature, most proficient and most enjoyable band in the movement and probably the best dance band in the country. (Only the NME could call them 'fast, young, smart and anthemic' and make it sound like an insult).

The Affair are so good that as the encore repeat of the titanic 'Time For Action' echoes round my ears I just can't imagine how the Purple Hearts could possibly follow them...

Yet the atmosphere of friendly competition on this tour is sharpening everyone up and the Hearts raised their game to deliver one of the finest sets I've ever seen them play. From the minute they powered into 'Steppin' Stone' you could tell tonight was going to be one hell of a tight showcase for their post-punk punch: well-rounded, pogo-promoting rock built on their impressive music muscle and embellished by Rob Manton's cocky Cockney holler and jumping jack stage antics.

Their other cover, pre-'Bowie' Mod Bowie's 'Can't Help Thinking About Me', is beefy attacking rock with handsome minor chords from Mr Stebbing and powerful percussive work from Gary Sparks.

MARCH O

Purple Hearts

BACK

The North
Wanstead

TOUR DATES

August 10	Scarborough —
August 14	Plymouth — Clones
August 15	Torquay — Townhall
August 20	Swansea — Circle Club
August 16	Birmingham — Barbarellas
August 17	Manchester — Factory
August 18	Cheltenham — Whitcombe L
August 22	Newport — Stowaway
August 23	Bristol — Trinity Leisure Cent

THE MODS

ZERO   SECRET  AFFAIR

August 24	W. Runton — Pavillion
*August 25	Dudley — J.B.'s
August 26	London —Lyceum
*August 27	Canvey Paddocks
August 28	Sheffield — Limit
August 29	Barnsley — Civic
August 30	Leeds — Fforde Green
August 31	Newcastle — Mayfair
September 1	Liverpool — Eric's

And the new numbers, especially 'Something You Can't Have', sound full of promise. But it's the old faithfuls that prove that the Hearts have got that elusive 'something'.

There's the stabbing attack of 'Frustration' with its immortal chorus: 'I get frustration, I wear it like a suit/But the jacket fits too tightly and there's le-e-ead. inside my boots'; the fine plea for individuality that is 'Jimmy'; the soulful feel and Jolt-like crushing chorus of 'Can't Stay Here' and best of all the single and raucous anthem, 'Millions Like Us' (OH YES).

And if the tour carries on this good, this united, this impressive, then there just might be…

Back To Zero, Purple Hearts and Secret Affair. Reasons to be cheerful parts one, two, three.

Unbeknownst to me at the time, the Torquay gig hadn't gone quite as smoothly as I'd imagined. While Secret Affair were on stage, Dave Cairns was repeatedly threatened by some creep in the crowd with a hammer that he produced periodically from inside his coat while mouthing the words "This is for you." The nut was removed by the band's ex-SAS security man Dave but even he had to sleep and that night the band's 'fans' ran amok at the band's hotel, causing chaos with fire extinguishers. They stole beer and dumped broken glasses in the swimming pool. Secret Affair were saddled with a £500 bill for damages.

The band did feel more secure when they played Barbarellas in Birmingham the next night. The club was two floors off the ground, with good security and the windows in the dressing room were all boarded up, too.

Dave Cairns says: "We thought at least this gig would be no problem... We were sitting backstage relaxing pre-show when I heard a banging sound outside the dressing room, which was two storeys up. I said, 'What the fuck's that?' The banging continued followed by a tearing and a ripping sound. I said, 'Jesus, there's somebody out there.' We all looked at each other. Then a fist punched its way through one of the boards – it was like a horror movie."

The whole board was ripped off the window and the face of veteran Glory Boy Crank (actual name Steve Borg) appeared, grinning from ear to ear.

"You can't keep me away," he said.

"You had to admire him," Cairns recalls. "He'd shimmied up a drain pipe like Spiderman, got on a ledge and smashed he way in. He was 18 or 19 and he was like an unstoppable force. He was beyond control and beyond our comprehension."

The Glory Boy imagined by Page and Cairns was rapidly turning into a monster worthy of Mary Shelley's Frankenstein.

Says Dave: "Trouble followed them around and they loved it. They were hooligans, a gang of guys from the East End who liked fighting. That was their lifestyle. And I guess that a few of them didn't realise that this wasn't just a bit of fun. It was our living, our vocation."

The hard core of the Glory Boys had fallen out of love with the band two months earlier, after the Huddersfield Polytechnic gig. Tom McCourt recalls: "The reason why me, Bernie, Bob, Rubble, John O'Connor and the rest of our mob stopped following the Affair was down to Huddersfield. The atmosphere was good during the day, but it got heated afterwards. The scooter boys started, a few (and I mean a few) of us did them and Page was on the coach back saying that it was all out of order about there shouldn't be violence at gigs blah blah blah. Then on the Monday at the Bridgehouse, on stage, he said something along the lines of we played Huddersfield and this is what we gave them and went into 'Time for Action' – to the cheers of people who hadn't been there! The fucking hypocrite! That was it for us and Secret Affair. The rest of the Glory Boys shifted to the Rejects later, mainly as a West Ham thing."

The Glory Boys weren't always innocent though. At Canterbury University that same month, a student who was taking the piss out of the band while they were playing was smacked around the head with a hammer by Crank. Police and an ambulance were called. There were no arrests but the bloodied hammer was discarded on the dashboard of Secret Affair's van.

"It was this kind of incident that eventually led us to hiring our own security," says Dave Cairns. "Most bands at that level would have done the same. We were letting fans into our shows for nothing who were more often than not winding up in fights or worse. No promoter would stand for that. We were warned by our agent and promoters that if we didn't contain the situation at the gigs, we wouldn't play."

The Affair filmed the promo video for their debut single 'Time For Action' at the Acklam Hall in Notting Hill, West London. The Glory Boys made up the audience (with a very youthful Eddie Piller standing in the shadows). The Ladbroke Grove Skins, led by Chris Harwood, got wind of it and turned up in force.

Dave Cairns recalls: "We were on stage finishing off the filming, doing retakes and so on, doing our job. We were away of a fracas outside but didn't know the extent of it. It was a full-scale riot. When we left the club it was like stepping in to a warzone. There were burnt out cars immediately outside and the smell of burning rubber in the air."

(Although Glory Boy Dave Lawrence empathetically denies both the suggestion that any cars were set alight in the fight, and the claim that the LGS had won).

Although the hardcore had fallen out with Page over Huddersfield, those who remained were still game for "action". There was more trouble on the March of the Mods tour at the Newcastle Mayfair gig on August 31st. Purple Hearts singer Rob Manton recalls: "We were a few numbers into our set when we started to get pint glasses of beer, some still full, thrown at us. They appeared to be coming from some older guys in their late twenties at the back of the hall. I said something like. 'There are some people here who want to wreck the gig, you know what to do'." At that point, although out-numbered the Glory Boys went in to action, and attacked the local trouble-makers. Manton remembers it as being "like a bar-room brawl in a Western." He goes on: "I believe the bouncers must have joined in on our side, because it was all over pretty quickly and the gig carried on without further interruptions."

As hits like 'Time For Action', 'Let Your Heart Dance' and 'My World' were swelling their live audience, Secret Affair knew they had to take drastic action to distance themselves from violence. They still employed a couple of the hardcore fans – Dave Lawrence and Chris Stratton - to sell merchandise on tour but they also brought in two ex-soldiers as security guards (ex-para Mick and the aforementioned former SAS man Dave) to keep the likes of Crank out. When a fan was knifed at their Portsmouth Pier gig that September, the band could at least say that no-one on their guest list was responsible.

"Most of the Glory Boys understood," says Cairns. "But one or two thought we were getting too big for our boots.

"They didn't think they were doing anything wrong. Fighting was just what they did. They didn't consider that he might be causing us problems but they were."

The aggravation caused by ruck-happy fans was to prove the worst of the Mod Revival's worries. The gig at the London Lyceum on August 26th also featured the nascent 2-Tone bands Madness and The Selecter. Like the Specials and Bad Manners, they were also providing a danceable post-punk sound…one that would ultimately prove far more successful.

SQUIRE

THE NEW SINGLE

WALKING DOWN THE KING'S ROAD

SEE 2

I-SPY RECORDS

CINEMA MOD-ERNE

Quadrophenia, August, 1979.

'WE ARE THE MODS, WE ARE THE MODS, WE ARE, WE ARE, WE ARE MODS…'

Brighton '64 and a proud, rowdy mob dominate the sea-front reveling in a riot, a white riot, a riot of their own…That's just one of the amazingly authentic scenes from Quadrophenia OUT NOW — a celluloid slice of a week in the life of West London Mods way back then; their sex, drugs, fights, clothes, transport, attitudes and life-style - and in particular one Mod, Jimmy, for whom the Brighton riots are a turning point in his fast-developing, drug-fuelled identity crisis.

For Jimmy, Brighton is everything, the highpoint of his existence as a Mod, the glorious pinnacle of the thrills, spills (and pills) of being SOMEBODY: "I don't wanna be the same as everybody else," he says. "That's why I'm a Mod. You gotta be somebody otherwise you might as well jump in the sea and drown."

But his certainty and striving for identity and independence bring him up against the law, fickle facile love, stuff-shirted bosses, and of course parents who don't understand why "he can't just be normal."

Director Franc Roddam has captured the spirit of the era. Phil Daniels is cast perfectly as the anti-hero. His scene with Steph (Leslie Ash) in a Brighton alley will stain sheets for years to come.

Quadrophenia is Jimmy's story and thousands of you who'll see it will know its part of your story too. It's as real as a kick in the bollocks but nowhere near as painful. It will undoubtably swell the ranks of today's related but autonomous Mod Renewal crack and serve as a superb monument to anyone dedicated to looking good, living fast and having fun.

The film of the year for the movement of the moment. And the jeans are by Levi. Who else?

Quadrophenia first saw life in 1973 as The Who's two-disc concept album. It was supposed to be the equal of their blockbuster rock opera Tommy, but in terms of sales and impact it couldn't compete.

If we're talking story-telling and song quality, however, I'd argue Quadrophenia is the better work. The narrative is simpler, but infinitely more realistic. There ain't no deaf dumb and blind pinball-playing Messiah here; no insanely over-produced pop culture fantasy. This is street life as it was lived…

London Mod Jimmy, his life coming apart at the seams, takes too much speed and blows his dough on a first class ticket to Brighton.

Here, Jimmy, a desperate mix of youth, ambition and fear, discovers the ace face Mod he once looked up to working as a lowly hotel bell boy.

The record ends up with Jimmy pissed, paranoid and stranded in the sea on a rock. (In the film, he comes off a scooter which flies off a cliff edge).

Maybe the horns and orchestration seem out of time, but the songs and many of the lyrics hit the spot.

'The girl I love is a perfect dresser/Wears every fashion, gets it to the tee/Heavens above, I've got to match her/I know just how she wants her man to be…' (Sea & Sand)

QUADROPHENIA

THE WHO FILMS
Present A CURBISHLEY BAIRD PRODUCTION **QUADROPHENIA**

Musical Directors ROGER DALTREY • JOHN ENTWISTLE • PETE TOWNSHEND

Screenplay by DAVE HUMPHRIES • MARTIN STELLMAN • FRANC RODDAM • Produced by ROY BAIRD & BILL CURBISHLEY

Directed by FRANC RODDAM • A POLYTEL FILM

RLD NORTHAL
CORPORATION

DOLBY STEREO ™

R | **RESTRICTED**

Under 17 requires accompanying Parent or Adult Guardian

THE POSTMEN

Canning Town, August, 1979.

EVERY week the music press subjects us to some pretentious fart spouting tedious, unintelligible guff about 'challenging rock 'n' roll practices' and 'redefining the limits'.

Generally all these articles achieve are big black print marks on the pinkies of any poor fool dumb enough to dig out a dictionary and wade through them.

What these self-satisfied rock intellectuals don't realise is that the real 'redefining' goes on in places they'd never dream of going to.

Like the Wellington at Waterloo last week, where street-poet Barney Rubble led a makeshift group recruited on the spot onto the stage: a right rowdy mob clutching drum sticks and recorders.

It certainly seemed like a real racket was painfully imminent. But they managed to blag some equipement and, with Hoxton Tom on a borrowed bass, John on guitar, Rory on drums, Kev on harmonica, Shaun on recorder and Tone on tambourine, a semblance of order was introduced into the chaos.

In fact, it sounded pretty good when the Modish looking band — they could call themselves the Fred Perry Five — struck up the likes of 'Al Capone' and various reggae and soul backing tracks for some indecipherable toasting from Mr Rubble on the alleged superiority of West Ham United FC.

'Look out, listen can you hear it?' the bard asked in one of his few defiantly coherent bursts. 'Panic in the CBL / Look out listen can you hear it? / Millwall up against the wall.'

The Postmen are similar. They work by word of mouth: an audience is assembled in minutes. Teenage gangs 'doing their own thing'. They choose a stage, empty houses, back gardens, parks and with makeshift instruments run a gauntlet of, strangely-unmusical songs such as

'Beardsmen' and 'Have A Cigar' held together by raucous singing and vulgar enthusiasm.

They've got no frameworks as such, they do it "for a laugh" and a real crack it is too. The Postmen's music is democracy run wild. Pogo and screw the pre-defined concepts of how groups work!

Back in the Wellington, Barney has led his mob offstage and five minutes later Six More Prophets are on; an Oxford six-piece making a rare London appearance. And, well it has to be said, the earth did not catch fire. For the first few numbers, I was particularly disappointed as the sound, though nicely driving, all seemed rather gutless and identikit. There was something missing.

In truth, the most interesting thing about the visual presentation was trying to figure out the point of having three guitarists. The band explained it as "None of us are powerful guitarists — we don't use power chords for example - but together the effect is powerful."

True, but all that's likely to lead to is a fresh over-manning scandal so prevalent in today's newspapers.

I was about to write them off until the fourth and fifth numbers, 'Not That Young' and 'Crime' when suddenly a rather ordinary band were transformed into a forceful punchy pop outfit with some fine guitar interplay. Now if all the set was like this…

Sadly it ain't. Their version of The Temptations' 'Ain't Too Proud To Beg', was appalling, while the slower 'Now I Know' was so drippy it must have taken days to dry the stage. They didn't get an encore.

GLORY BOYS!

August Bank Holiday, 1979.

11.15am. A car-load of West Ham skinheads from Grays, Essex, pulls up on the forecourt of the Five Bells pub at Southend-on-Sea. As they get out stretching their legs they are surrounded by a gang of eight older Rockabillies who have been laying in wait. It's a rat-trap, baby, and they've been caught. Or so the leering Rockabillies think. They don't realise that their intended prey are the front-runners of a twelve strong convoy of skins, Glory Boys, Mods and assorted hooligans. Parka-clad terrace legend Kevin 'Wellsy' Wells in the car behind spots what's happening and stands up through the sun-roof, re-directing the other cars back round the roundabout to the pub forecourt like a determined general. Rockabilly faces drain of colour as the cars circle them and park. An awesome away-team spill out; among them are Hoxton Tom McCourt, Barney Rubble, ace face Bob 'Bovril' Baisden, Gary Hodges, and a plethora of hardcore West Side combatants including H, Bernie, Kenny, Frank and Grimsby. It's the Sweeney of street-style. If there ever was an A-Team of hooligans, these guys are it.

The Rockabillies don't run, but they're not happy. The ambushers have been ambushed themselves. They shrink into a circle. Hands reach for coshes, chains and knives. They aren't nearly enough. It's all over very quickly.

Bank Holidays and beach-fighting go together like pie and mash, strawberries and cream, bovver and boot. This very English tradition has been revived this year in the wake of the exciting Mod renewal that has shaken up London and the Home Counties. Lots of youth tribes are heading for Southend – mostly Mods and Skins, with sub-sections of suedeheads and Glory Boys, the hard Mods who follow Secret Affair, along with a sizeable proportion of terrace tearaways... I'm just hoping they don't start steaming into each other – last weekend's scooter rally got called off after Northern Mods clashed with their Southern rivals and then the Old Bill. Mods against Mods. Everyone agrees that this is bad news. There's no need for it.

I'm here as an interested participating observer – a low-rent Hunter S. on beer and speed - to record the day's events for posterity, in Sounds, the music paper which has become the thinking Mod's rock weekly of choice.

The car I'm in reaches the Essex coast at 10.35am. We follow the signs to Southend sea-front, past the Kursaal arcade and the Minerva pub. Christ, there must be fifty bikers and Teds here already and we ain't seen a Mod yet. We sink in our seats, turn up the collars of our Harringtons and keep driving. Well, what do you know? We turn the corner and see a sea of new wave sons and daughters. The seafront is crammed with Mods and Skins surging down towards the Minerva and getting repelled by a thin blue line of Essex cops. The mood is good, buzzing. The chants are loud and persistent:

"We are the Mods!"

"Skin'eads!"

"We are the Mods!"

"Skin'eads!"

"We are, we are, we are the Mods!"

Let's park this car, find that pub on the seafront where everyone is meeting, the Hope, cos life is a drink, and you get drunk when you're young...

STAND outside the pub, sinking lagers – "Forsyte Sagas" – in the humid sunshine. About 200 Mods are gathered on the seafront opposite. Sporadically they charge down the road towards "the Grease" and get turned back. They look good. No-one thinks it odd that so many late Seventies teenagers are deliberately setting out to re-live the kind of seaside mayhem that so excited tabloid headline writers in the Sixties. "That was then, this is now," says Eddie, a 17-year-old electrician from Hackney. "Now it's our turn."

A train load of Skins with a smattering of punks turn up from Southend station. The two crowds size each other up and cheer in mutual celebration. They cheer cos they're smart and they're clean and this is the time to be seen. Time for action...

And a good old Cockney knees-up, in the groin.

By mid-afternoon there are close on 3,000 here, although the police and the press say 1500. The activity consists mostly of mixed Mod and Skin regiments making random charges in the direction of the opposition in the Minerva, spreading over roads like spilt soup on a kitchen floor, and holding back the traffic in mass displays of strength. And I'm in there with them, swept along by the mob and the excitement…when you're in the crowd, you don't see any problems; you don't fear anyone or anything. It's all jubilation - just crazy smiles and the feeling of being unshackled; of POWER. It's like the first time you invade a football pitch. There's nothing anyone can do to stop you. For the first time they – the cops, the authorities – are afraid of YOU.

Paul Weller won't approve, but inevitably his lyrics are running through our brains: 'Feeling so brave, you can't be stopped when you're young…'

THE funny thing is it's not that violent. It looks worse than it is. And naturally it will be portrayed in the newspapers as being far worse than it was. But I've been caught up in violence before, at demonstrations and this is small beer compared to Grunwicks or Lewisham or Red Lion Square. All that really happens is a couple of hundred kids at a time charge down the road, a few coppers say "You can't go no further" and the kids turn back. Revolution it ain't. But no-one seems to care. Being there, that's what counts. The laugh, the crack: tribal rival rebel revelry. A young Tilbury skinhead who paddled out a hundred yards into the sea to kip in a boat was the hero of the early afternoon.

The feel-good mood does not last. As beer flows, fights erupt like teenage spots. The skins are the most daring and also the prime targets for random arrests. One time a rocker drives his car past a gang but it gets caught up in the traffic. Skins swarm around it like angry hornets. They yell abuse and kick at the panelling with their steel-capped Doc Martins while the driver shoots v-signs at them, his fingers festooned with cheap, lairy rings. The cops materialise and the gang leg it. Undeterred a uniformed officer grabs a young skinhead who had been watching from a wall and shouts, "You're nicked!"

"I ain't done nuffin," the kid protests, accurately. The cop knees him in the bollocks and drags him off.

Gangs rarely attempt to rescue mates who are nicked, although the arrested themselves put on a show. One skin, handcuffed in the back of a van, puts his feet on his burly captor's chest and sends him flying through the door. Another cuffed crop-head makes a run for it to mass cheers before he falls arse over tit and is retrieved by the ever-angrier Essex constabulary.

Bet they both got a good going over down the station.

Stories of individual bravado buzz around the pilchard-packed pub, becoming instant mythology, embellished and magnified through noisy repetition.

THE MOD REVIVAL

The police eventually identify the Hope as hooligan mission control. The hardcore are here, and so are the pill-pushers and the kids flogging snide t-shirts. Just after 2pm the cops decide to shut the place down. This is the only time serious violence seems a possibility. A lot of the older West Ham chaps are in here and as the cops mob up outside glasses smash and the pub explodes in raucous defiance: "Kill the Bill!", "I'm forever blowing bubbles!", "Harry Roberts is our friend, he kills coppers!" "I like punk and I like Sham, I got nicked over West 'am"; "Maybe it's because I'm a Londoner…"

Why don't you all f-f-f-fade away…don't try to dig what we all s-s-s-say.

I'm in the midst of it, swept along with the defiance, intoxicated by the danger, a feeling of invincibility fuelled by speed and lager.

"Come on then, cunt-stable," says Gary Dickle. "Come and have a go…"

THE cops think they can defuse the situation expertly by clearing the pub with dogs. No-one fancies taking on snarling Alsatians, so people move out slowly, moodily spilling on to the pavement. It's counter-productive. Angry now, the mob storm towards the Minerva like they mean business. We pass the Wimpy Bar with its smashed window – a skin girl is said to have thrown a Ted girl through it a few hours earlier. About a hundred yards ahead of us, the Grease have swelled to about 200 strong. A Glory Boy platoon suddenly breaks away from our flank and surges up the hill to the left. It makes the charge in Quadrophenia seem as threatening as Annie Walker shambling across the Coronation Street cobbles. The tactic is obvious – hit the Minerva from the rear. A classic pincer movement. But the cops are smart. They see what's happening and head off the breakaway mob at the pass. Once again, the ragged army of Mods, skins and football herberts is turned back before they reach their target. There will be no mass beach fighting today.

THE two sides stare uneasily at each other, with the cops in between. I doubt it even occurs to any of them to wonder why exactly they are "at war". It's just accepted as natural. The Rockers – the Grease – are the eternal enemy whose presence has united all the different gangs. But what are they really? Just other working class English folk with wildly contrasting ideas of what constitutes a cool look and a good night out…

Maybe that's just the way it is; everyone's gotta hate someone. That's how people are.

Inevitably my mind goes back to my own youth, eleven years earlier. It was June 1968, I had just turned thirteen. I was at the Dreamland amusement park in Margate, Kent, with an older cousin and my friend

Kevin from Charlton. There were gangs of left-over Mods and Rockers dotted about, along with a few mobs of younger skinheads. The Mod girls looked gorgeous with their bobbed hair and slacks or skirts that came just over their knees; but love was most definitely not in the air this day. The out-of-town Mods eyed the local Rockers with contempt. Their displeasure was returned with a side-order of venom. The tension fascinated me. The Mods were more numerous, the Rockers fewer but older and probably harder. The first fight kicked off. I wasn't scared, it was exhilarating, but my cousin bundled me and Kev into an arcade. Opposite, a fella with Ted side-burns leapt over his hotdog counter to join the fray. An older kid saw his chance and seized it. He vaulted the counter, opened the till and helped himself to the takings, taking to his heels just seconds before the police arrived. Years later, the comedian Malcolm Hardee confessed to me that this opportunist tea-leaf had been him...

To the papers, politicians, and the TV news hooliganism is all just pointless – either mindless violence or empty bravado. But they only see youth cults from the outside, from a distance. They see the boot go in or the window smash but they don't see the creativity and culture – the art, the music, the style, poetry, literature, friendships and the feeling, goddamn it, the feeling of being part of something, something now, something happening, something that matters. It's like judging a rhino by its horn or the work of Dickens by the misogyny of Bill Sykes.

Back in the heady here and now, I contemplate the opposing tribes. Aside from the sartorial differences, the biggest rift between them is age. The Rockers are generally older. They're also scruffier and tooled up; some have quiffs but mostly they have long greasy hair, a mass of leather and denim sheltering under an American Confederate flag. Some of their trousers are flared.

The Mods hoist up a Union Jack with The Who emblazoned across it as a counterpoint. "They're history, we're now," says a spotty teen, the irony completely lost on him.

Sharp young Londoners start to banter. "Look at them spotty hairy-faced bastards – and the blokes are just as bad."

"What about that grease-bag? 'E's got enough oil on his barnet to solve the fuckin' petrol crisis."

"Look at that fat cunt, he'd 'ave to go to school to be an idiot..." and on it goes. And it's the same with the Rockers, who think the Mods are effeminate "girls", and the skins are "thickoes". "My brain hurts!" yells a fella in a drape-jacket pointing a heavily ringed finger at a skin. "Look! 'is brain hurts! Migraine! The fuckin' gumbie. Where's yer hankie, gumbie? Mum forget to pack it? Have a look! His fuckin' strides have had a row with his shoes."

Heated slogans and obscenities are hollered before the bored cops begin to push the Mod-Skin crowd back again.

The Enemy is never engaged. They're never even reached; and it seems to me that most people prefer it like that. It makes them all the more perfect: Pantomime baddies to hiss and boo. It's something to define yourself by: we are not THEM.

This separation makes the few isolated skirmishes of the day seem all the more dramatic, and they are re-told frequently. The arrest of West Side terrace warrior Kevin Wells is a favourite with Wellsy being said to have taken an ever larger number of cops out with him.

It's now gone 3.15pm and the Mod and skin battalions have been pushed back towards Southend Pier. Opinions are split between the hardcore who think the day has been a waste of time because there wasn't much fighting, and the majority who have just enjoyed the sheer anarchy of a good old English show of strength in the sun.

IT'S all downhill from here. Slowly the police push these teenage tickets back along the seafront. Hundreds line the hill up to the town centre: an army without a cause, or a general. Everyone agrees that lack of organisation and co-ordination are the only things that stopped the mob routing all opposition – Grease and cops. But no-one does any organising.

Frustrations boil over. Small incidents with the police detonate along the front. 75 people are arrested today, but there are no serious injuries and the mood is now largely positive: the kids, united, will never be defeated.

We cheer the few flotillas of scooters and clock famous faces from the new Mod scene: Grant Fleming, the three lovable baboons from fanzine Maximum Speed, suede-head legend Hoxton Tom and his entourage, Billy H from the Chords, Yeti, old mates from Greengate, Back To Zero...these are people who have been with the movement since the start, months and months before the Quadrophenia film came out. I just wish every jaded hack who sat behind a desk in London dismissing Mod as a commercial hype could see this now.

I can see for miles...

THERE are a few sporadic charges to alleviate the boredom, but most of the crowd accept that it's over. The afternoon is winding down. Nothing more is going to happen. By 4pm, the majority are leaving; either drifting home or towards Canvey eleven miles away for tonight's gig. We reach the island in 20 minutes and start looking around for Long Road where the show will be. See a Parka-clad kid sitting with his girl by his scooter. It's a beaut, a real handsome P-reg Vespa festooned with extra headlights and wing mirrors. Both the bike and the kid look familiar, and they should do – he's Robert E. Lee who graces the front cover of the Bridgehouse 'Mod Mayday' live album. He obliges us and the van containing r'n'b herberts the Little Roosters with an escort to the Canvey Paddocks. We kill time eating Wimpys and playing 'Love Me Tender' on the pub jukebox for a laugh. All newcomers are greeted with exaggerated accounts of the day's action, and are suckered along long enough to get the drinks in until they twig you're taking the piss and shout "You cunt" without exception. At one stage, Hoxton Tom convinces a dimwit that the police had called in army reinforcements and the skins had linked up with some Navy lads on shore leave. "It was the people walking on the water who got me though and when the Pope turned up on a Lambretta…" "You cunt!"

The turn-out for the gig is a let-down; only five or six hundred in. We were expecting a capacity crowd but it seems most people have headed back to London. Still, the bands are on top form, with promising sets from Squire and Back To Zero building to stunning performances from Secret Affair and the Purple Hearts. A perfect conclusion to an indifferent day. As ever, the Affair's cocky lyrics mirror the mood of the crowd: 'Glad just to be alive…so much I wanna change…' But what, Ian? What do you wanna change? And what are you gonna put in its place? He never says. It's more the thought of change he's embracing, the need to make room for "the young idea" whatever that might be. Or more likely it's just the faces on Top Of The Pops he's referring to. Bye bye Cliff, see ya later Bee-Gees…make way for us? Well, there are worse ambitions.

But Paul Weller caught the grim reality for the audience more accurately when he said how hard it is to understand why the world is your oyster but your future's a clam. Yeah. Because days like today let you think you're a king, when you're really a pawn. We don't care though, we're still buzzing from the glory pills. So much to say, so much to do. We shake hands all round and crawl out into the darkness. We fought the law and went home, we fought the law and we went home. A day in the life of a movement.

Poxy work again tomorrow.

(Reprinted from the book Hoolies by Garry Bushell, with the permission of John Blake Publishing.)

NEWS OF THE WORLD
GOSSIP AND LETTERS...

Arista have signed London Mod band **Secret Affair** to a deal which enables them to have their records released on their own I Spy Label. Their first single under the deal 'Time For Action' will be in shops August 17. The band's forthcoming 'March of the Mods' tour with **Purple Hearts** commences at Scarborough Penhouse on August 10 and ends at Liverpool Eric's on September 1. **Secret Affair** are due to appear in a film called Stepping Out, which documents the rise of the current Mod scene.

The originals and still the best. **The Jam** who are currently recording an album at Virgin's Town House Studio in West London and have a single 'When You're Young'/Smithers-Jones' out on Polydor on August 17. The album is likely to appear in October coinciding wiht a tour by Weller and Co.

True Love: Seen leaving the recent **Barney and his Rubbles** concert at the Wellington, Waterloo - Barney himself hand in hand with Yeti of the Look. Malicious gossips make of that what you will... meanwhile at the same gig we discovered an anti-fanzine called **Minimum Sloth** circulating. Wonder what **Maximum Speed** will make of that.

DETAILS OF the **March of the Mods** tour, featuring **Secret Affair**, **Back To Zero** and **Purple Hearts**, have now been finalised and the bands will play the following dates@ Scarborough Penthouse (August 10), Plymouth Clones

(14) Torquay Town Hall (15), Birmingham Barbarellas (16), Manchester Factory (17), Cheltenham Witcombe Lodge, (18), Swansea Circles (20), Newport Stowaway (22), Bristol Trinity Leisure Centre (23), Cromer West Runton Pavilion (24), London Lyceum (26), Canvey Island The Paddocks (27), Sheffield Limit Club (28), Barnsley Civic Centre (29), Leeds Fforde Green Hotel (20), Newcastle Mayfair (31) and Liverpool Erics (September 1).

MODS FALL OUT HORROR: The first national New Mod tour starting this week has come into a bit of bother already with Essex band the **Little Roosters** getting the boot from their co-headliners Secret Affair and the Purple Hearts in favour of **Back To Zero**.

An irate **Rooster Gary Lammin** told us "We have been dropped because we below **Secret Affair** off-stage at the Marquee and they knew we'd do the same all the country.

Several leading Mods find this very hard to swallow and that the elbow stems from **Back To Zero**'s higher rating in the mod hierarchy than the Roosters, whose music is more late sixties Rolling Stones inclinded.

Secret Affair's Dave Cairns himself said: Gary Lammin's talking drivel, they've never come close to blowing us off stage. **The Roosters** were originally suggested for the tour because they put up a lot of the money. However the other headliners, ourselves and the **Purple Hearts** decided that **Back To Zero** deserve the tour more.

"Besides if **Back To Zero** do the tour **Maximum Speed** will have a proper distribution which is what we all want. We're even holding a private benefit for the paper this week."

Secret Affair incidentally, are also making a short promo film for their soon-come mighty single 'Time For Action'.

the film will be shot round the East End and will hopefully according to Dave, try and explain the hows, whys, whats and wherefores of Mod as a '79 street movement.

Purple Hearts 'Millions Like Us' single is now expected in September, as is **Back To Zero**'s 'Your Side Of Heaven', while **Secret Affair**'s 'Time For Action', as previously announced, will be available on the band's own I-Spy label on August 24.

After the **Little Roosters** were dropped from the March of the Mods tour at last moment, **Roosters** guitarist Gary Lammin rang in to blame 'fellow' MOMT band 'We blew them offstage at the Marquee, and they knew we'd have done it on the tour. They just shit themselves." Ian Page of **Secret Affair** replied that the band wouldn't be dragged into a slagging match he felt that the **Roosters** would hae done nothing to add to the harmonious atmosphere that is needed on such a package...

Squads of Mods Love Quad: Zillions of good reports hitting our streets correspondant on the alleged excellence of 'Quadrophenia'. Modsters giving approval include the unanimous **Chords**, Bridge House Manager **Terry Murphy**, and a raving **Grant Fleming** who commented "It could 'ave been about us - knoworimean".

THE TEENBEATS, who have just released their first single, the Troggs' 'I Can't Control Myself,' on Safari Records, have lined up a series of gigs over the next few weeks. Having played dates in Liverpool and Ramsgate and London (where they supported Chris Farlowe at the Marquee) last week, the band continue at London Rock Garden September 19, London Harrow Road Windsor Castle 21 and then playa matinee at the Fulham Greyhound on the

22nd. It will be open to anyone over the age of 14.

Other confirmed dates for the band are at London The Wellington September 23, High Wycombe Nags Head 26, Blackpool Norbreck Castle 27, Halifax Good Mood Club 29, Canning Town Bridge House October 1, Sheffield Limit Club 2, Middlesbrough Teeside Polytechnic 3, Hayes Adam And Eve 11, Manchester Polytechnic 13, Kingston Polytechnic 20, Nottingham Sandpiper 25.

The LONG march of the mods, led by London band **Secret Affair** who recently signed as exclusive marketing and distribution deal with Arista, plus Purple Hearts and Back To Zero, continues at Birmingham Barbarrellas (Thursday), Manchester Factory (Friday), Cheltenham Whitcombe Lodge (Saturday), Swansea Circles (Monday) and Newport Stowaway (Wednesday).

MEET the Glory Boys. The latest in the line of modern musclemen have lifted their handle from **Secret Affair**'s mod anthem in praise of natty dress. Look out for those tell-tale signs - the squarely-shorn barnet, the 'keyhole' logo emblazoned on the biceps, the word 'Mod' tattooed on the inside of the lower lip. The bruisers in question have exchanged their East End stomping grounds for a stretch of The March of The Mods tour. They claim to be Secret Affair's personal protection service, though without them muses a sceptical journalist, the bnd probably wouldn't need any. In fact, theres been occassions of late when the band have had to protect the Glory Boys. Indeed after the Factory gig in Manchester, Affair hired a troop of taxis to ship the GBs to safety with alien factions seemed to have them outnumbered. At Torquay, Affair and the **Purple Hearts** were left with a sizeable bill for a trashed hotel bar when their fearsome followers droped in for a late night jar. And worse... when Affair played a rcent Acklam Hall gig for the purpose of making a promo film, the unsuspecting GBs were sprung on leaving by a rival army, with a couple of cars getting totalled in the process. Honestly, you can't slink off for a quiet night out anymore now can ya?

MOD MISERY

I AM not a particular Sixties or Mod music freak but after getting pissed off with punk I thought I'd like to become a mod. But my Mod friends made me puke. They inferred that to become a Mod you have to spend £30 on a suit and £12 on a parka then have all the right records and practically a certificate signed by Paul Weller.

And now there's the article practically by the wankers of Maximum Speed. Well MS tried to be the gospel of mod but I've never known such narrow-minded big heads in my life. All the 'hip' groups, the Purple Hearts and Back to Zero hate the Merton Parkas just because the Parkas have got the talent and have released an excellent single.

The groups on the Bridge House LP just play the same old tuneless punk but without the drive and energy that made punk succeed. I thought that Sixties music was tuneful and a bit poppy; not this wimpy punk that the hip bands play. My mate is now a mindless zombie who reads Maximum Speed three times a day and cannot think for himself. I was going to become a Mod cos I like the fashion but I have obviously failed my entrance exam. Long live the Merton Parkas and all the talented mod bands. Up Yours Maximum Speed – **Quentin Cook. Reigate, Surrey** (Quentin went on to be known as Norman Cook aka Fat Boy Slim and Mr Zoe Ball.)

WALKING DOWN THE KINGS ROAD

SEPTEMBER-OCTOBER 1979

UNK WAS TO THE MOD REVIVAL WHAT SKIFFLE
VAS TO THE BRITISH BEAT BOOM - A PRECURSOR
AND A MOTIVATOR - I.E. WITHOUT LONNIE
ONEGAN, NO BEATLES - AND WITHOUT THE
ISTOLS, NO PURPLE HEARTS

imon Stebbing

BACK
TO
ZERO

September 29, 1979.

THE NEXT decade will kick off with this decade's movements – the new wave of Heavy Metal, the old punk, the new punk, the latest crop of over-rated 'head' bands and of course New Mod, the current whipping boy for every worthless hack in the business.

Naturally a lot of Mod bands aren't worth talking about – it's the same with any new musical tide. But our old friends in the press, the usual whining fannies, have been slit up a treat this month by vinyl goodies delivered by the movement's cream – Secret Affair's 'Time For Action', the Purple Hearts' 'Millions Like Us' and 'Now It's Gone' from the Chords. The tastiest threesome since Phil Lynott met those twins… but that's another story.

And behind this triumphant triumvirate - the proof in plastic that New Mod needed and deserved - comes 'Your Side of Heaven', a single from Back To Zero released this week on Chris Parry's Fiction label. It's a potent slice of 70s rock, influenced strongly by 'Can't Explain' period Who, which merits being mentioned in the same breath of its aforementioned contemporaries.

THE MOD REVIVAL

BTZ band have just completed the well-received March Of the Mods tour with the Affair and the Purple Hearts with enough grit and gusto to confirm that their form is definitely not suspect. But that name had always bothered me.

Why should anyone wanna go back to anything? We should be moving forward! After all if New Mod is going to mean anything, surely it's as a Renewal, as a progression from that sublime 60s base.

"Oh yeah, that's right," BTZ's diminutive vocalist Brian Betteridge affirms. "But you've got it wrong. The name ain't supposed to mean anything. It's not a corruption of 'Less than Zero' and it's nothing to do with coming down off speed as different people have suggested. We just wanted a name that wasn't 'The Something'.

"In fact the original slogan was 'Back To Zero? Forward To The Eighties!'"

Hmm. Quite a mouthful, as even Linda Lovelace would avow.

Actually, in the very beginning the band were going to be called Maximum Speed and that famed mod zine was to be Back To Zero; the band and the 'zine's fates intimately entwining because Clive of MS was doing likewise with BTZ guitarist Sam Burnett's sister. And the three illiterate Xerox monkeys have managed the band since their humble North London beginnings last Christmas when comprehensive kid Brian Betteridge, a Sixties soul fanatic with a large vinyl inheritance from an elder ex-Mod brother, finally tied the musical knot with his grammar school educated partners, Burnett, Mal (bass) and Moore, Andy (drums) – all recent converts to the embryonic and still independent North London Mod scene.

Sam, the band's composer, was irresistibly drawn to New Mod. He'd liked punk music but not the image, and was set on the parka trail after attending an early Purple

Hearts gig.

"We didn't consciously set out to be a Mod band," he explains. "But we were all committed to Mod and so naturally we became part of the movement."

Influenced by Costello and early R&B, Burnett developed an individual sound accurately characterized by the managerial trio in Sounds as "catchy, melodic and moody". Translation? Well, whereas the Chords hit like a runaway steam engine, BTZ's numbers are less instant, and tend to mature with repeated hearings.

"Maybe we're the thinking man's Mod band" laughs Brian.

Their current set contains some infectious gems which augur well for future development. Like the haunting 'Modern Boys' which they wisely swerved as a single release to avoid getting drawn into the spurious race to produce a Mod anthem. No need to be so…obvious.

Instead 'Your Side of Heaven' has a stab at following their contemporaries into the nether regions of the charts (even if the B-side 'Back To Back', the hardest number in the set live, is marred here by poor production.)

My only real reservation about the band is that they aren't charismatic characters either on or off stage and given their lack of musical clout this could cause problems. But then again, it does mean that they're cheerfully egoless. Lord knows there are enough big heads with bigger gobs in this business…

Maybe I'm over-cautious. After all, they've done well this year, slowly building up much Mod respect that the recent tour enhanced and though they've been off the road since due to the departure of drummer Moore ("musical differences" – he was a closet Deaf Barton). The imminent recruitment of a new beat keeper and a planned spate of gigs to coincide with the single should see them consolidating their high position in the Mod league table.

Bearing in mind the sheer enjoyment of their best numbers and the changing shape of Sam's writing – a gradual departure from the obvious power chord trappings – the boys could be maturing into one of the most rewarding new bands at the start of the new decade.

Back to Zero? Nah. Forward to the Eighties!

*This article originally ran with the sub-heading: 'The thinking man's Arthur Mullard - Garry Bushell - meets the thinking man's Mods – Back To Zero'. Mr. Mullard, for those who don't remember, was of course a renowned British intellectual whose version of 'You're The One That I Want' – a duet with feminist icon Hilda Baker – was a supreme exercise in ironic subversion. Probably.

sounds

The Face of '79

PAGE 32

THE MODS

Bridgehouse, Canning Town, September 29, 1979.

THE Mods got to headline tonight's show after winning the toss of a coin with Beggar, who proceeded to go down like a cup of cold sick with a bored East London audience. Faced with crowds this jaded, Beggar would be best advised to invest in double-headed coins. Let some other poor sods warm up the Billies...

Once a cover band, the Mods still throw in the likes of 'Substitute', but original numbers like 'Party Land' suggest this Edgware-based combo are worth taking seriously.

And what's that you say? Their name is a cynical cash-in? Untrue. The Mods christened themselves thusly in the summer of '78, many months before the Revival took shape. By the time the buzz about the Purple Hearts had started, the still teenaged Mods had already played Dingwalls.

The band consists now of Neil Cox on guitar and vocals, Alan Robson (guitar), Dave Ross (bass) and Ian Guthrie (drums). Original singer Mark Casson left last month to form called Catch 22 just for the Heller it (literary gag, sorry).

The Mods started of playing Tamla Motown classics spiced up with songs by the Small Faces, the Kinks, the Who and the Beatles – so a far more sixties sound than the Chords or the Hearts.

By January this year, they had introduced three original ditties including the foot-tappingly populist set-closing tour de force, 'One Of The Boys' which is generally accompanied on stage by the destruction of a TV set. Punters love this, venue managers generally seem less impressed.

Chaps, put Thomas & Sarah [Naff Upstairs Downstairs Spin-off - Square Eyed Ed] on screen when you do it, and I'll jump up and help you.

The band doesn't shy away from playing to the crowd. Dave Ross happily pounded away on his bass to accompany the Bridgehouse crowd's chant of "Mods! Mods! Mods!" lest anyone mistook them for the long raincoat brigade...

Tight and confident, the Mods are a hard-gigging band who first came to the outside world's attention with their tracks on the Bridgehouse Mods Mayday compilation album. They sound much better in the flesh.

PS. Always popular live, the Mods never really caught on with other bands and by the end of the year their London shows were suffering from the fashionable disease of mindless crowd violence. Their staunch and vocal North West London following seemed to irritate local mobs and the band increasingly shied away from the capital, building up a decent following in the Midlands. Record companies never came a-sniffing, however – the band's name wasn't their stepping stone - and after soldiering on with gigs the Mods finally demobbed in August 1981 after playing bottom of the bill at the Finsbury Park Rainbow.

NORTHERN MOD: THE SHOCKING TRUTH

Yorkshire, October, 1979.

n October, 1979, I thought that I ought to explore the Northern Mod scene for myself. You could subtitle this piece: 'I thought all Northern Mods wore flairs, and Parkas blitzed with beer mats until I discovered The Killermeters…'

I CHANGED TRAINS at Leeds, leaving the relatively plush Inter-City behind to board the Huddersfield connection, a vehicle so archaic I half expected to find Robert Stephenson stoking the boiler (lovely woman, name of Doreen, 18-stone in her stockings).

Settling back, the grim words of the last Cockney voice I'd heard echoed around my brain again – a stern-faced Southern Mod advising me strongly against going on this mission of discovery to industrial Yorkshire.

THE MOD REVIVAL

Grimly, the youth repeated old prejudices about Northerners and their alleged obsessions with Stranglers stick-ons, 40-inch flairs (referred to in hushed tones down here as 'the trouser problem') and Parkas covered in beer-mats and sewn-on bar towels.

He poked a finger at my Harrington, tastefully bedecked with CAFC and Secret Affair badges, pointed at my straight jeans and functional Fred Perry and told me, in no uncertain terms, that I'd be about as welcome "up there" as a dose of clap on honeymoon.

He also reckoned that I'd make a mighty fine target for Northern retribution for supposed Southern crimes. Risky or what? Sod it, I thought, I ain't getting paid danger money, why don't I just jump back on the old John Wayne and go on the Tom & Dick for a week?

But don't fret, faithful readers. Sounds scribes are made of sterner stuff, and, hiding behind Ms. Turbett's skirt, I trundled on...only to find that the Southern Mods had got it all wrong and that their view of the North has been based on premature sightings of their Northern counterparts...from June, in fact, when Secret Affair had brought a coach-load of lairy Londoners up for a gig with the Killermeters, the Huddersfield band who form the musical mainspring of the whole Northern Mod scene.

For the first time, that night the local scooter clubs had decided to turn up in force, displaying the aforementioned fashion embarrassments, and it was their alien presence that had led the Southerners to pre-judge and write off the Northern scene. But that's not to say, North and South have much history in common. Although very similar in essence now, the two scenes are miles apart. Whereas Southern Mod took off in earnest in February this year, with embryonic roots stretching back to mid '77, Mod in the North has a more direct link with original sixties Modernism.

By their own admission, the North caught onto Mod later, but hung onto it longer, although some would argue more as a parka and scooter thing than a posey/state of mind affair. In the south, the original Mods split into hippies and suits (who begat the skinheads) and scooters fell rapidly from grace. In the North, however, change was slower and different, and the scene was still flourishing long after trend-setting London townies were into acid or aggro.

Mod DJs everywhere had prided themselves on their ability to search out new artists and new labels, developing their sets beyond the standard Mod soul soundtrack music of Tamla Motown and Stax. They sniffed out over-looked gems on smaller labels. Naturally when Mod persisted in the North, the DJs continued this trend, and (I'm oversimplifying like crazy) this eventually evolved into the distinctive sound of Northern Soul - fast, brassy, often bootlegged and found on labels like Ric-Tic, Shout and Golden Records.

Based round all-nighters in Wigan and surrounding areas such as Cleethorpes, Manchester, and Blackpool, Northern Soul developed in the early seventies as a Mod off-spring with marked differences. Primarily the cult made such a fetish of obscurity that musical values went increasing by the board, while for practical reasons suits collars and ties were replaced by vests and wide bags (the new scene was also a lot straighter than its predecessor, less the prerogative of the sharpest kids). Clubs such as the Wigan Casino, the Twisted Wheel in Manchester and the Golden Torch in Stoke-on-Trent became Meccas for this emerging scene.

Aside from sweet soul music, the other constant in the North's evolution were the scooter clubs for whom Wigan all nighters were a danceable alternative to the staple diet of cross-country scooter runs. These clubs span the years between Sixties and Seventies Mod, and even though at times club membership might have been down to five or six enthusiasts, the tradition was not allowed to die.

New Mod has swelled their ranks again. One informed observer tells me that there are currently around 2,000 scooterists north of Birmingham organized in clubs like the Fugitives and Revival in Huddersfield, the Red Lion Club in Heckmondwicke, the Yorkshire Roadrunners, the Scunthorpe Road Rats, the Preston Wildcats, the Crewe Jaguars… and many more (the South's 5-15 Club from Sevenoaks, Kent, aren't too well respected it would seem however and prejudiced put-down tales abound about how they bring their scooters on runs in the back of lorries; an outrage of course).

This summer, the Scooter clubs discovered the New Northern Mod scene and for the most part fell in love with it. Many of the scooter boys have now discovered the fashions too and a casual observer would be hard pressed to tell the two tribes apart on the clothes front. (One club incidentally is completely infatuated with the Jam and have customized their scooters with the 'Strange Town' single sleeve picture).

At the same time, much more so than in the south, Northern Mod music fans have shown a corresponding interest in the scooter clubs. But where, you might well ask, did they come from?

THE ANSWER in a word is the Killermeters. The 'Meters began life in mid-77 as a punked-up r&b combo then called the Killer Meters. They were influenced by Dr Feelgood and the Stones, and lasted until the beginning of '78 when disillusionment set like plaster. They reformed

West Runton Pavilion

Tuesday Sep. 25th	SPECIAL GIG BY THE FABULOUS **PENETRATION** at a special price of 80p
Saturday Sep. 29th	To continue the march of the mods - **THE CHORDS** Plus guests **ONE EYED JACKS**
Friday Oct. 5th	To consolidate it : **MERTON PARKAS**
Saturday Oct. 6th	**SOUXSIE** and the **BANSHEES** Plus special guests **THE CURE**
Friday Oct. 12th	**SLAUGHTER & THE DOGS**
Saturday Oct. 13th	**SORE THROAT**
Thursday Oct. 18th	**Judie Tzuke**

the following October and consist now of vocalist and bassist Vic Vespa – formerly Vic Vomit, actually Vic Szczenowicz (not much of a name, but a brilliant score in Scrabble); then there is lead guitarist Mick Moore, drummer Graham 'Jez' Jessop and the Ruttle brothers Sid and Tony on rhythm guitars. Their sound today is very different.

"We were all pissed of with straightforward basic punk material which is why the band split up," jez explains. "We wanted to play something with a bit more melody and technique hence the type of songs we started doing in October."

Coinciding with their change in musical direction was the band's increasing association with Paul Nicholson, a Sixties Mod who'd never lost his cool and who would talk at length about Mod as he'd lived it. Northern Soul never floated Nicholson's boat. "Mod didn't die here till about 1969," he explains "and Northern Soul to me didn't have any identity, stupid baggy trousers and… Well I never had any time for it."

Inspired by Paul Nicholson's recollections, and their own musical ambitions, led the 'Meters to decide that Mod was the image they wanted to adopt, and this at time when the Jam aside, only the Purple Hearts were blazing the parka trail dahn south.

In short, they began totally independently from the Southern scene playing their first gig last December and gradually building their own following who, perhaps more jocularly than the South, have congealed into a movement of their own, calling themselves the Jolly Boys.

Aptly Paul is known as King Jolly but I spoke to one of his deputies, a guy by the name of Evil Roman. It's true! I'm not making this shit up. He had his name changed by deed poll, and went from writing fanzines and poetry to being the Killermeters' biggest fan. This guy is nuts. He once walked ten miles to get to one Killermeters gig and took an Aladdin over-dose the one times he missed a performance. Believe me, no-one ever did that for the Merton Parkas...

According to the slightly unnerving Evil, Jolly Boys have a much more challenging mission statement than the Glory Boys of London town. Their one aim in life is to get steamed out of their boxes every time they go out; in other words, inebriated, legless, pissed...so drunk in fact that skunks notice. In short well and truly, jollied up. (Blues incidentally are virtually non-existent up here; beer is the drug of choice).

OF ALL the bands to have emerged in the North in their wake – The Name in Peterborough, the Moving Targets in Leeds, The Scene in Bradford, Handsome Jack & The Casualties (cough) also in Huddersfield, and the punky Two Tone Pinks in Manchester –

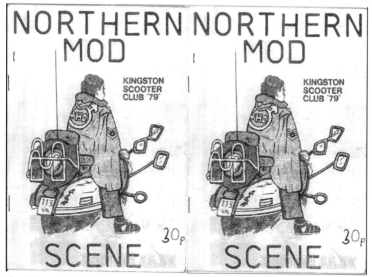

the 'Meters have undoubtedly established the biggest and best scene around them, as amply illustrated by tonight's gig at Huddersfield's one Mod venue, the Albion (once the location for a punk disco that was dropped as punks became virtually extinct up here, replaced by a Mod movement which has been expanding steadily ever since the 'Meters bridged the gap between Mods and Scooter Clubs in May).

Fact is, Mod is far bigger now in Huddersfield than punk was at its coinciding stage of development. It's also a solidly working class movement, as reflected in the 'Meters own day jobs – two engineers one carpet fitter, one cabinet maker and one building labourer.

Most of the local scooter clubs have shot off to Wigan tonight – it's the first all-nighter for about a year – but there are still enough eager punters to pack the place out. I take the opportunity to chat to fans, the band, King Jolly and Scooter boy Bob Monkhouse (no relation) who is a member of the 15-strong and growing Fugitives Club.

Bob's been riding scooters for six years now and he lives and breathes them, forming his own club yonks back and currently owning ten of the beauties, all of them personally customised by his own fair hands. His eyes glaze over at the mention of the Arthur Francis Extra S-type 200 and he affects a heartfelt sneer at the mention of Vespas ("Lambrettas are scooters," he says. "Vespas are Vespas.")

"I used to listen to Northern Soul," Bob admits. "But I didn't start going to Wigan till '76. I started listening to the Killermeters about two months ago. I don't really rate many new Mod bands but the Killermeters are definitely going places. Now you've got Northern Soul one way and Mod bands the other, and Scooters are in the middle linking the two together."

The worst aspect of the current Northern scene is the growing police interest in scooter riders, and just as many people testify to police victimization as condemn violence between North and South, something Paul Nicholson gets particularly uptight about. "It's ridiculous," he opines, "A load of shit. North or South, its all working class kids, that's what it's all about and what's the point of working class kids punching shit out of each other?"

None at all I'd say, none at all. I wondered how he felt about now the sixties, being part of both and all.

"Well it's different, it's not the same at all now really. We used to blow all out wages on clothes and now it's all second hand clothes, and they've got their own thing now, their own music which is great, especially Secret Affair, the Teenbeats and the Killermeters. The only bad thing when the Southerners came up was you had some of these Glory Boys wondering about going 'Sieg Heil' and that really annoyed us here."

And that is another gratifying thing about the North – there's no obsession with violence, and no hint of suspect politics.

Downstairs tonight the dance-floor makes Wembley on cup-final day look like a two man audience in the Albert Hall. I wouldn't say it was packed but it took me six attempts to reach the bar and then I only succeeded by yelling 'Fire' in a strange high-pitched voice.

The first chilly fingers of lager were just finding their way into my belly when stage front the pilchard-packed mob's chants of 'Joy-joy-joy-joy-JOLLY BOYS!' reached a crescendo and the five Killermeters trotted on stage to a riotous reception. Yeah, I know it was a home crowd and all that but no way was the crowd's ecstatic reception the result of excess beer or misplaced loyalty. Simply the band play one hell of a fine blend of sixties derived (cynics in the office claimed my tape recalled everyone from George Harrison to Wayne Fontana) modern pop; a creamy twelve song recipe that puts them well up in the Mod's Division One by my humble reckoning.

Best number for my money was the next single (either on Psycho this month or EMI/Din Disc/Phonogram etc if they've got the suss to sign 'em up snappy) called 'Twisted Wheel', a superb hymn to Manchester's famed early sixties Mod mecca to be coupled with the faster scooter song 'SX225' – and up till '68 that was THE scooter to have.

An unhealthy fixation with the past sure but it doesn't permeate the whole set where matters of the heart predominate (like it or not Eros is replacing Anarchy on all the best-selling banners these days).

Basically the songs are strong and well-structured, oft-times perfect pop having none of the 'wimpiness' live that is sometimes wrongly attributed to their recorded work, the fine Psycho single 'Why Should It Happen To Me'/Cardiac Arrest'. Edwin Starr's 'SOS' and The Who's 'Legal Matter' are covered particularly well, while the tender 'Rhona' sees their first proper exercise in dual guitar work.

Theirs is a sparklingly fresh pop sound that finds a receptive sea of clapped hands and hungry, joyous faces bucking about in a sweaty human mess in front of me. It's exhausting even to watch. The band manage two encores before idiot bomb hoaxers (McCullough and Barton?) get the place closed down and I'm left pondering how much further they would have got by now had they been based in the Smoke instead of grimy old Yorkshire…

The band talks with a genuine excitement about their music and their movement. "We're totally into the idea of Mod here," Jez enthuses. "Having a good time and looking after yourself, it's great. The punk thing was defeated by the commercial market. It started as a reaction but ended up as business. But the Mod scene up here is really healthy. No way is it a business thing. Up here it's ordinary kids and Oxfam shops and everyone's really into scooters, and the music and the look."

"Obviously it wouldn't have happened without punk," Vic Vespa interjects, "But it's a new movement. It's more melodic and danceable. And we're building something of our own. Something fresh. Usually something happens in the South and the rest of the country follows but with Mod the Southerners seem to be trying to change something that's our own, and that won't happen because we've got something special here.

"But thankfully the antagonism between North and South is starting to cool down now and I believe it's got to, otherwise the whole movement will collapse."

What do you reckon will happen with Mod then? "Obviously it'll go the same way as punk eventually. Anything that comes from the kids on the streets is taken over and made commercial but at the moment the whole scene's going well."

A glazed look comes into his eyes. "Someone said last year that 1979 was gonna be the year of Mod" (it was me – GB; oh and Alan Lewis) but I reckon 1980 will be the real year of the scooter. Next summer it's gonna be massive."

"You know what my ambition is now?" Jez asks rhetorically. "It's to play Manchester Apollo and pack it out with Mods instead of Rush fans." "That'd really be something to achieve."

And I'll see you there Jez, I'll see you there.

JEZ never did play Manchester Apollo. The month after I wrote this piece, with an Observer magazine front cover in the pipeline, the band got far too jollied up before their showcase gig at London's Moonlight Club. Record company interest evaporated. The 'Meters finally signed to Gem, who were to the Mod scene what Aquaman is to mountain climbing. Their 'Twisted Wheel' was feebly produced by Sulsh & Leathwood (of Cliff Richard fame/shame!) and failed to chart. A promo tour supporting Eddie & the Hot Rods was equally badly thought through. And the band's turn to psychedelia failed to find a receptive audience. By 1981, the boys had evolved into Soldiers Are Dreamers. They sounded great, but debts accrued from the Killermeter days stopped them from taking off...

As mod declined, the fashion sense died with it. Scooter boys became openly contemptuous of mod and by 1984 mods were organising their runs entirely separately to the scooter boys.

NEWS OF THE WORLD
GOSSIP AND LETTERS...

Living Past: We hear that even as the **Purple Hearts** excellent debut 45 "Millions Like Us" rockets into the Top 75 the enterprising Romford innovators have already nipped in the old recording studio and recorded 'Frustration' as a follow-up.

The Jam are featured in the BBC2 television programme 'Something Else' which gets its second screening this Thursday at 11.30pm.
The band perform their latest single, 'When You're Young', and its follow-up 'Eton Rifles'.

Speedball a Southend three-piece band will be releasing their first single this wekend. It's called 'Is Somebody There?' and its issued on No Pap Records.

The Mods Mayday 79 album featuring five London mod bands recorded live at Canning Town Bridge House, which has been released by I-Spy Records has now been picked up by Arista. The album features fifteen tracks by **Secret Affair**, **Beggar**, **Small Hour's The Mods** and **Squire** and all 2,000 of the first pressing have already been sold out. It was recorded on May 1 and will have a recommended retail price of £4.00.

The Lambrettas - they could just be a mod band - play London Marquee September 22, Brighton Buccanneer 23, Canning Town Bridge House 24, Camden Music Machine October 2, Brighton Alhambra 6 and 18.

TIME FOR ACTION

THE MERTON PARKAS will be undertaking a British tour in the wake of their second single for Beggars Banquet called 'Smile' and their first album, 'Face In The Crowd'.
They start at West Runton Pavilion on October 5 and then Halifax Good Mood Club 6, Jacksdale Grey Topper 7, Cardiff University 9, Nottingham University 10, Bath Pavilion. 11, Keel University 12, London Chelsea College 13, Poole Wessex Hall Bristol Romeo And Juliet's 15, Nottingham Trent Polytechnic Blackpool Norbreck Castle 18, Dundee University 19, Glasgow University 20.
More dates are being finalized; including, a major London gig.

In September 1979, incensed by the one-sided, irrational and downright unfair reviews the New Mod bands were receiving in the rock press, I wrote this furious and possibly inebriated piece 'naming the guilty men'.
We reproduce it here in its ferocious entirety.
IF MOD was exposed much more it'd be had up for indecency. Let's face it, you have to queue up to slag it off nowadays. Every single silly ponce employed by the music press stands poised to unload some smart arse, inaccurate one-liners about the movement - as long as that entails reviewing a record or venturing somewhere 'nice' like the Lyceum. Go down the Bridge House? Good heavens old chap, don't be daft, they drop their aitches down there.
Credit where credit's due, Dave McCullough started the ball rolling reviewing the Purple Hearts and the Chords at the Cambridge Hotel in May on the strength of one number a-piece and several spins of 'Strange Town' in the bar.
Since then Secret Affair have become his favourite target for sly digs (thus sparing the Ruts and the Members), even

though he has never ever been to a Secret Affair gig - a mere detail obviously.

The target seems so easy that every other half-witted bore has jumped on the bandwagon - well known has-beens, non-gig attendees and bottle jobs like the NME's star writer Tony Parnsip (wonder when Julie will have her go) and tedious self-important pseuds such as Jon/Savage (the Cambridge educated dullard). And, now the precedent had been so famously established, virtually every man jack of those Numerous Mundane Egocentrics down there in Carnaby Street has followed suit.

Mod is "a business hype", we are told. "Conservative". "Power-pop" (the Purple Hearts and Secret Affair are Power-pop?!?! Clean your ears out, fellas.) "You can't dance to it." (S'funny, kids must have been jogging down the Wellington).

"No way is this anything to do with rock 'n' roll rebellion," chimed 'CSM' and Danny Baker recently, proffering Dylan and disco as the alternative voices of the barricades...

Quite why Mod is politically reactionary has never been explained, the claim has just been repeated so often that they all accept their own lies without question (the old Hitler technique).

Actually the NME tossers have been well dealt with by their own readers so let's turn to their worst offender, a chubby little hippy who works for Step Forward, sorry the Paul Yates Weekly, and, despite the fact that his physical contact with the Mod scene is less than zero, continuously and ignorantly resurrects the hoary old "Mod as Big Biz" hype chestnut so he can join the android league in heralding their nice safe little psychedelic revivals and revel in all those great revolutionary messages that only post-graduates with long raincoats can understand. The truth, the indisputable empirical truth is that New Mod was the creation of such merrily aristocratic and entrepreneurial figures as Billy Hassett a Deptford-bred non-millionaire, Grant Fleming an East London born non-tycoon, Brian Betteridge a North London hatched non-magnate and a host of other aging 'moguls' disguised as street kids and Jam fans. Sinister huh, pop-pickers? When Sounds first brought Mod to the world's attention we said the obvious: that the Biz would move in to corrupt, just as the media would, just as a bunch of no-hopers would jump on the bandwagon.

It was common sense to assume that the fashion and music businesses and the popular press would endeavour to side-track the whole affair into a mere revival and suck every penny out of it at the same time. If they succeed totally, as it sometimes seems to me they will, the trite, idle, conservative and complacent music press will have to bear a sizeable portion of the blame.

GARRY BUSHELL.

SEPTEMBER 29, 1979

THE MOD REVIVAL

WACKY WACKERS

MR BUSHELL, who do you think you are, you Cockney idiot?
With regard to your article on Mod 11 /8/79 you state that
Northern Mods wear wide flares and Stranglers regalia.
Living in Liverpool I consider myself, and so do my pals, as
being Scouse mods. Liverpool is situated in the North of
England so therefore we are Northern Mods and no-one in
Liverpool wears flares. Nobody in Liverpool has worn flares
for a good four years. Yet you maintain that we have "come
round of late".

To put the record straight people in Liverpool are extremely
trendy and have been wearing Fred Perry's, loafers, drainpipes
and fastening the top button of their shirts for years. In
Merseyside there are a number of scooter clubs like Cloud
Nine, Phase 2, White City and Glitter Mods who have been
wearing Parkas and drainpipes for years.

As for your 'supposedly' Mod music it is on the whole shitty.
The best group out of the lot is the Merton Parkas; although
Secret Affair and the Chords do one or two passable numbers.
As for that star of stage and screen, Grant Fleming, he is a
renowned West Ham prat, and that person from Dagenham
who gets his lip tatooed must be one head case.

The Northern Wollyback* scooter clubs that do wear flares
and go to Wigan Casino are more original than you Cockney
wimps and they will still consider themselves Mods after
you Cockneys have progressed into hippies, beatniks and
psychedelia because they were Mods before Anarchy came out.
Your article made us (namely the Park End at Everton,
the Rad End of Liverpool and the Birkenhead and Liverpool
Scooter Clubs) very angry. — **The Scouse Mods**.

*A woolyback is someone who wasn't born in Liverpool.

TIME FOR ACTION

MILLIONS LIKE US

ON FRIDAY 21st I listened to a few minutes of 'Kid Jerkin's Roundtable' and I heard Ian Page of Secret Affair saying that 'mod' (regd trademark) was revolting (sic) against punk. He went on to say that 'mod' was a positive thing; it was the complete opposite of punk. Mods wanted to build and create, whereas punk wanted to 'destroy' (regd trademark).

Later in the evening I went to see XTC at Newcastle's Mayfair. When I got inside I wondered where all the tables and chairs had gone. I discovered later that they had been removed by the management because of all the trouble at the 'March of the Mods' gigs (remember they want to build and create) where during numerous fights, chairs were thrown around the Mayfair.

I don't know how Ian Page can have the cheek to say on Radio 1 that the Mods are a positive force, when he was actually in the Mayfair when his created Mods were throwing the furniture around and kicking hell out of everyone. Now, thanks to them, everyone else has to lean agsint the wall or sit on the floor. They make me sick. -

Roger Judd Gateshead, Tyne and Wear

THE MOD REVIVAL

MODS SHOULD STICK WITH MODETTES

In Answer to the punkettes from Tyen and Wear letter.
Me and my mate are punkettes as well and recently we hve
been noticing smoothie girls leeching onto our punks and
we cant understand what out punks see in them.

We go to loads of mod gigs cos one of our mates is a
modette and we go to loads of skin'ead gigs cos loads of
our mates are skins. We've noticed that skins and mods
(rather than punks) are in real demand amongst smoothie
girls. These girls, who wear pencil skirts up to the eyeballs
and low plunging v-necks, skake rattle and roll over the
place very indiscreetly placing themselves on the view of
their unsuspecting victim. They really have a ball at mod
gigs cos they can really shake rattle and roll in their boob-
tubes.

We don't invade their discos so why should they spoil the
atmosphere of our concerts? They have no regard for the
music, dress or what the punk skin'ead or mod movement
stand for, it is very obvious that they're only out to see
how many blokes they can pull and you can't talk to them
because they are so stupid, ignorant and giggly in the
prescene of their 'heroes'.

If a bloke becomes a punk he shouldn't associate with
smoothies. If he wants a smoothie girl then be a smoothie.
Our boyfriends (punks) agree with this.

We'd never dream of going out with a smoothie etc.
Punks should stick with punkettes, mods should stick with
modettes, skins should stick with skinettes and smoothies
should stick to smoothettes. **Cindy and Janice Battersea**.

TIME FOR ACTION

GARRY BUSHELL are you trying to be funny, you Elton John resembling turkey!
You had better start a punk band or become a designer of studded dildos for bored housewives! Your column is a disaster. **Rund Jonkers, Rotterdam Holland**

CONGRATULATIONS to Mr G Bushell on some fine reporting of the new 'Mod' scene, bands and live album. However, I would be extremely interested where I fit in to all this. Having been a skinhead in the early '70s I've kept my love for ska, Trojan and soul (not disco) music. I still enjoy early Pistols and Clash music and I wouldn't miss a Damned or UK Subs gig for nothing. I've liked the Jam for as long as they've been, even when they (as in early 1978) it was extremely un-hip to utter a good word for them.
Since early '78 I've been wearing sta-prest, loafers, two-tone suits etc. But now I find myself being called a Mod but as I understand it, Mods dressed nothing like that. However, these clothes I like and when the Mod thing has come and gone I'll still be wearing them.
I also like good music, Ian Dury, Kwesi Johnson, Dr Feelgood and most of the new bands now doing the circuit in London are excellent - Madness, Merton Parkas, Specials, Squire, Back to Zero etc etc. What I'd like to say to everybody who's reading this is, don't play at being a Mod, or a punk unless you really believe in it. I've seen scooter boys from East and South London. Mods who look like Mods, camel hair suits, Harry Fenton jackts. I wouldn't insult them by trying to call myself a Mod.
And now I've got something to say to ALL you skins who come to Mod gigs and shout 'Sieg Heil'. If only you knew how stupid you looked, you only come to the gigs that are

badly attended cause if you tried that in a bar full of Mods you'd be slaughtered.

Lastly, to everyone who's enjoing all the Secret Affairs and Speedballs of late, stand up for yourselves, all the 'Sieg Heil' skins are true cowards at heart, when the football season's back they'll all clear off anyway. More on Teenbeats, Purple Hearts, In the Shade, Mods etc. For all true skins, Mods punks and true skins, Mods, punks and music lovers - **Anonymous Angry Coward (just like the skins). London.**

BEAT BOYS IN THE JET AGE

NOVEMBER-DECEMBER 1979

SIXTIES & '79 SOUNDS SOUNDED SO GOOD. I THINK
NOT ONE SUBCULTURE COULD EXIST WITHOUT A CULTURE
OF SOUND PLAYED BEHIND IT. MUSIC HAS GOT AN
IMPORTANT ETCHING IN LIFE, MINE IS MOD

Celia Luccita - Italian '79 Mod

THE CROOKS: ROBBERY WITH INTENT

Manchester, November 10, 1979.

L ate one night in Chelsea, a crook jumps a well-dressed geezer, holds a knife to his neck and says: "Give me all your money!" The bloke is furious. "You can't do this to me," he says indignantly. "I am a British MP." "In that case," says the crook. "Give me all MY money!"

ARRIVING IN a Manchester staggered en masse by the shock news that it had been secretly owned by Sir Matt Busby for years, I strode out of Piccadilly station (or Manchester Busby as it's now known) only to be set upon by a ragged street urchin who, with a mind-buggering impudence, demanded a "penny for the guy", his snotty finger indicating a tatty heap of refuse at my feet.

THE MOD REVIVAL

When I, with some wit I fancy, replied "No but I'll give you a ha'penny for the whistle" the youth assumed the sort of distant blank expression that you'd normally associate with Dave McCullough when he's reminded whose round it is. But now look at me, hours later, gigging it about at Salford University (or Sir Matt's College as it's now officially described) with that self-same out-to-lunch look blessing my own boat. And the reason is the band on stage. The Crooks.

Now to you that handle probably summons up thoughts of faithful old felons like Fletch and Godber floundering in some mythical flowery dell exchanging thoughts on screws and snout and Mr. Barraclough's sex life. But to me the name The Crooks evokes unfortunate visions of bearded bandwagon-jumping geriatrics feebly donning Ben Shermans et al in a cynical attempt to pass off their weak-kneed pop slop as Mod, and jacking in jobs as teachers and librarians to do it.

This vision, nurtured over the past months by several chaps who are normally more on the ball that one of Sir Matt's protégées, was about as true to what I was watching on stage as the idea of the Pope – the real one, not Chris – flogging Durex on a stall down Romford Market.

Fact is not only did they look pretty young but they sounded pretty nifty too, and when a quick rabbit established that the 'bandwagon' bit was about as historically accurate as Pravda to boot, the fact-hungry newshound in me — as buried 'neath the breast of every Sounds scribe — thundered into a Lou Grant-style fact-finding orgy of oh, at least five minutes, in order to establish: THE TRUTH ABOUT THE CROOKS (fanfares blare, man cheers, women weep, Nuns orgasm etc.).

Chief tunesmith and guitarist Jim Fingers (real name Tim Parry) and vocalist (and now second guitarist of ten weeks standing) Dino Dean formed the Crooks Mark One at the end of '77, meeting at Middlesex Poly from where they eventually qualified as teachers (although they never got round to teaching).

By the end of '78 they reckoned they'd got as far as they could with that line-up and enlisted the present rhythm section in November: bassist Chris Brod, an old mate of Jim's who he used to play Who covers in a school band with, and shit-hot drummer Mick Sparrow who joined via the small ads in Malady Mawker.

REJIGGED, THEY soon established themselves as nabobs of the North Circular via interminable gigs at the Pegasus pub in darkest Stoke Newington. At this stage they were a rugby-shirted semi-comic combo playing the likes of 'Beans On Toast' and 'Oral Sex', but they also became an invaluable focus for the then embryonic North London mod scene, as well as playing an important role in inspiring and aiding the development of bands like the Scooters and Back To Zero.

The Crooks' first single 'The Modern Boys' released last month was written in these '78 days as a tribute to the young Mods they were attracting and perhaps inevitably, these lads' fashions and passions rubbed off on them in return.

Off went the rugby shirts, on went the Fred Perrys, and out of order went the opinions of finicky Mod trendsetters. Because let's get one thing straight - all this was happening long before there was any bandwagon to jump on.

How many Mods bands now can honestly say they weren't wearing safety-pinned schmutta or similar this time last year? And if being influenced is a cardinal sin then even the hippest Modster stands accused.

So what else? The age jibes are bullshit too — 19, 23, 23, and 23 don't exactly spell Methuselah in my books. And as for the music, well New Mod is so musically diverse that I find the 'not Mod music' accusation hard to take too, especially as their particular brand of dance music has all the requisite Kinks/Who/Small Faces roots...

No I reckon the Crooks have unfairly borne the brunt of misplaced elitism. Tonight they were supporting the poor old Merton Fartas and frankly they blew them off stage with a bouncy brace of energetic punchy pop songs ('Thousand Faces', 'Sound Of Today', 'Modern Boys') wherein contagious choons wrestle with stirring, snappy anthems stamped with body and identity.

CRITICISMS SPRING to mind like the obvious sameness of their sound (like most first albums in fact), and their vision is strictly Funnsville, Arizona. No dealing with the nastier side of life. The Crooks are firmly into unleashing the hairnet and dancing the night away. And tonight's audience — a strange blend of raucously enthusiastic Liverpool Mods with their needle stuck on Quadrophenia chants, 'typical student types', token snappy dressers and horsey university ladies after a little bit of rough — seem happy enough with that.

Let's face it, any band that digs out obscure numbers such as the Small Faces' 'Understanding' and the Kinks' 'I Need You' and bung in one of their own called 'Trying To Make Love To You Is Like Banging My Head Against A Brick Wall' can't be all bad. 'Modern Boys' is a great song too.

DUKE OF
LANCASTER
Approach Road, New Barnet
(Beside B.R. New Barnet)

Thursday November 30th
CROOKS

Friday December 1st
64 SPOONS

Saturday December 2nd
EARTHBOUND

Sunday December 3rd
BABY GRANDE

Tuesday December 5th
TAKEAWAY

Chatting to the chaps apres gig, and inevitably back in London Town chez the Wh*te L**n, a man couldn't help noting that for Arsenal fans they were, and I quote Ian Penman here, a bleeding great bunch of geezers (and let's face it, Arsenal come from Woolwich originally anyway).

Sure Jim Fingers looks too much like Dave Higgs for anyone's good but he pens some sharp old sing-along pop pearls as exemplified by their Pye subsidiary Blueprint single 'Modern Boys', produced and generally sharpened up by ex-Advertising bod Simon Boswell, who even as you read this is working with them on their debut album which will hopefully be retailing in a shop near your own bedroom by next February. Along with a second single, a headlining tour, a trip round Europe . . . yep, the Crooks are pretty sussed people.

Forget boring snobs everywhere, get your arse out gigside pronto and experience their rich bundle of poppy fun before they're charging three sobs a ticket for the pleasure, 'cause I reckon the Crooks are ace enough to be on your box in the months to come, and I don't mean Police Five either. Even though I've always found that show to be a very useful guide to what will be coming tound the estate over the next few weeks (cont. Shooters Hill Nick).

JOHN'S BOYS: WEST ONE RIFLES

London, November, 1979.

THE Jam played a secret gig at the Marquee as 'John's Boys' on Friday 2nd November which ended in a brief but vicious sea of fists and bottles outside as frustrated fans clashed with heavy-handed club security men.

The trouble had started earlier in the evening when the bouncers – some of whom had been drafted in just for the night – used what was felt to be excessive force to clear ticket holders out of the entrance corridor and were met with rowdy resistance.

The cops were called in, and attempts to trace the rowdiest of these resisters in the packed crowd resulted in one person being escorted out of the building. Later a second man was ejected on the rather shaky grounds that he "knew the trouble-makers."

I was unable to trace the exact cause of the after-show fracas, but tension was evident as I left. Many of the bouncers hurrying punters out of the building seemed to be in possession of cut-off snooker cues and the like. They didn't look like they were in any hurry to rack up snooker balls either.

As kids were pushed and prodded into the street, the whole front of the Marquee club was then showered in bricks and other building debris from a building site opposite. In the course of the chaos, the Marquee's windows were smashed and a couple of the bouncers were cut and bruised.

One youth told me that he had been hit by a security man wielding a piece of wood with nails jutting out of it and proffered a suitably ravaged forearm as proof. He claimed that the fight had been provoked by bouncers who were "tooled-up."

When I put these allegations to the Marquee the next day a spokesman replied: "The trouble was caused by a bunch of skinheads who'd come looking for trouble. None of our employees were in any way responsible." (A disingenuous answer as the temporary security staff responsible for the roughest over-reactions were hired help not employees).

A second John's Boy gig, set up Saturday the 3rd at the Nashville was called off following violence during an Angelic Upstarts show at the venue.

There was a little more to that story than made the paper. When I rang up the Marquee to ask about the incident I was told that the trouble had been caused by "Garry Bushell's mates" – not a quote I felt obliged to add to the report. It's certainly true that the ticket-holder unfairly thrown out of the gig was known to me, and to the terraces of West Ham United. Here is my review of the actual show…

THE Jam's secret gig naturally turned out to be as secret as the outbreak of World War Two. The 'House Full' sign was up by 6pm, leaving hundreds of pissed-off punters morosely moping around outside. The crush inside made the average sardine tin seem blissfully roomy.

The Nips played a pretty fine set I'm told — missed half of it meself trying to crow-bar myself through the door; but what I saw was shambolically impressive and impressively shambolic: a mix of ramshackle r&b plus rowdy punk tunes served up by scrawny, bug-eyed Shane.

Any band who trample all over 'Downtown' and write a song called 'Maida Aida (She's Got Big Knockers)' are okay with me. (There y'are, didn't compare Shane's lugholes to the FA Cup once).

Before the Jam's set, a troop of Old Bill put in an unwelcome appearance due to an early contretemps between bouncers and punters which later approached near riot proportions outside. But when John Weller's stocky figure appeared onstage all thoughts of drug-busts and 'police oppression' evaporated and eyes were fixed firmly stage front.

If I was Paul Weller, I would be praying that someone somewhere was going to start making constructive criticisms soon. I was straining my brain to find faults, but I kept coming up against a brick wall. I couldn't detect so much as a hint of weakness or dishonesty or musical laxity.

No, this review reads 'WOW!' in 48-point type. And that ain't idle sycophancy, son, that's a calm considered critical conclusion – an acknowledgement that the band in front of me mean business, and are the business.

The Jam are probably the only one of punk's original 'big four' to have emerged from the frantic furor of the last three years with their credibility intact and their music still maturing. The singles this year — the smart, insightful 'Strange Town', the spit and irony of 'When You're Young', the pessimistic power of 'Eton Rifles' — testify to Weller's steadily flowering creativity and easy way with anthems.

The new numbers played tonight, especially 'Private Hell' and 'Saturday Kids' (who 'live life with insults / drink lots of beer / And wait for half-time results'), combine a rock-hard freshness with typical Jam melodic strength. No surprises sure, but no letdowns either; and no more clues from me, kids, wait till next week for the proper reviews…

The set was a brave, adventurous mix of the old and the new which left me reeling from the squeeze and the stench of sweat and spilt lager and the wham-bam succession of killer choons, everything from the driving menace of 'Down In The Tube Station At Midnight' to the rolling class awareness of 'Mr Clean' with almost the entire crowd mouthing and punching bitterly along with the heartfelt 'I hate you and your wife / And if I get a chance FUCK UP YOUR LIFE' lines.

Then there was the subtler commuter consciousness of Foxton's finest composing moment 'Smithers-Jones' and the slow, meaningful accusation of 'Butterfly Collector', off-set by the fire power of 'Eton Rifles' and 'David Watts'.

Gig of the year? No contest. It's just a shame that the rip-roaring encore of 'A Bomb In Wardour Street' so neatly predicted the brick and bottle uproar outside afterwards.

maRquee

90 Wardour St., W.1   01-437 6603

OPEN EVERY NIGHT FROM 7.00 pm to 11.00 pm
REDUCED ADMISSION FOR STUDENTS AND MEMBERS

Thur 1st Nov (Adm £1.00)

ORIGINAL MIRRORS
Plus support & Ian Fleming

Fri 2nd Nov (Adm £1.50)

JOHN'S BOYS
The Nips & DJ Ian Fleming

Sat 3rd Nov (Adm £1.00)

THE BOOKS
Plus Bauhaus & Ian Fleming

Sun 4th Nov (Adm £1.00)

THE VAPORS
Plus support & Mandy H

Mon 5th Nov (Adm £1.50)

THE PRETENDERS
Plus guests & Jerry Floyd

Tues 6th Nov (Adm £1.00)

LITTLE BO BITCH
Plus support & Joe Lung

Wed 7th Nov (Adm £1.75)

THE LURKERS
Plus friends & Jerry Floyd

Thur 8th Nov (Adm £2.00)

BUZZCOCKS
Plus friends & Ian Fleming

HAMBURGERS AND OTHER HOT AND COLD SNACKS AVAILABLE

SECRET AFFAIR: TUNES OF GLORY

November 17, 1979.

HE TIME comes when cheery everyman theories and haughty highbrow hignorance have to be put aside; when all the spouting, strutting and counter-cutting become secondary to the few grams of vinyl revolving on the office Sanyo, when the proof of the pudding is in the playing…and for Secret Affair that time is now.

Ian Page must be the most sorely abused geezer in the world what with the constant stream of jibes he attracts — "Evil Knievel uses his mouth for practice jumps", "He's got more rabbit than Watership Down", "Mod's answer to Jimmy Pursey" and so on, you know how it goes.

And even his most fervent admirers would have to admit that he talks himself into a lot of unnecessary hassle. Yet the biggest irony of all is that Secret Affair's songs say it all.

This album, featuring nine SA originals and one cover, serves as both a lyrical New Mod manifesto and the musical proof in plastic that Mod is more than just 'a bunch of silly kids playing power-pop.'

The Affair's 'new wave soul' formula that 'Glory Boys' both reflects and sharpens up via smooth production and wider instrumentation is essentially simple: Put crassly, the band combine old style Motown influenced dance rhythms with Dave Cairns' powerful biting rock guitar and Ian's hard-hitting, often bitter lyrics, the whole recipe mixed into irrepressibly catchy sing-along dance numbers.

Side one kicks off with a mess of street sound, disco snatches and stirring orchestration building into the gentler guitar-picking intro of the title track, the band's hymn to their followers, wherein punchy verses give way to the anthemic chorus - 'We're the Glory Boys/So scared of getting old/Yeah, we're the Glory Boys/We may look cold but our hearts (hearrrrtttsss) are gold'.

The Glory Boys, in Affair mythology, represent the most Mod-conscious of the New Mod movement, coupling street suss and hardness with fun 'n' fashion loving narcissism, as neatly captured by Page's simple verse: 'You're looking at me boy/ Trying to match my stare/Don't you know I'm a Glory Boy/I could cut you down by combing my hair.'

Elsewhere the lyrical manifesto is widened to argue for danceable change, themes already expounded in the excellent two single hits included here — the sharp, irresistible anti-apathy assault of 'Time For Action' and the current groover with a bullet, 'Let Your Heart Dance'.

Yeah who needs stay at home, po-faced, scared to dance critics? Music is primarily about FUN and if that's controversial or reactionary than screw your revolution, chum, we'll make our own.

'Let Your Heart Dance' sums up the New Mod mood — 'Goodbye to pogo/Tired of the disco/Time for a little more style'. While, as Giovanni Dawop so rightly said pissing over hacky 'Resurrection Shuffle' comparisons, the song is a driving two-fingers to the joyless clichés and musical mires that we'd got bogged down in.

'New Dance' ends side one with a bang, exploding with rock-hard guitar into a crashing chord progression experts term 'Townshend-esque', before giving way to the gentler jogging verses and a mighty diamond of a chorus. Verse two captures some of Page's acidic attitude. 'Faceless clowns without a stage/ Don't try and trap me in your plastic cage/I'll take off your make-up with a razor blade...'

Kicking off side two, 'Days Of Change' is another archetypal slice of catchy contemporary popular music, driving along with a mightily contagious chorus: 'Cos these days of change are here to stay/And the need for change will find a new way' - probably the healthiest sentiment expressed this year. Say no to complacency. Say no to star-trippers. It's up to you.

Despite the lies and jaded cynicism of jealous gumbie critics the Affair are anything but a business hype. Fact is, only a fool could avoid noticing the anti-business bitterness which underlines this entire album.

And I ain't gonna get into that 'changing the music biz' hippy red herring either because you will never change that outside of changing the socio-economic structure of society as a whole, my friend, and quite frankly I can't see the Fall doing that, maaaan.

The missing tracks are their harder version of the Miracles' silky, sinuous but probably somewhat understated 'Going To A Go-Go', the soul-suffused anti-Biz swinger 'Don't Look Down', another sharp dance ditty in 'Shake And Shout' with its Spencer Davis throwback of a bass line, the classy maturity of the newest number 'One Way World' and last of all the extended seven minute saga of a has-been star-slag, 'I'm Not Free (But I'm Cheap)' with its neat trumpet/guitar interplay.

THE MOD REVIVAL

And there you have it. An album of startling strength, ripeness, and self-assuredness, which virtually single-handedly justifies the New Mod explosion and places Secret Affair firmly in the vanguard of today's hungry new new wave of bands.

It is an excellent testimony to their strengths and abilities; a modern pop album that sparkles with righteous anger, tight instrumentation, and snappy singsongs. A manifesto you can dance to. Page, Cairns, Smith and Shelton should ignore the ignorant critical holocaust which is undoubtedly about to come and treat themselves to a few bottles of vintage shampoo and some fat, juicy Joe Blakes. You deserve it, boys. See you on the road. Right?

SMALL HOURS

TEENBEATS

Bridgehouse, Rock Garden, November, 1979.

I'VE spent the last few days on groove manoeuvres checking out bands I'd heard good things about but hadn't got round to seeing… First, toads, we'll talk Teenbeats, a five piece band from Hastings, who I saw without the benefit of a set-list last Sunday; and found to be possessed of pleasant pop promise not to mention a vocalist called Huggy Leaver who reminds me of my old mate Nick Tesco from the Members.

Forget that 'Farewell To The Roxy' past and the bleached blonde look, Huggy has just got to be one of the ace-est of faces around today. Readers of Jackie should be warned that your rag will probably be jam-packed with that boat race in the not too distant future.

The Teenbeats specialize in poppy R&B, of which the supercharged Hot Rod-style number with the '1-2, 1-2-3-4' chorus was easily the catchiest, as well as being an essential educational tool for the innumerate.

They have attitude as well as style. And as with all the best Mod bands, Sixties influences and Seventies energy make for a hugely enjoyable dance recipe.

Live gems included their excellent fiery cover of the Troggs' 1966 smash 'I Can't Control Myself', which should never have been a

THE BRIDGE HOUSE
23 BARKING ROAD, CANNING TOWN, E16

Thursday November 22nd 50p **THE MO-DETTES** + Wasted Youth		**Monday November 26th** 50p **SMALL HOURS** + The Face	
Friday November 23rd 60p . **THE BRAKES** + The Stickers		**Tuesday November 27th** 50p **LONESOME NO MORE** + Prime Movers	
Saturday November 24th 60p **O.T.'s** featuring Jo-Ann Kelly + Chris Youlden		**Wednesday November 28th** 50p **WASTED YOUTH** + Industrials	
Sunday November 25th 50p **SPECIAL BRANCH** + The Streets FACE		**Thursday November 29th** 50p **FLEXIBLE DUSTBINS** + Shiner	

single, and the next 45, their own 'The Strength Of The Nation (Is Youth)', which is even better.

All in all then, as Robbi Millar would have it, 'a nice band, this'.

Small Hours on the other hand are more than just another promising young band. To cut a long story short they are simply the best new band I've seen since Secret Affair, coupling a genuine gritty Sixties soul/Memphis R&B sound with Neil Thompson's appropriately rough-edged vocals tight instrumentation, and a strong, well-structured set which at times embraces an epical Springsteen feel.

If you've got the Bridge House 'Mods May Day' album you'll be familiar with three of their numbers already, but it must be said that in the flesh they're rougher, tougher, earthier and all together more convincing...

It's New Wave soul delivered with passion and pizzazz.

If you wanna know more you'll have to tune back later kiddiwinks. A feature in your favourite paper is as inevitable as the encore they got tonight.

LONG TALL SHORTY: IN TIME WITH '79

London, November, 1979.

' They call me Long Tall Shorty, cause I know what love is all about' – Tommy Tucker

JIMMY Pursey gave Long Tall Shorty their name and their first record deal, but did he also destroy their credibility in the process?

Certainly rock press snobs have used their association with the touring 'Pursey's Package' bandwagon as a stick to beat the hard-working young Mod band. And their debut single 'By Your Love' – produced by Jimmy P – earned them a proper critical kicking from the unfeasibly angry Dave McCullough in the pages of Sounds.

'Long Tall Shorty's effort is indescribably ugly,' he seethed, his mouth foaming with indignant rage. 'A kind of Mod-churn, produced by the dreaded Pursey who I hope one day shall be put in front of some sort of r'n'r equivalent of the Nuremburg Trials' (...alongside me!)

Which ain't bad going for your first review...

Mind you, McCullough also had a go at the Purple Hearts' excellent 'Frustration' – which he dubbed 'even worse' than Shorty; and the Low Numbers' 'Keep In Touch', which he called 'embarrassingly badly produced', again by Pursey, so it looks like his real target was the lanky Sham singer all along.

Div Mac is the least of Shorty's worries though; their big problem is that they seem to have pissed off Lady Luck as well.

Misfortune has mounted for them like an over-keen porn star. 'By Your Love' b/w '1970s Boy' was originally scheduled to be released on Polydor, but then the record company dropped Pursey's entire label. Warners finally brought the single out after a couple of months and then promptly decided to withdraw it just one week later.

The boys, understandably, are wearing their frustration like a suit.

Fresh-faced guitarist Tony Perfect explains: "Jimmy's JP label, which was for all the bands involved in Pursey's Package, originally had a deal with Polydor. But then Mensi" – pug-ugly Angelic Upstarts singer – "had a ruck with a security guard in the record company building after he'd thrown an aborted foetus out of a top floor window and the whole package was dropped." (How unreasonable – Ed).

Tony goes on: "So after much delay, Pursey's Package jumped ship to WEA. But then a second disaster hit. Just after our single got released the A&R man responsible for it all, Dave Dee got the tin-tack, and the whole of Pursey's label was dropped. All of the singles were withdrawn after just one week, which in our case meant after 200 sales..."

A collector's item, then. They'll be laughing about it one day, probably... as long as the unlucky bastards steer clear of open man-holes, level crossings and busy road junctions.

Long Tall Shorty are actually one of the earliest of the Mod Renewal bands, originally forming in August 1978 as the Indicators, from the wreckage of obscure punk band Ben E Dorm and The Tourists (putting the pun in punk, by order of Ma Beya.)

Although he doesn't make a song and dance about it, Perfect, born plain Anthony Morrison in Tulse Hill, Lambeth, South London, was one of the first of the new Mods. "I was a Jam fan who started dressing like Weller," he recalls. "I didn't meet any of the others though until I went to the Great British Music Festival in December last year."

The Jam were headlining. This was when all Mod-inclined teens, such as Grant Fleming and Tom McCourt, became aware of each other's existence.

Tony recalls: "I was wearing a Union Jack jacket which I'd bought off Bruce Foxton for £35. I had no idea that there were any other Mods in the UK at all. But that night I bumped into about forty. Foxton recognised the jacket and invited me backstage where I met Grant. I ended up watching the Jam from the side of the stage which was a real thrill."

The first line-up was Perfect on guitar and vocals, Jimmy Grant (sometimes called Colin Clitheroe) on bass, and Mark Reynolds on drums; Keith Mono took over as singer two months later.

Tony, born on 25th January 1961, grew up loving bands like the Small Faces. Jimi Hendrix is his guitar hero, but when I ask who their biggest influence is, he replies "the mirror."

Live the band play powerful, punk-tinged rhythm & blues in a set that includes gems like 'Cheap Girls', 'Long Time' and 'Lit Up' as well as covers of Sam Cooke's 'Shake' and The Who's 'Legal Matter'.

Pursey caught the likeable likely lads in action when they supported Sham 69 at the Electric Ballroom in Camden, and the rest is tragedy. Jimmy, no doubt advised by his batman, Grant Fleming, was impressed enough to invite them down to Polydor's studios in February 1979 where he asked them to run through their entire set for him.

Says Tony: "We played the lot and he didn't seem too impressed so then I said, 'Wait, we've got one more' and we played '1970s Boy' which was the first song I'd ever written. I hadn't wanted to play it because it was only about ninety seconds long, full of swearing and very punk. As soon as he heard it, Jimmy was leaping about the studio going, 'That's it, that's the one.'

"We recorded it there and then; it was supposed to be the a-side. But when we went back a couple of weeks later to record the b-side, me and Keith had written 'By Your Love' (actually based on our earlier song 'Lit Up') which Jimmy decided was even better; because at that point don't forget the Mod Revival wasn't even being written about in the press, and he'd signed us as a pop band."

It was Pursey who persuaded the band to change their name to Long Tall Shorty, taking it from a song recorded by the Kinks (but written by Don Covay).

Shorty's aggressive edge meant they could support the likes of the Upstarts and appeal to punks and skins as well as the fledgling Mod scene. "Up until then we'd always played to a Mod audience," says Tony. "I'll always be a Mod in my attitude to life, but anyone can come and see us, except hippies."

They've gigged pretty much everywhere in the capital – the Wellington, the Marquee, the Nashville, the Greyhound and the Music Machine. Mod zine Maximum Speed picked up on them after they played on the pavement in Carnaby Street, outside the Carnaby Cavern, where Mark kicked over his drums, Tony smashed his guitar on the ground, and Jimmy Grant "just looked pissed". The zine described singer Keith as "the only sane member of the band."

They're not fighters though. "It's a waste of time and effort," snorts Tony. "I like going to the seaside but I go for holidays, not rucks."

Style isn't an obsession, either. "We like to look smart, but we'd rather spend their money on rehearsals than clothes," he says.

Why are they in a band? "That's easy," Tony smiles. "We want Rollers and 'cheap girls'. Why else?"

With their luck they'll probably end up with cheap girls in hair rollers.

"Hey," Feedback says. "If the kids dig it we'll keep playing. Everything we do is for 'the kids', man." And there's enough irony in his tone for that to have been a John Lydon quote.

*Shorty never did beat Lady Luck. They'd already recorded a follow-up single ready to release on the back of 'By Your Love' but that went by the wayside when the debut 45 was canned. They got the chance to support the Chords on their first UK tour, but pulled out after the opening night in Middlesbrough. "We were poor because our manager took all our money," Tony recalls. "We ended up sleeping in the transit van in the freezing cold, and the manager had his feet out because they stank so much, making it even colder. It was fucking horrible. We were all eight stone. We hadn't eaten. He wouldn't feed us. We never saw any of the gig money. After that first indignity, we decided stuff the North, and we pulled out and fell out with the penny-pinching manager."

The fall-out didn't stop there. Mark Reynolds and Jimmy Grant left the band – Perfect quipped that they'd kicked him out "cos he had acne" - but Tony decided to keep Shorty going. He moved to bass, they had Keith Mono on vocals, Stewart England on guitar and Mike Morrison, Tony's brother, on drums.

Shorty recorded demos for CBS in the summer of 1980, but nothing came of it. The line-up changed again, with Perfect moving back to guitar and vocals, while John Kiely joining on bass. Their second single 'Win Or Lose' b/w 'Ain't Done Nothing Wrong' was released by Ramkup Records. It didn't chart.

Still riding a tidal wave of ill-fortune they secured a slot at the 1981 Reading Festival only for their performance to be over-shadowed by a crowd riot. Four smartly dressed geezers took the stage and the 8,000 long-haired rockers and scruff-bags present responded with friendly cries of "Piss off you Mod wankers" and a welcoming hail of empty beer cans.

Shorty responded with a piss-take version of Black Sabbath's 'Paranoid' followed by The Who's 'Substitute'. The crowd's mood switched to furious. New drummer Derwent started shouting "We are the Mods" over the PA and was quickly struck on the head by a full can of Fosters (which naturally he pocketed for later). Chaos ensued.

Another crowd punch-up followed at a Chatham gig and Shorty were banned from the Marquee. Shortly after, John quit and Stewart went off to join the Foreign Legion which appeared to offer less hardship. By November 81, even Tony Perfect had had enough. He changed his name to Tony Feedback and joined the Angelic Upstarts, replacing Glyn Warren on bass. Mensi's opinion of their political song, 'Anti CND' has never been recorded. Shorty's first drummer, Mark Reynolds, ended up playing for the Oi! band Infa-Riot.

*AN LTS compilation '1970s Boy' was released by Captain Mod in 1997. Shorty reformed in 2000, releasing the album 'A Bird In The Hand' on Countdown Records. Tony Perfect continues to tour Europe with the band and continues to write and record hard-edged new rhythm & blues songs. Shorty now consists of Perfect on guitar and vocals, John Woodward on bass and Jim Piddington on drums. They call their sound 'giffer punk'.

NOVEMBER 10 1979 20p

sounds

Mods vs. The World
THE GREAT DEBATE: PAGE 31

MODS
& SODS
THE MOD
DEBATE

Covent Garden, November, 1979.

"MOD IS VERY SHALLOW. THERE'S VERY
LITTLE IN THERE"
– DAVE CAIRNS

I n early November, 1979, a bizarre debate about Mod was held at the offices of the weekly rock paper Sounds in Covent Garden, and later reported in hysterical terms such as 'MODS vs THE WORLD', 'THE GREAT DEBATE', 'WAR OF THE WORDS', 'IS THERE LIFE AFTER MOD?' The discussion asked whether Mod was just a media-manipulated fad, to which the simple and obvious answer was no. However this didn't prevent the stern-faced Dave McCullough from leading the assault. In his mind, Dave was Robespierre defending the punk revolution and the Mod bands and their apologists and chroniclers were either record industry tools or reactionary fools.

For McCullough, Mod represented (accurately) a retreat into the bad old days of dressing up and having fun.

THE MOD REVIVAL

We assembled in the Spartan office conference room. There were two clear sides. In the pro-Mod corner, were me, Goffa Gladding from Maximum Speed, Billy H from the Chords, and later Dave Cairns from Secret Affair. Not exactly the Brains Trust. Pitted against us were Mayo Thompson from Red Crayola, the near mute Chris Westwood and McCullough. Rock photographer Paul Slattery was taking the pictures. The Chairman was Phil Sutcliffe, an elder statesman of rock journalism from the North East.

I GOT the blame for it all, naturally, but in this case deservedly. The previous month I had written a 'Cruelty Corner' article in which I not only defended New Mod but branded office cynics 'silly ponces', 'bores', 'has-beens', 'non-gig-goers', 'bottle jobs', and 'tedious self-important pseuds'. Although quite why I held back so much escapes me...

Dave McCullough, who scowled and frowned through-out the 90 minute encounter, picked up the gauntlet and led the attack. To Dave, Mod was "harmful" because he claimed it was "the continuation of the outdated idea that rock 'n' roll is merely a business or some sort of economic lifestyle." He went on: "I've heard no Mod records that light any spark in me...I think the idea of perpetuating something that's ten years old..."

"Twenty," shouted someone slightly better at maths.

"Is boring," McCullough concluded. But he said the discussion would be worthwhile as it might illustrate the machinations of the biz and explain why and how "this so-called phenomenon Mod has managed to claw its way into our lives."

I stepped up to the plate, to put the case for the defence, arguing that living in London gave us a perfect vantage point to see how everything punk had set out to do had been distorted and destroyed. "Bourgeois values have crept back into what was essentially an anti-business thing," I claimed.

Punk had sold itself as anti-commercial and as an explosion of ideas from ordinary kids, but it had turned into a profit-making machine. Cash from chaos. I then mentioned everything from rip-off bondage gear to the charts dominated by the New Wave - the likes of Gary Numan, the Police and Blondie. "Punk has opened up the market to these people who have become the new establishment and they're exactly the same as the old one," I said. (Although in fairness, I always liked Debbie Harry). Punk, I argued, had become "just another uniform, just another way of dressing.

"Punk was supposed to be about individuality, encouraging people to think for themselves" and oppose the status quo. That sense of free-thinking had been eroded and punk had become a Kings Road caricature of itself. Many were disillusioned, and a large number of them at street level had created the Mod movement by themselves and for themselves.

Mod wasn't the creation of people in boardrooms, music business entrepreneurs and fashion entrepreneurs; it was the creation of ordinary kids who wanted something of their own that was vivid and lively and not the toy of somebody who was trying to manipulate them at all."

Adopting my best Rumpole of the Bailey pose, I went for the big finish. New Mod didn't have importance or the meaning that punk had, I said. It had never thought in terms of any sort of revolution. But it had been criticized in the rock press for entirely false reasons. People have said that it's Power-Pop, which it patently isn't, that it's a big business hype which is isn't because it began in the Bridgehouse and the Wellington, places like that. But I concluded that Mod's chance of mod growing and achieving something of importance was threatened by the business and the cynical rock press.

McCullough, whose default setting was feral sarcasm, pretty much ignored my entire tirade. His only response was to snort derisively. "I can't understand why Ian Page isn't here anyway," he sniffed. "Maybe he's washing himself."

We pointed out that Ian was actually working on his album and hadn't got to bed until eight o'clock that morning. His ablutions were not of our concern.

"It's a pity he's not here to defend the baby he's brought up," McCullough snapped.

Page's paternal claim on the Mod baby was immediately questioned loudly by the rest of the room. Phil Sutcliffe moved to restore calm by bringing in Mayo Thompson, an intellectual Texan, who agreed that "the substantive issues raised by punk" were never dealt with. He could understand why people want to keep some energy going, he said.

Asked to define those punk issues, Mayo raised the level of debate. "Socially, that the access to the means of producing music didn't belong to the people who wanted to make it," he said, losing half the room. Mod would be appropriated in the way that punk was appropriated, he argued, accurately as it happened. He continued: "Punk was never a well-formed movement and I don't think Mod will be because the grounds on which it is proposed are too shaky. Garry, you raised the bourgeoisification of punk rock and it seems to me that punk actually never sorted out the way it was going to stand against that happening. The individualism never got beyond an individual being for himself. We see the same thing with mod."

Of course one of Mod's main areas of self-expression is fashion. And, he said "as clothes become a uniform they can lead to factions and conflicts" — none of which anyone present seemed to favour. Mayo finished by saying: "How anyone can get worked up about what people wear completely baffles me."

Sutcliffe took this line straight to Billy Hassett. Did he get worked up about what people wear?

Billy replied that it didn't matter to him whether the Chords had Mods or punks in their audience. "As far as I'm concerned people come out just to enjoy themselves. If they come to see us it's a compliment."

Goffa took this ball and ran with it. "I don't give a monkey's what people wear to be quite honest. Three years ago I was possibly seen wearing spiky hair" (at which point, he blushed prettily) "but at the same time, without going into much, greater depth about it, I don't really see what that's got to do with it."

McCullough scowled some more and said that Mod fashion was only important because "it indicates the kind of unimaginative, repetitive, unadventurous character of Mod."

Mayo agreed adding that it was dangerous to give people the impression that all they have to do is get a shopping-list of clothes and features right. "It's in none of our interests to perpetuate that."

It was all getting a too anal for Billy. You go to a gig to meet your friends, and think you'll wear a Fred Perry to look smart, he said.

Mayo muttered darkly about fashion coming from above. I argued that most youth cult fashion was initiated by the participants and had been since the dawn of the Teddy Boys. The businessmen came in later. Talk turned from the Mr Bigs of street couture to their equivalents in the record industry. The 'opposition' is disconcerted by Mod's apparent haste to sign itself away to the highest bidder i.e. the major companies. (So unlike the Pistols and the Clash...).

Mayo Thompson, who was also representing the Rough Trade label, asked why the bands deal with record companies? Was it because they felt they had to?

Billy adopted a defensive stance. "A geezer, right picking up the guitar and starting to learn it, he dreams of being in a group and he dreams of being on Top Of The Pops. Then you say to him 'Ah, credibility. You shouldn't be playing on TOTP.' But all he wants to do is play to an audience, make records and gain a bigger audience. That was the reason why he picked up a guitar, that's why everyone I talk to got started."

Mayo went over the same ground, asking if bands should go on Top Of The Pops or not, should they put out records on coloured vinyl? Should they sign to record companies who maybe have an arms division?

Ethics. According to McCullough: "It all comes down to your basic idea of what you are doing. What is rock and roll?"

Mr Sutcliffe claimed that Mod sounded like "surrender, waving the white flag and being happy beneath it."

Surrender to what, though? Reality? I argued that it was a question of knowing your limits. "Will music ever change the world? I don't think so. I don't think pop groups have it in them to even change the music industry because it's part of present day society. With record companies all you can decide is whether you're going to sign to a big capitalist or a small capitalist. If you're in a group you have to ask which one will promote your recordings more efficiently and distribute it better. All the small capitalist amounts to is inefficiency."

McCullough immediately accused me of me "very negative" (pot! Kettle's here) and "a bland cop-out." Mayo asked whether realism meant "making the most lucrative deal". He also argued that bigger companies were less efficient, saying: "Look at their profit margins, look at the cries going round the industry right now. EMI is obviously in serious trouble, a lot of these people are and they're getting ready for a recession. But I think it's pessimistic to say there's no way you can change this system. If I didn't believe there was some different possibility there would be no point in carrying on."

At this point, Dave Cairns arrived and was instantly set upon with accusations that Mod is presenting a 'clothes-maketh-man' delusion. Billy H was enraged. "You can't understand!" he said angrily. "What we're really on about is just going out and having a good time."

This enraged McCullough. "How can you possibly say that rock 'n' roll is about going out and having a good time?" he fumed. "Only that! How can you? Nothing to do with threatening the economies through which rock 'n' roll is being siphoned..."

We really were talking in two different languages, and to prove it Billy replied: "There's geezers up there right and they've got all the money and the y decide. Not us."

"Do you accept that?" asked McCullough incredulously. "That they decide the way you're going to live?"

Sutcliffe accused Billy rather poetically of "papering over the cracks of despair."

Mayo accused Bill of propagating "the ideology of common sense." Common sense "tells you that the best thing to do is get your head down, get a deal, make a lot of money, go out and give the kids what they want, entertain. Common sense tells you to do that kind of stuff

when in fact all of your instincts, all of your social relations tell you to tear that down if you can."

Dave Cairns leapt in and blanket-panned independent labels as a whole, before claiming that Secret Affair's own I-Spy label, distributed through Arista Records, was different because they had secured "artistic control."

Thompson asked how much control they'd have if they stopped having hits. An argument about contracts and labels ensued, with McCullough claiming "Bands like Swell Maps have proved that the whole system isn't really necessary."

Swell Maps hadn't troubled the charts though; Secret Affair had.

"You're right in that if we have a flop record people might turn around and say 'You can't do that'," argued Cairns. "But there again we've got that much confidence..."

Phil asked if Mod was inspiring?

I said that it inspires a lot of people to make music, write fanzines and go to gigs. Dave Cairns argued that Mod was positive, unlike punk. "A lot of things that punk stood for was great but it became so negative very fast. I mean kids on the street getting into the idea of 'no future' and tearing things down and not putting anything up instead..."

Phil asked Cairnsy what Mod inspired in him. He took a while to answer.

McCullough mocked him: "It's a long pause." (It was)

Cairns: "It's a difficult question." (It was)

McCullough: "For someone who's been in a band for so long and ranting and raving about being positive and building things up. It's a hell of a pause!"

Finally Dave Cairns said: "I wrote a song called 'Time For Action' which was purely for some of the kids who had been Mods out on the street and been pushed around and now they've come together with a lot of people and they don't get beaten up which is great. But I'm very confused about the people who follow us now. What does it all mean to them? The philosophy we've set out doesn't seem to have any reaction."

Is that it then? asked Sutcliffe. "By wearing the same clothes they've been able to identify one another as a gang and therefore they can protect themselves?"

Cairns: "No, it's not that. Some kids have really picked up on the idea, the fashion' scene/ smart-dressing, the whole attitude. Even the attitude to work of some people I know has improved. They're into working hard, earning a good wage packet and enjoying what they do."

Was this why Mods get labelled "Thatcherite", Phil pondered?

Cairns said aspirational was a better word. "What interests me is that friends of mine who got into punk gave up their jobs and went on the dole whereas now Mods are going out and getting jobs which is pleasing to me."

Billy disagreed. "Mod is about getting money for clothes," he said. "Look better than your boss and that'll frighten him. You want to look better than the next geezer."

Why, asked McCullough, who was a scruffy bastard at the best of times. "You're associating Mod with buying things," he said, accusingly.

"No, it's being one over the next bloke," Billy said, prompting McCullough to call him "very elitist."

Billy protested that the first Mods were an elite. "Why not? Why can't you have that?"

McCullough: "Why can't you have elitism? How can that be fun, recognising that somebody's better than somebody else? Surely you're moving into very ugly areas there."

Mayo Thompson took up the Marxist baton: "If the world worked that way it would be just great but it doesn't. Capitalism doesn't inspire all of us to have a lot of capital. It just inspires us to be very opportunistic with respect to our neighbours. If capitalism worked it would be ducky, man, because capitalism is full blown right now. Capitalism is based on the self-interested individual aspiring."

I argued that looking good was about pride in yourself, which rattled Dave McCullough's cage again.

I also went on to say that you're taught to feel inferior to your boss, that he is better than you and that you're just a dreg. The first stage in fighting back is to take control of how you look.

McCullough: "But what Billy was saying about the early Mods being superior to the later Mods completely defeats that argument."

Mayo: "We live in a welfare state and the main issue is the right to earn a living, the right to access to the means of production, the right to continue to exist...those are basic questions and this is an attempt to deal with it in some way. The main problem is that the ideas are half baked, nobody thinks anything through, nobody is willing to organise in the way that things have to be organised to actually consolidate that ground and win that space that's why we always give it up over and over again."

At this point, Billy gave up to catch a train for a gig in Birmingham. I rounded on the prosecution and demanded to know what their alternative was?

McCullough: "There's not just one, you have to think of loads of them... steps forward that have been made by the independent companies and by certain groups. The growing awareness of the groups, their hesitancy about signing for major labels — which apparently mod doesn't share. In general we're going forward with bands like Swell Maps. And even

Stiff Little Fingers, the way their album was paid for, produced and distributed."

As an alternative New Faces for Chrysalis, I snapped.

Mayo: "It worked out that way I agree."

McCullough: "But it didn't have to. It was their choice."

It was because falsely or not they thought Chrysalis could ship more units for them.

McCullough: "They retrogressed, it was their fault."

Mayo banged on some more about Swell Maps and "their task is to win space" with the backing of Rough Trade. The words 'ontological' and 'reification' cropped up. It all sounded very dippy hippy to the Mod boys. I suggested that Mods were "creating something for themselves, scenes of their own. Mod has been identity and it's been a lot of fun and

that's probably the end of it and if you want to criticise it, it's probably valid to say that it's not going to bring about any changes. But then if you are talking about social change you've got to start thinking about political parties and trade unions which is a whole wider thing altogether."

Phil Sutcliffe asked: "Can you only have an identity by being like other people? Did Mod raises its followers' awareness of society, the position they're in?"

A dispirited Dave Cairns didn't think so. "The people who come to see us, they don't see beyond five yards. It's really dispiriting. They're not into it as anything more than the style, something pretty to wear. It's disappointing."

Ian Page tries to make them think, he said, but often in vain.

Dave then defined the debate as "you guys over there searching into the ideals and the philosophy, what it all stands for, while we're coming out with, like you say, long pauses and, Mod is very shallow. There's very little in there, after all that."

Ian Page was infuriated by this debate, branding it "inane", "negative" and "unjustified." He wrote a passionate piece defending Mod from its intellectual detractors, which was published the following week.

'WHAT'S WRONG with being teenage and naive?/To be a cynic all the time leaves you nothing to believe/You criticise everything we say/ You say you've heard it all before, but we're saying it today/I'm ready for your labels, the sour taste of your doubt/For you to stand still and shake your head, I knew you'd take the easy way out.'

The year was 1977. I was sixteen when I wrote the lyrics above for a song called 'Just Another Teenage Anthem' which was the debut single from a group called New Hearts for whom I also sang. Nobody listened then. Few listen now.

Zero in on a moment's intensity young man, sharp look, street corner, a cold stare from old eyes in a young face Pride/dignity – self respect.

Near the end of 1978 there were young men like the character of the previous paragraph living near men in the east end of London. They gave me a priceless and rare gift. The realization that I could be special, important, positive and constructive, by being those things for myself not for my mirror. Not to the world or flashing cameras or ...Sounds (music papers, newspapers, television ad nauseum).

These, friends were good to me, and as a member of Secret Affair they inspired me to try to give that realisation to others. These people were called Mods. I called them 'Glory Boys' and some of them liked the name, because it was a title not a label; a representation of their choice of self expression. THEIR CHOICE.

The names 'Glory Boy' and the more popular 'Mods' (an abbreviation of the word modernism, which is defined in my Collins dictionary as 'any movement which aims at expressing the mind of emotions of the present day') are terms that serve to unite the shared thoughts of many young people. A verbal flag or banner. To share an ideal with someone is not unoriginal or unimaginative. A shared ideal is harmony.

Speaking of unoriginal and unimaginative brings to mind the Sounds feature of last week entitled (in order of appearance): MODS vs THE WORLD, THE GREAT DEBATE, WAR OF THE WORDS, IS THERE

LIFE AFTER MOD? Blah blah waffle waffle. That's a lot of titles for an ideal that 90 per cent of the music press claim to be meaningless. I think my favourite is MODS vs THE WORLD as an example of what the feature wasn't about.

I mean, where was the world when this "great debate" took place? Unless of course I missed the rise to power of Dave McCullough (mis-informed journalist), Chris Westwood (bad journalist) and Mayo Thompson (bombastic waste of space) who took it upon themselves to represent every living being on Earth who isn't a Mod/Glory Boy.

So there they were, two journalists and a part-time dictionary compiler from Rough Trade opposing 'Mods', versus a journalist, a fanzine journalist, and a musician from a Mod group. This human menagerie is later joined by Dave Cairns who rarely speaks to his friends, let alone bicker with strangers. The bias towards journalists (I use the term loosely) was rather strange I thought, if you consider that the issue is by choice opposed to the media's 'contribution' to society.

Some inane personal attacks were directed at me during the course of the 'debate' and some negative, unjustified criticisms were directed at Mods. Many of the questions and challenges were, I think, left unanswered. I was unable to attend the pantomime, sorry, 'debate' as I had an appointment with reality that day, but I'd like to answer some of those ambiguous questions myself.

They say that empty vessels make most noise, so I'd like to start by answering the loudest. Cue lights. Curtain.

Dave McCullough: "My attitude towards Mod is that its harmful because..."

Hang on a minute! Harmful? How is it harmful, who does it harm? Who is this bloke? What are we discussing here, Cambodia, the arms race, drug abuse police brutality, Martian invasion? He's discussing cause without effect.

"...harmful because of its continuation of the outdated...".

Outdated? Does this man report trends or create them?

"...of the out-dated idea that rock 'n' roll is merely a business or some sort of economic lifestyle."

If by the term rock 'n' roll he means contemporary music, then he's missed the point already. Mod is an attitude shared by all kinds of people, bank clerks and bricklayers, working class and middle class. They do not necessarily deal in the business of music though they may. be customers for the music businessmen who try to sell them, for instance music papers like Sounds.

It is a music business that Dave McCullough earns his living from and also provides him with the 'economic lifestyle' he claims he wants discontinued. The continuation of rock 'n' roll as a business is much more in evidence through Sounds. To say that Mod continues an environment or situation that Dave McCullough so comfortably conforms to is incorrect. Furthermore I question his qualification as judge and jury for those very reasons. However . .

"I've heard no Mod records that light any spark in me so far ..."

I have no cause to complain since I have similar opinions of his work.

"I think the idea of perpetuating something that's ten years old is boring. I think this discussion is worthwhile because some useful points of view might come out of it on why this so-called phenomenon mod has managed to claw its way into our lives."

Ha! This is the easy bit. This bloke is arguing with himself now. A worthwhile discussion on something boring? What a contradiction. As for "clawing its way into our lives". People like McCullough are clawing their way into Mods' lives. And we don't need them, their opinions or their mental masturbation spewed onto the pages of every paper on the music scene.

Mod was going eight months before the press soiled it with its cynicism and disdain. At the moment our second single has sold more than thirty thousand copies in two weeks. Thirty thousand people.

I'm sure there are that many Mods in the country but that's a lot of people for Dave McCullough to argue with.

"I can't understand why Ian Page isn't here anyway. Maybe he's washing himself."

Christ! How petty I wasn't there because I didn't regard the 'debate' as pertinent or relevant. I don't see why I should be answerable to anyone.

"It's a pity he's not here to defend the baby he's brought up."

It's not my baby — it's my belief.

"He's more or less championed it in the music papers."

All I ever did was answer questions and dare to voice my opinions. In doing so I evidently have broken some music biz rules, bloody good job too!

Later on Dave Cairns arrives and is asked what Mod inspired in him. He takes too long to answer the question and is mocked by McCullough.

McCullough: "It's a long pause." (it was)

Cairns: "It's a difficult question." (It was)

McCullough: "For someone who's been in a band for so long and ranting and raving about being positive and building things up. It's a hell of a pause!"

TIME FOR ACTION

The longest pause of all was the voice of self-opinionated derision and the shallow rantings of a room full of people taped, typed, and overstated on the cover and three pages of Sounds. "THE' GREAT DEBATE": Hmm.

Rich kids and poor kids selecting a style of dress which represents a certain look that can only be achieved from the inside, means the rejection of material/financial division. It transcends politics, right or left wing. It is a social comment and a young philosophy. Music is a universal language. It reaches the heart and touches the mind. Music as communication is its priority.

For me, there are only two types of music. Good and bad. Mods are people. But my music is for all people. If you don't agree with what I have to say, fair enough. But make sure you understand before you indulge in the prejudices of people like Dave McCullough. Find faults in yourself before you find fault in others.

A millionaire could spend a fortune, on mohair, tonic suits with thin lapels, cut by expert tailors and still be a fool. Meanwhile, Joe Soap in his dry-cleaned, re-textured second-hand Oxfam suit struts past old Max the Millionaire slob and rejects Max's right to feel superior, or treat our Joe like a soiled pound note. Powerful people — businessmen in suits, take their clothes, retain your identity.

It's a small glory agreed, but it's a situation that could have a more profound effect on the way some people think. A re-evaluation of the difference between spiritual and material achievement could destroy the way politicians, the media and technology predetermine our lives before we're old enough to realise what's happened.

I do not believe that everyone is equal. I believe everyone should have equal opportunity to be top dog.

Mod is just a way of trying to contribute. What's yours?

'Faceless clowns without a stage/ Don't try and trap me in your plastic cage/I'll take off your make

THE CHORDS

London, Marquee. November 1979.

WHATEVER happened to the Chords? You remember them. Mod band out of South London who, as recently as four short months ago, looked set to rocket into the hearts of the nation's pop kids.

The lads seemed to have it all: songs, grit, respected fans in the shape of Paul Weller and Jimmy Pursey, a glowing feature in Sounds, a record deal. So what happened?

Ah, there's many a slip between huge and hip...

In short order, the band fell out with their record label in a much publicized row with Pursey, a few daft apeths instigated an anti-Chords campaign; the ignorant wrote them off, and then malicious gossips claimed they were on a star trip...

Which, frankly, is the biggest load of old cobblers this side of the retired shoemakers' convention.

The only way the Chords have changed is that their cynicism quote has upped considerably and that's not necessarily a bad thing. Live they are hotter than ever.

From the minute they hit the stage, you realise they've lost none of their drive, none of the things that so impressed me four months ago, which is presumably also the reason so many record companies are currently battling to possess them.

So, let's talk facts, malchicks. The Chords are a South East London band comprised of charismatic Billy Hassett on vocals/guitar, moody Chris Pope on guitar, solid Martin Mason on bass and diamond geezer Brett 'Buddy' Ascot on the skins.

The eight original numbers in their present set are a more than adequate showcase of their talent and appeal. And because you thrive on comparisons, I'll point out that they're

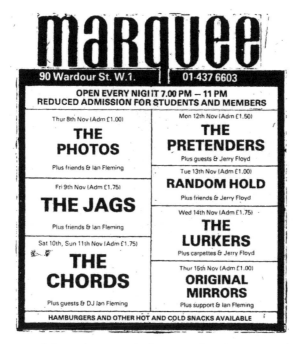

reminiscent of the early Jam, which means that the bulk of their songs manage to combine the attack and power of punk with a strong pop sensibility.

So anthems like 'Don't Go Back', 'I Don't Wanna Know' and the single-to-be 'Now It's Gone' are assertive, punchy, sinewy numbers with powerful, catchy hooks hollered by an earnest looking William and embellished by some neat spunky guitar from Mr. Pope with his new Paul Weller barnet.

I'll tell you once more: this band mean it. They've got the energy of a thousand squaddies. And though success for them is merely a matter of time it's worth re-iterating their value to the whole mod movement.

So thank you God, thank you John Peel, thank you Maximum Speed and thanks to everyone who have realised that The Chords are STILL one of the most exciting and important of today's Mod bands.

Forget movements and the moaners, let's hear it for The Chords Revival.

THE SMALL HOURS

East London. December 1979.

'In the wee small hours of the morning / While the whole wide world is fast asleep / You lie awake and think about the girl / And never, ever think of counting sheep...' ('In The Wee Small Hours Of The Morning' immortalised by Frank Sinatra)

BRIDGE HOUSE business blossoms a goal kick or three away from the molten lead murkiness of the river, and the dying dockland industry which once gave the East End so much of its heritage and character(s).

Past the towering electric pylon, along the boulevard of broken dreams and dropped Hs, punters shunt into the pub for another Mod full house. Among the buzzing 400-strong clientele, a cluster of blank generation die-hards loll about in scruffy contrast to Glory Boy stand-easy sharpness, all Oxfam flash and cash transactions, and the less finicky fashions of passing West Ham herberts and other live music revellers.

Outside, the weekly turn-out of spotty school-kids who've picked up their parkas at inflated prices and their Mod ideals ready-pressed and bastardised from the mass media, are told firmly that their Levi-clad under-age asses are about as welcome as herpes on honeymoon. And walking dipstick doorman John the Chin earns himself a new intake of heartfelt spidery hate mail.

Inside the clatter and cherry chatter drown out the clicking of the pool table as jowls froth with lager and chewed-out Wrigley's and I take advantage of an offered vantage place behind the bar to wait as the band get ready to roll.

Just another bog standard 'Mod' band I'd reckoned, the sort of sixties over-fixated twerps who have embarrassed the genuine gutsy core of this mislead and over maligned movement. Nothing likely to drag my attention from the ocean of lovely liver rot all around: brandies, whiskey, rums and hey wonder how she got that arse into them strides, wonder if he knows he is going bald, wonder how long I'll have to wait for the mini cab, wonder... KERRAMMMMMM!

Suddenly and quite as dramatically as it sounds my nomadic interest is grabbed and bagged by the band on the boards. The Small Hours have exploded into their set opener 'The Kid', a powerful driving soul excursion building on a gritty Springsteen-like formula as Neil Thompson wraps his rough gruff vocals round an ardent account of teenage tribalism:

'When we wore the clothes and made it known/Just whose side we were on/It felt supreme, like a perfect dream/No longer on our own/It felt so good to be understood/Just to be part of it/We had to run or cry and spit in the eye/Of whoever posed a threat.../Sometimes I wanna go back there/Cos things right now are hard to bear/That's what I'm TRYING to make you see/It's just the kid in me...'

This sounds like the best song the Boss never recorded.

Neil is the charismatic visual magnet of the band, looking a touch like a less alien Joe Jackson. He is flanked by the less obtrusive be-shaded axe-man Armand Hand and bassist Kym Bradshaw to his left, and cool, continental looking keyboardist wide-eyed Carol Isaacs, who adopts a Gary Numan-style stare for the duration of the set, while ex Jolt man and canny scot Iain Sheddon plays hide and seek behind the beat boxes at the back. Now you see him, now you canny.

Writing credits are liberally sprinkled among band members, and the result is an impressive multi-flavoured stew of stirring, rough and ready R'n'B rubbing infused with an authentic 60s soul feel; all underlined and informed by vigorous, up-to-date energy. Amphetamine grooves indeed.

Their three covers, The Four Tops' 'I Can't Help Myself', Doris Duke's 'Can't Do Without You' and J.J. Jackson's 'But It's Alright', are delivered with genuine affection and authentic flavour, while, that man again, Bruce Springsteen's moniker repeats a few more times in my drunken doodlings like an ill-digested curry, in particular the impressive 'Underground' which like 'The Kid' is a Thompson/Hand composition. There's a touch of early Georgie Fame about them too, before he got into jazz and disappeared up his own Aristotle. But probably the most accurate points of reference for the Small Hours' modern soul attack are names like Graham Parker and The Rumour, and New Jersey's Ashbury Dukes – themselves caught in Springsteen's long shadow.

Being part of a vibrant movement of the moment should make recognition, packed venues and hits that much easier to come by. Shouldn't it?

Point is, I hadn't been so pleasantly surprised since Mike Bailey took up the managerial mantle for Charlton AFC. But wary with the next morn's hangover that I might have just been swayed over much by the, ahem, free-flowing bonhomie I made a date to catch the band again at the Marquee with their biggest fan Charlton renegade Woolwich Mark of Upton Park infamy.

I'm pleased to report that in front of a smaller audience and confined to a shortened set, the Hours' musical magic was just as stunning. They delivered a set of tight and passionate, heart-tugging, high level R&B for hardcore fans whose strange, feet-glued-to-floor 60s dancing style makes for an entertaining side show.

Neil, Carol and Armand began musical life in a soul band called Street Chorus who attracted an errant Kym Bradshaw from Aussie punk legends The Saints as a fan for the last few gigs of their existence. The four went on to form the Small Hours in March with Iain, still living a double life as a Jolt, helping out and eventually staying on as they set out to develop as a "Motown/Stax-influenced modern band."

Their third ever gig was on May Day this year at the Bridge House and their premature, not to mention poorly mixed (albeit historically interesting) offerings 'Hanging In The Balance', 'Midnight To Six' and 'End Of The Night' are to be found gracing the famed 'Mod Mayday' collection.

The band's name reflects their basic philosophy – enjoying yourself, getting a bit merry, and generally dancing and partying into the wee 'small hours' of the morning. Risking embittered retribution from the divvy end of the Sounds spectrum they rabbit on regardless about music as Fun rather than Art; embellished only by Kym's considered opinion that Mod and in particular the Small Hours are the true continuation of the Punk live music tradition – and he ought to know. Listen to The Saints' 'I'm Stranded' for confirmation of their spiky genius.

"I'd been trying to find something," Kym admits. "And to me the Small Hours are that. The music may be different but it's the same SPIRIT..."

"Rock 'n' roll is exactly about that though," Iain interjects controversially. "It's about spirit and enjoyment - having a good time. That's why 99.9 per cent of people go to gigs, to have a good time."

"And to kill Millwall," adds Woolwich dubiously. Mark, you're not helping here, mate.

"Which is what 'Midnight To Six' is about," say Kym, side-stepping claret and blue bravado neatly. "Working all week for Friday night and then going out and enjoying yourself - living for the weekend. Like in Brisbane right, where I come from, you would go out to enjoy yourself and the police there are really heavy. Resisting arrest means you didn't roll fast enough. Young kids would get beat up really badly. I did..."

"That's why his brain has been permanently damaged," quips a passing manager.

Kym ignores him and concludes: "'Midnight To Six' is like the young kids' alternative."

Kids. Fun. Unpretentious good time music. Enjoying yourself. In an industry when name-dropping obscure French philosophers is de rigueur, such base concepts sound dangerously revolutionary.

*SADLY, the Small Hours released just one e.p. before calling time on the band, the excellent 'Midnight To Six' in 1979; although a recently released anthology stands as a testament to their promise. They are one of my favourite groups who never made it. Carol Isaacs now plays with Indigo Girls. Kym Bradshaw runs a farm in Shropshire. Armand Hand is a writer. Neil Thompson is a TV director. And Iain still plays drums, with the likes of 13 Frightened Girls. He is a music critic on The Australian newspaper.

NEWS OF THE WORLD
GOSSIP AND LETTERS...

New Mod Mag All right Shock: Latest mod fanzine in the world is called Get Up And Go. Issue Two is just out for 20p plus SAE from Wough Twade and features stuff on Secret Affair, Selecter, Squire and the Specials.

Back to Basis: **Back To Zero** bassist Mal is currently starring in his school's production of Midsummer Nights Dream, As King Of the Fairies of course.

Pursey's Package, whose dates at the Kensignton Nashville last month were cancelled in the wake of skinhead violence, will now make their London debut at West Hampstead Moonlight Club on November 19 and 20.

The bands are **Jimmy Edwards**, **Long Tall Shorty**, **Kidz Next Door** and the **Low Numbers**, all of whom have singles scheduled for release by Warners (and produced by Pursey) shortly.

The Jam have sold out dates on their forthcoming tour at Wolverhampton, Glasgow, Newcastle (both nights), Edinburgh, Portsmouth and all three nights at London's Rainbow, so fans need not bother to apply for tickets at these venues.

The Teenbeats from Hastings follow up their first single, 'I Can't Control Myself', with 'Strength of The Nation', which is released by Safari this weekend. The group have gigs lined up at ST. Ives (Hunts) Scout Hall November 21, Bradford Palm Cove 23, Nottingham Sandpiper 24, Huddersfield Coach House 25, Manchester Pips 26, Reading University 30, Hastings Queens Hall December 13.

THE MOD REVIVAL

MORE VIOLENCE AND SAVAGERY: The one-off secret Jam gig as 'Johns Boys' at the Marquee last Friday (the planned Sturday Nashville one being called off following the Upstarts' troubles) ended in a brief but vicious sea of fists and bottles outside between bouncers and punters.

Trouble started earlier when the bouncers - some drafted in for the night - roghly tried to clear the entrance corrridor of ticket holders and were met by rowdy resistance. The police were called in to gry and trace the 'resisters' in the packed hall and they escorted one person out. Later another person was ejected on the grounds that he 'knew the trouble makers'.

We were unable to trace the exact cause of the apres-gig fracas but some friction was evident as punters were leving under bouncer supervision most of whom seemed to be in possession of cut-off snooker cues and the like.

Almost instantly the whole front of the Marquee was showered in bricks and rubbish from a tip opposite and in the course of the uproar the Marquee's windows were smashed and a couple of the bouncers cut and bruised. One youth claimed to have been hit by a bouncer on the arm with a piece of wood with nails jutting out of it and proffered a suitably ravaged forearm as proof. he claimed that the fight had been provoked by the bouncers who were 'tooled up'.

In a reply a spokesman for the Marquee replied "The trouble was caused by a bunch of skinheads who'd come out just looking for trouble. None of our employees were in any way repsonsible for what happened.

Whatever the fact that wat with the Upstarts/Sham/Specials troubles are now The Jam we cold rename this column 'The week's ruck' and that ain't funny.

TIME FOR ACTION

The Purple Hearts, who came close to charting with 'Millions Like Us', begin a British tour at the end of this month and release their second single 'Frustration' on Fiction REcords this week,.

They start at Farnborough Tumble Down Dicks November 27 and then paly Lincoln Drill Hall 29, Blackpool Norbreck Castle 30, Wolverhampton Polytechnic December 1, Bishops Stortford (venue to be confirmed) 2, Exeter Routes 4, Birmingham Underworld 7, West Runton Pavilion 8, Birkinhead Hamilton Club 10, Sheffield Limit Club 11, York Oval Ball 12, Manchester Polytechnic 13, Scarborough Penthouse 14, Middlesborough Rock Garden 15, A London date is being lined up for Christmas.

The Hearts will be using support bands on all dates and they'd like to hear from mod bands who feel they could support them at various venues. Those interested should send tapes and a picture to the Purple Hearts, c/o Fiction Records, 14-16 Chaplin Road, London NW2. And send a stamped addressed envelope if you want the tapes returned.

The line up at for the Islington Hope and Anchor R&B festival has now been finalised. The festival kicks off next Monday November 19 with **Little Roosters** and is followed by **The Pirates** 20. **The OT's** (Dingwalls house band) 21, **The Inmates** 22, **Wilko Johnson's Solid Senders** 23, the **Blues Band (featuring Paul Jones)** 24, **The Bishops** 25, the **American Blues Legends** 26, **The Untouchables** 27, **Stepaside** 28, **Red Beans and Rice** 29.

Tickets are priced at £1.50 per night. Members of the bands have taken a personal interest in ensuring beer supplies throughout the festival, but there's no truth in the rumours that 'Johnny B Goode' is to be rationed among the bands"

THE MOD REVIVAL

Purple Hearts, recently signed to Fiction Records and suported by a variety of new bans on their first major tour, have confirmed dates at Lincoln Drill Hall (Thursday), Blackpool Norbreck Castle (Friday), Wolverhampton Polytechnic (Saturday) and Bishops Stortford Triad (Sunday). More details next week.

Beggar the Leyton based mod band who appear on the Mods Mayday album have gigs at Manchester New Osbourne Club November 29, Bradford Palm Grove 30, Sheffield Crazy Daisy Club December 7-8.

Small Hours have lined up gigs at West Hampstead Moonlight Club November 29, harrow Road Windsor Castle 30, Nottingham Sandpiper December 1, Islington Hope and Anchor 3, London Notre Dame Hall 6, Nottingham Lincoln Collge 7, Clapham 101 Club 8, Manchester New Osbourne Club 13, Bradford Palm Beach 14, Newbridge Memorial Hall 16, Crystal Palace Hotel 21, Clapham 101 Christmas Party 22.

Direct Hits and **The Scene**, northern mod bands who are signed to Manoeuvre REcords, have lined up a series of dates at Hull Wellington Club November 29, Sheffield Limt Club December 4, Manchester Osbourne Club, Retford Porterhouse 7, Middlesbrough Rock Garden 8, Blackburn Kings Hall (supporting the Jam) 12, Yor De Grey Rooms 12. Rainham has a new rock venue opening on December 1st. It's at the Chalford Hall in Lamb's Lane. As well as providing two bars and catering, the promoters have also organised low cost local transport from the gig to various local districts.

TIME FOR ACTION

The opening acts on December 1st are **Little Bo Bitch** and **Little Roosters**.

AN EX-KILLERMETER WRITES

I WOULD like this brief opportunity to clear the air of suspicion concerning my split/sacking from the **Killermeters**. This is not meant as a last attempt at hitting the national press headlines but an informal thank you to all who helped us along the way (including Garry Bushell) and the Northern Mods and scooter clubs whose loyalty I personally greatly appreciated.

I had no intimation whatsoever about this happening and must admit it deeply grieved me after all the hard work we have all put into the band the last 12 months. I can only think/hope that this was instigated by some power in a record company's office.

I feel deeply sorry if my personal performances have restricted the band's onslaught to success, and can only hope that with a replacement the boys go on a further glory (get it). Best of luck in the future lads, and can anyone lend me a fiver? — **Graham 'Jez' Jessop**

PS I still want Virginia Turbett's socks. Phone Huddersfield 24948 if any Mod bands want an enthusiastic drummer.

What a farce the 'Mods vs the World' debate was. So Dave McCullough says rock and roll isn't about enjoying yourself and that the mod attitude is regressive, a business attitude. Well, let's take it into perspective thern shall we? For a kick off, when I go to work (yes I work - y'know you hae to, to get money, right) for 5 days a week - come the weekened I want to go out (I feel sorry for kids who aint got jobs etc, but what can I do?). I might dress up a bit, see a band maybe - but basically have a good time - I don't want some Mayo Thompson type telling me how to change society against a tunelss twang in the backgroun, which is supposed to be interesting or different.

Then of course we're told mod is regressive - a business attitude - not '79. Well I want to go to my local record shop and buy so and so's single. A 5,000 single on Fast or Rough Trade means buggar all to me - I just want the record. If McCullough has the grudge against business then why pick up your wages this week eh? I maen you don't want to buy food, pay for travel and heating and succumb to the business world do you?

I mean, it is a business world! Very few people do things for nothing - they'd be fools to do otherwise. Music isn't going to change that - ever! Maybe it's a shame - I don't know. Mods dont buy clothes for the sake of it y'know - the clothing is basic and comfortable and yes, sometimes I do get a lift out of being smart - tht doesn't mean I'd vote for Maggie Thatcher though.

Of course paying £12 for a park, £40 for a suit and £7 for hush puppies robs me - almost as much as £18 for crepe soles, £40 for a leather jacket and £20 for bondage trousers.

I don't give a - about musical differences nor what clothes people wear. In the end, does it really matter? We're the same people under the clothes so why analyse, examine, put down and worst of all categorise kids' attitudes, dress and music? Goodnight -

Chris Green. Worcester.

FRUSTRATION

1980

INFORMATION

WHEN I SAW THE CHORDS I
KNEW STRAIGHT AWAY WHAT I
WANTED TO DO WITH MY LIFE.

Gary Wood

THE CHORDS: MAYBE TOMORROW

January 19, 1980.

J ust as Mod was shaping up to be the Bermuda Triangle of pop, with blinkered philistine scribes shooting down all-comers like the Home Guard on speed, and even yours truly begining to believe I'd been a victim of some mass hallucination over the summer, the Chords have finally come up trumps on vinyl.

Blessed with clean uncluttered production, courtesy of Andy Arthurs, 'Maybe Tomorrow' manages to combine the power and the urgency of the bands sizzling stage show with a sure-fired, guaranteed wimp-free sense of hard pop, aggressively spitting in the face of the Eighties instead of dumbly looking back at the lobotomised cretin to some lost and probably mythical Sixties golden age.

Catchy opening chords lead into meat and two veg body of the song with its contagious chorus that points an angry finger at everyone from thug bouncers to truncheon-happy cops who try and keep us safely 'in our place': 'Imagination, or real sound?/From the streets, from the towns/Silent footsteps, whispers unfound/It's too late, the deadly underground/It's reality – or just lies/From those who talk with lead/Be good now, and don't do nothing/Cause if you do/Bang-bang, Bang-bang, you're dead.'

Like 'Time for Action' and 'Millions Like Us', 'Maybe Tomorrow' is a contemporary pop classic for contemporary people – in particular, real Mods who haven't been drowned by the commercially castrated 'movement'. It's out in six days and if it isn't a hit, I'm going to start believing in conspiracy theories.

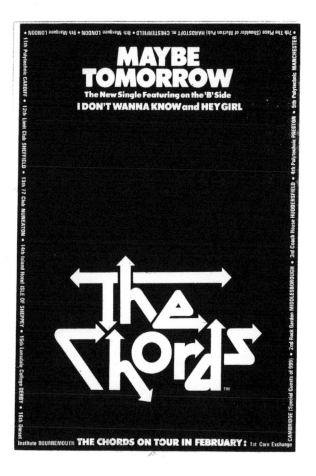

OF
ANOT

THE CHORDS: DEFINITELY TODAY

February 16, 1980.

"HEY GAL, it's forty-four, forty-bleedin four..."

I must be dreaming. I think I'm seeing a naked man at the end of my bed yelling at me. I blink but he doesn't go away. "Forty-four" the spectre continues and unless he's talking millimetres I can see he ain't discussing the vital statistics.

"That means Top Of The Pops and we'll have to drive down to London after the gig tonight. Forty Four! Screw me with a ragman's trumpet" (He didnt actually say 'Screw me with a ragman's trumpet' but I believe thats the sort of phrase Sounds ought to be encouraging) "Whatdyareckon about that then?"

I never got the chance to reply cos before I could open my mouth the figure, who I eventually placed as Chords road manager Paul Halpin, had bolted out my hotel door yelping those magic numbers and hysterically knocking on doors. Whether the fact-leaking steaking was an expression of pure joy or a desperate attempt to interest members of the opposite sex in his puny particulars I couldnt tell you.

THE MOD REVIVAL

Even with ten tag teams working out in my head (due I should add to lack of sleep rather than one over the eighteen - alcohol and I have parted company thaks to a bumbling quack's inability to distinguish an attack of wind from alcoholic gastristis, and not as the Chords would slanderously have it cos "Garry's got the "clap hands)") I can work out that Halpin is referring to this morning's new chart placing for the Chords' excellent second single 'Maybe Tomorrow' which has just leapfrogged up 26 places loking cert to penetrate the Dirty Thirty by the time you read this.

It's a formidable forty-five, a power and convincing slice of hard pop firmly rooted in today. It's angry and relevant and it makes me feel good, even vindicated about my championship of the Chords since their dingy Deptford beginnings. More importantly it shows that the Chords will survive the messy demise of what Mod became.

Mod, what a tragedy you turned out to be... not that it needed to be that way and not that I intend to drown this very alive band in obituries, but seeing as the Chords', assocation with Mod has positively held them back up to now we better hold an impromptu history lesson.

The Band were formed by two cousins, Billy Hassett and Martin Mason, who graduated from school bands to plaing Who and Beatles covers in varoius humble South London frontrooms.

the arrival of guitariest and main songwriter Chris Pope in January 1978 saw them beginning to evolve heir own sound while they played a predominantly New Wave/Who cover set in local pubs. The final line-up change came a year later when Brett 'Buddy' Ascott left South London punkies the Meat (now variously in the Jump and Splodgenessabounds) to replace Paul Halpin on drums.

You can trace the sound they developed through their own musical preferences. If they all woke up as their heroes tomorrow Chris would be Joe Strummer, Billy would be Paul Weller, Brett would be Keith Moon and Martin probably McCartney. The music they played was hard and frantically paced, as furious as a bee trapped in a jam jar but with a pop sting. Early on they sounded like the young Jam but then they shared the same roots.

The Chords and the Purple Hearts were the first of the New Mod bands and the ones who most closely fitted the idea of a Mod Renewal as a New Wave development rather than a silly sixties revival. The fledgling Mod movement at this time ¬– February, March, April and May – was exciting and promising and the Chords were riding the crest of the wave.

Paul Weller rated them. through Sonds I was waxing enthusiasm on their behalf and through leading Mod Grant Fleming, Jimmy Pursey snapped them up for his label and everything was geared for a summer single debut.

Things soured quickly. There was the much publicised Guildford incident with JP and Fatty Jones which resulted in the band and the label parting company. This set them back months and when the debut singl 'Now It's Gone' did finally come out on Polydor in September it was a feeble affair with the great stage song sabotaged by limp-wristed production job.

By this time the worst elements of Mod, stoked up by trite mass media coverage, had come to the for fore. Gutless power-poppers, conservative family entertainers, and small-minded revivalists abounded while music journalists instead of seeking out and encouraging the good roundly condemned everything 'Mod' as hopeless. Needless to say few had bothered to desert the Cheapo's run to actually see the bands.

Quadrophenia fuelled negative angles and in retrospect the fact that Ian Page with his fluent but flawed 'fashion first' philosophy became the loudest voice on the scene was also unhealthy.

But by the end of October the 2-Tone bands had hit the charts to stay. New Ska became punk's danceable mass successor and the original Mod argument was all but six feet under and with it some great records notably from the Purple Hearts, BTZ and the Low Numbers.

The Chords were not killed that easy. Up against the wall last year they recorded a fiery John Peel session that rally showed their worth (and won them the Polydor contract).

Sustained by Peel, Sounds, and Maximum Speed the band soldiered on with Pope reacting to general disillusionment and negative press by going awa and writing some of his most convincing numbers to date, which I got to heart first hand last week on the current 13 date plug-the-hit-sing tour.

By Their standards this tour finds the Chords unusually restrained. Not for them the 'Now Its Gone' tour execcesses like vicious tea-bag fights and beds hurled out of fourth floor windows. Which ain't to say it's passing off without incident.

Meeting me at Preston station, Paul and Buddy relayed the news that the whole band hd just done a runner from a ramshackle hotel devoid of residents run by a wizened bible-bashing Hitchcockian manageress full of such worldly knowledge as "You come from t'London? Ee, that's a den of iniquity. Yer going t'Manchester t'morroa, ee that's a den of iniquity."

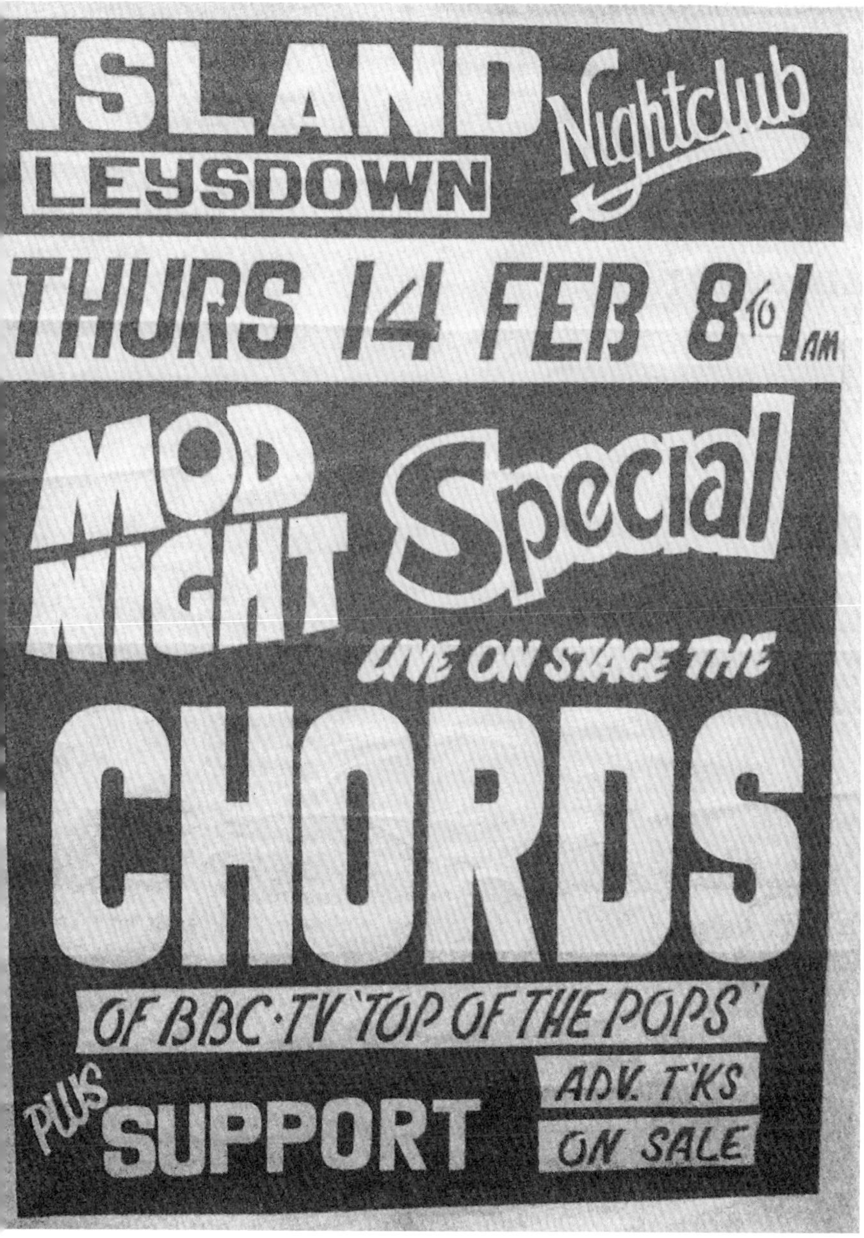
ISLAND
LEYSDOWN
Nightclub
THURS 14 FEB 8 TO 1AM
MOD NIGHT
Special
LIVE ON STAGE THE
CHORDS
OF BBC·TV 'TOP OF THE POPS'
PLUS SUPPORT
ADV. T'KS
ON SALE

Yer going down t'Millwall, eee that's the Den (she probably didn't say that one).

Hurling bangers out of the van window at innocent passers-by, Bud gives a viciously accurate imitation of the skinheads who had threatened to ruin the Middlesbrough gig two days before, after which the band had got ejected from their hotel for harbouring London fans on their floors.

Today they're playing Preston Poly and we're stretching the budget to stay at the Crest hotel, also host to Uriah Heep – the early 70s hard rock band, not the Dickens character. Very 'eavy, very 'airy.

The Chords all seem good humoured coves, but Bud is the funniest and is prone to discussions of Pam Ayres' little-known sister Pubic and unusual renditions of classic hits - paralleled by the band's hilarious sound-check covers of punk standards, impromptu HM readings and indescribable 'Dave McCullough specials.'

All of our party are faithfully betrothed except for Paul and Buddy who couldn't pull the proverbial bog chain. At Preston Poly I catch him giving student fillies the 'Ascott slow burn' which involved pursing his lips twisting his face into a life-like impersonation of a pensioner with chronic piles. It didn't work, he denied it and the la-di-dah girls were more interested in giggling "Oh I say we're all supposed to be Mods tonight." Laugh? I almost bought meself a copy of Militant.

Preston Poly is clean and new but the 130 punters look a touch pathetic in the big pit-like hall. I couldn't help wondering whether it was an audience or the queue for the bar. A handful down the front were well into the band, but most of them were more into music as a spectator sport, tapping feet and nodding heads like those little dogs you get at the back of Cortinas.

But they were a noisy bunch and with the Chords tending to encore on the strength of anyone down the front coughing, three encores were the order of the day. At the next gig, at the cosier Manchester Polly where 'Solidarity With The Steelworkers' posters vied for attention with Vegetarian Cafe ads and essential bulletins on the socio-economic structure of Iranian society, the crowd danced more but clapped less so you can never tell.

Both gigs were decent showcases for the band's musical muscle. The older songs still hit like a sledgehammer in a velvet cover, being memorable pop-with-backbone excursions delivered at a frantic pace. The songs seem altogether more together after the band's productive studio experience with produce Andy Arthurs. Chris's new songs are superior to the old both musically and lyrically.

These include 'Happy Families' with is slower than usual Undertones-like feel; 'Tumbling Down' with its aggressive build-up and chunky reggae-influenced passages; and best of the lot the probable next single 'So Far Away' with a riff redolent of the Skids, spirited drive and catchy chorus. The Chords are broadening their sound away from out and out thrash while retaining their power and energy.

On the stage though, they are still a visual mishmash. None of them are sartorially elegant though Martin always looks sharpest and adopts a classic statuesque/comatose bassist pose. Buddy, who is one of the 'if it's miked-up hit it fast' drumming school, periodically sheds his shirt, probably in a pathetic attempt to interest women in with some imagined naked ape appeal. Unfortunately his ever open mouth makes him look more like a stranded goldfish.

Bill is small and plays a Rickenbacker. He's always on the move but either taking tiny steps or making giant leaps he looks earnest and up for it. Chris Pope just looks aggressive. He sports a Gibson SG embellished with multi-coloured Op Art tape. Thankfully he doesn't wear his Gang Of Four raincoat on stage.

Chris is 19 this April. He's the son of a telephone operator, hails from Catford, South East London and looks a little like a leaner, younger, slightly more sober version of Chris Difford. He's one of the most promising song writers of his generation, certainly one of the best to come out of Mod. Contrary to NME misinformation, he doesn't sing on 'Maybe Tomorrow'.

Like Billy and Martin, Chris went to a strict Catholic school; his was St Joseph's at Blackheath. Except the only gospel he learnt was the one according to Strummer and Orwell. He left for a full time Chords career eight weeks before his 'A' levels.

"I wrote 'Tumbling Down' about St Joseph's," he reveals. "About the way they ram religion down your throat..."

'You're the kind not supposed to think or talk/Never run just walk/When they're around/Do what they say/When to work and play/You'll be someone, someday/Or come tumbling down...'

"'So Far Away' is about responsibility and 'Happy Families' is a piss-take of families who stay together 'for the kids' when there's no feeling left and they convince themselves they're happy.

"A lot of our older songs I wrote when I was 17. I know more now and I think I tend to write about more relevant things now. I've never thought of Mod as an inspiration - how can anyone write about the Kings Road? And anthems are a waste of time...

"'Maybe Tomorrow' is a sort of 1984 thing," he says. "It could happen..." The sleeve is a picture of French riot cops attacking demonstrators in 1968 when it seemed like the workers and students might overthrow the establishment. The lyrics say: 'Be good now and don't do nothing/ Cos if you do/BANG BANG, BANG BANG - YOU'RE DEAD'.

"We don't wanna present ourselves as a political band," Chris says. "I don't think political songs are worth a toss unless they bring out what could happen instead of saying 'Do this or do that'."

All the new songs will be on the debut album, out around Mid-April. It'll have twelve tracks with a give-away 2-track single with the first 10,000 pressed.

'Maybe Tomorrow' also has that classic line about New Mod at the beginning: 'Imagination? Or real sound? From the streets, from the town...'

"Mod could have been much more positive," Chris reckons. "It was positive at the start. The bands were there and the atmosphere was there. I don't know what swamped it. We did feel part of the movement and our beliefs are still the same. Everyone made a lot of mistakes.

"The whole 'looking good's the answer' bit really seems naive to me. I don't think you've got to wear this or that to be a good person, it's stupid. We were just wearing what we wanted to wear, the casual Fred Perrys and jeans. Kids can't afford flash ninety quid suits and all that shit."

Martin and Buddy are pretty much in agreement. Bud summed the whole obituary thing up thus: "Too many wimpy bands, too many revivalists, too many elitists. The best two things that I've got out of Mod is a love of soul music and white socks."

Billy Hassett is the best known of the Chords. He was born nineteen years ago in Whitechapel, the son of working class Irish-Catholic parents. He grew up in Deptford and went to St Thomas The Apostle Catholic school in Peckham.

"The first band I ever saw was the Who at Charlton," he reveals. "And they knocked me out. I got all the later stuff. After I got into the Jam I started listening to the earlier stuff. But my favourite band of all time, don't take piss, were the Beatles. John Lennon was my hero. He was great. I never forget when they played the Palladium and he said 'Those of you in the balcony can sing along, the rest of you just rattle your jewellery.'

"When I was at work I got into punk. I was a clerical trainee at LEB and I used to go to work right normal and there'd be pictures of punks in the papers with safety pins through their bollocks and everyone'd go 'Disgusting' and I loved it. I got banned from the LEB Social Club for playing the Sex Pistols..."

Whereas Chris was into the Clash, Billy was captivated by the Jam. He and Buddy were on the original Jam fan pilgrimage to Paris at the beginning of last year from which Mod as a movement grew.

"At the beginning it was different," Bill recalls. "It was music not fashion that mattered. I made a lot of good mates out of it. When it got soppy a lot of my mates turned Rude Boy. When it started, Mod was more Clash and Jam influenced, influenced by the late seventies sound rather than the Seekers or even Motown. We go to gigs now and all the Mods expect us to be Ska or jangly power-pop, and we're too hard for 'em. Yes at Middlesbrough the punks might have liked us but they wouldn't move and show it because we were 'Mods'. It's so dumb.

"We're squeezed and you either give up or do like us and the Purple Hearts have done, go away and come back with better stuff."

He goes on: "Chris is really improving as a writer; he's learning how to say things in his songs, the pressures on us have made us think about how to express ourselves.

"We've got something to say about the shit everywhere and the stupidity, about why should a Mod hate a Punk and vice versa."

Understood, and quite right.

"We're trying to comment on what we see around us," says Billy. "And all the stupid rules, you can't like this if you're that and you can't like that if you're this.

"Tear up the rule book, tear down the barriers. Kick over the statues!"

the **LAMBRETTAS**

THE LAMBRETTAS

new album
Beat boys in the jet age

The Lambrettas debut album
'Beat Boys in the Jet Age' is going places.
It includes their new single 'DA-A-A-ANCE'
which is already a hit, as well as their
previous hit single 'POISON IVY'.

'WATCH THIS ALBUM GO!'

Lambrettas on tour.

LP TRAIN 10
MC SHUNT 10

 phonogram

THE CHORDS: MOD CLICHES CRUCIFIED

May 10, 1980.

AFTER the Affair's 'Glory Boys', this is easily the most impressive album to come out of the exciting Mod explosion of the last year, and it testifies powerfully that the Chords will be one of the few bands to survive the gumby-fication (a technical term) and misdirection of that movement with their honour intact and their relevance unquestioned.

Already, the band captured here are at a transitional stage with the older aggression-fuelled material, the three-word-title crowd-pleasing faithfuls that so excited sweaty London clubs interspersed with Chris Pope's more varied and convincing later songs. If the earlier songs show why cynics dismissed the band as a less inspired and more one-dimensional version of the early Jam, the newer ones illustrate how they are developing real identity as a sinewy modern pop combo more in line with the Undertones than the Lambrettas.

The title track is a case in point, opening with a decorative Skids-style riff and then building into a contagiously catchy, handclap-embroidered, muscular-pop pearl. In similar vein, come the two latest singles, the mighty meaty slice of righteous young anger 'Maybe Tomorrow' and the solid current chart prospect 'Something's Missing' hopefully a Nifty Fifty entrant by the time you clock this.

Acoustic guitars open two other Pope new numbers, the slower-than-usual 'Happy Families' with its bitter ironic lyrics, and the excellent 'Tumbling Down' - Pope's angry two fingers to his strict Catholic School upbringing, with its powerful build-up, catchy backing refrain, strong chorus and pointed lyrics: 'Do what they say / When to work and play / You'll be someone someday or come tumbling down'.

These numbers show the band developing from their thrash and bash beginnings, and building on that energy and excitement while broadening their sound without losing one iota of vitality or punch. Of the older material we get Pope's 'Breaks My Heart', 'I'm Not Sure', 'It's No Use', the Hassett/Pope 'Dreamdolls' and Bill H's 'What Are We Gonna Do Now', and it must be said that a couple of these tend to re-inforce a general office accusation that the album's a touch grey-sounding. My one real criticism is that the album could have done with sounding a bit brighter. Maybe Andy Arthurs's production is to blame or maybe the sameness of the earlier stuff. Either way the new numbers don't reflect the problems nearly so much so it's not really anything to worry about.

There are also a couple of good covers here, a powerful rendition of Sam & Dave's 'Hold On I'm Coming' and an interesting run-through Lennon and McCartney's 'She Said She Said' – like the Jam, the Chords marinated their tough punky pop with their influences, the Beatles and US r&b.

The album comes with a free EP. Mine has been half-inched already but I can assure you it includes a superior version of the poorly produced debut single 'Now It's Gone.'

Fifteen tracks then which show these South East London youngsters firmly set on the Deptford to Destiny path. If I were Chris Pope I'd lock myself in my Catford mansion (cough) and start writing NOW. If the band's next batch of songs are anywhere near as good as the last few, the Chords' success should be assured.

THE
LAMBRETTAS

Lewes. July 5, 1980.

East Sussex band The Lambrettas had the biggest hit of all the Mod Revival groups with their cover of the Leiber & Stoller smash, 'Poison Ivy' which peaked at Number 7 in March 1980. But it wasn't all rosy. In their short career they managed to fall foul of both the Sun newspaper and, even scarier, the Cockney Rejects...while hardcore London Mods were inclined to refer to them as the Lame-brettas. Was it just jealousy?

Founder members, singer/guitarist Doug Sanders and guitarist Jez Bird, who'd both been in a local Lewes power-pop band called Shakedown, recruited bassist Mark Ellis and drummer Paul Wincer to form the Lambrettas in 1979, taking the name from the iconic Italian scooter make.

Doug recalls: "There were only a few Mods locally in Brighton and Hastings; we had no idea there would be a Mod revival on the scale that it grew into. That's why when we formed we decided to call ourselves The Lambrettas to make it as obvious as possible, so that people would know what we were about."

Their first gig was bottom of the bill on Hastings Pier; promoter Peter Haines offered to manage them that same night. After a few months of gigs, including a Music Machine support with the Purple Hearts and a South Coast special bill at London's Dublin Castle with The Teenbeats, the Lambrettas were snapped up by Elton John's Rocket Records.

Their debut single 'Go Steady' generated reasonable airplay and helped secure more bookings. Their second single 'Poison Ivy' – which Pete Waterman suggested they should cover - was the band's break-through song. But their self-penned follow-up, 'D-a-a-ance' was a hit too, peaking at Number 12.

Their fourth single 'Another Day, Another Girl' conked out at 49, however. The song had originally been called 'Page 3' but The Sun newspaper took legal action to force them to change the name. The tits. The court ordered the destruction of all the manufactured sleeves.

It was while they were on Top Of The Pops with 'D-a-a-ance' that the incident with the Cockney Rejects occurred.

In his book Cockney Reject, singer Jeff Turner recalls: "We were mooching about backstage and the Lambrettas come walking along to do their slot with their manager who was only about 5ft 4, a proper little Hobbit. So for a laugh we started singing 'Poison Ivy' to them. They were all right about it but the little short-arse manager was bang out of order. He said: 'If you could ever be as big as these boys you won't be taking the piss.' Here we go! I said 'Who are you fucking talking to, you ignorant cunt?' Well his bottle went and he kept going, but because we were all really lagging we couldn't let it go. To our minds, the geezer was taking a fucking liberty so we followed them all into the studio. By now the band was up on the stage and the cameras had started rolling but we were so pissed we didn't care. We all bowled over with the intention of doing 'em. Mick went up to the manager and jerked him by the shirt. This fella's going 'Fuck off, get away from me, get away from me.' One of us, I won't say who, stuck a cut-throat up to his neck and said 'You dirty little cunt, you fucking mess with us and I'm going to put this right in to your jugular.' Well the geezer started crying. He was quaking. There was no-one to help him. His band was on stage and I'm looking about to see if there are any cameras on us. There weren't, which was a relief, and I quickly calmed it all down. I said: 'Leave it, he'll have us fucking nicked! We've made our point. We're not bullies…' And our fella let him go. He just ran. The geezer absolutely wet himself. He'd brought it on himself by being rude in the first place, not that it merited the cut-throat. It got out of hand."

You never had that with the Goombay Dance Band.

The Lambrettas' album, Beat Boys In The Jet Age, came out in the summer of 1980, spent eight weeks in the charts and climbed to Number 28. After less successful singles and a second album called Ambience, which didn't chart, The Lambrettas disbanded in 1982 following personnel and image changes.

*JEZ reformed the band in the 1990s, but sadly died of cancer in 2008 aged just fifty.

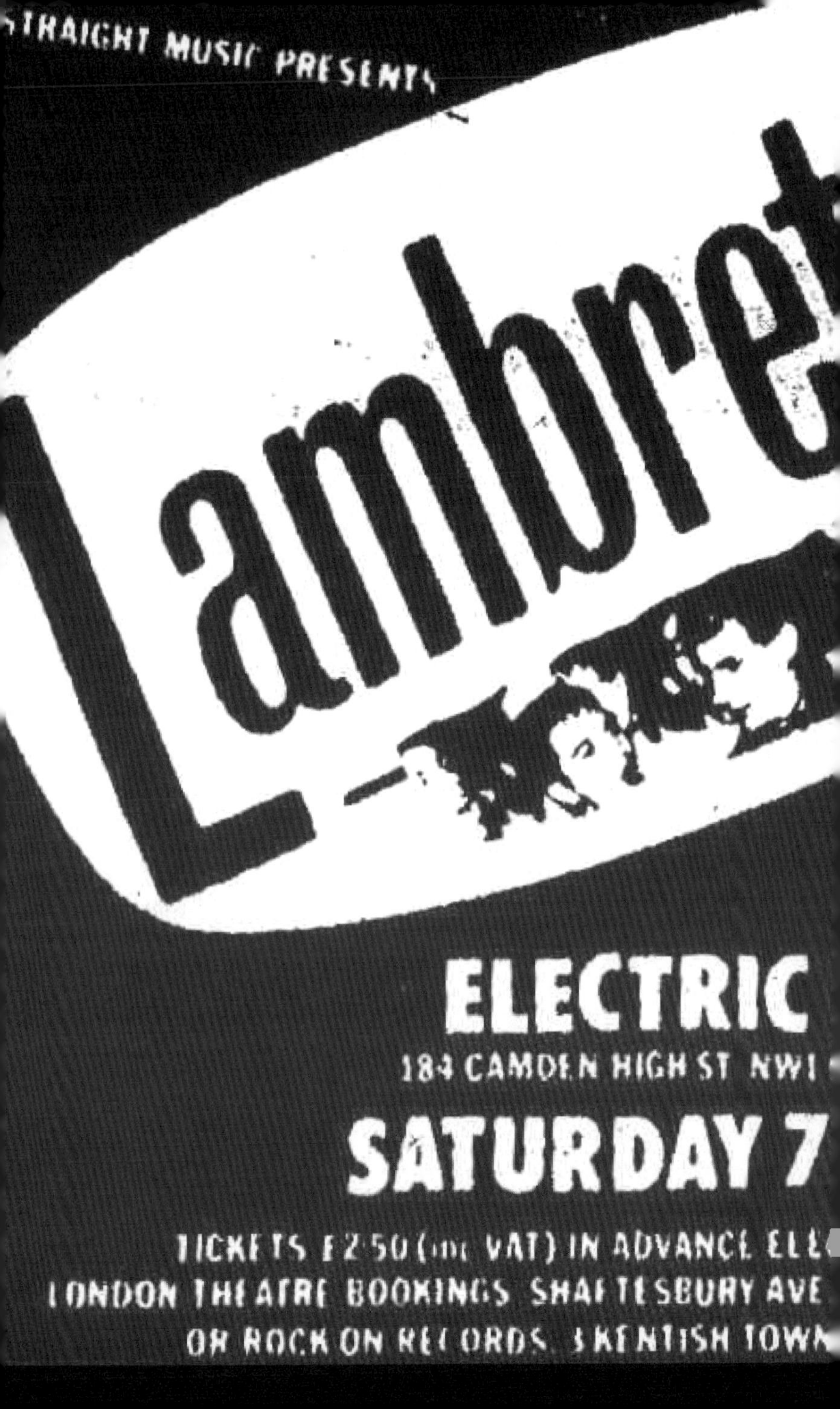

STRAIGHT MUSIC PRESENTS

Lambret

ELECTRIC

184 CAMDEN HIGH ST NW1

SATURDAY 7

TICKETS £2.50 (inc VAT) IN ADVANCE ELE
LONDON THEATRE BOOKINGS SHAFTESBURY AVE
OR ROCK ON RECORDS 3 KENTISH TOWN

ias THE **V.I.P.s**

DOLLY MIXTURE

ALLROOM

(EST TUBE CAMDEN TOWN)

JUNE at 7·30

BALLROOM BOX OFFICE, TEL 485 9006,

439 3371 PREMIER BOX OFFICE TEL 240 2245

NW1 TEL 485 5088, OR £2·50 ON NIGHT

THE MODETTES: OTT IN THE OC

Orange County USA. September, 1980.

The Cuckoo's Nest club in Costa Mesa, about fifty miles south of Hollywood, was the largest punk venue in Orange County. It claimed to have the world's first mosh pit, and every West Coast band worth its salt would play here, including Black Flag, the Vandals and TSOL. Everything seemed fine when we pulled up outside. I was travelling with the all-girl pop band the Mo-dettes. Virginia Turbett was taking the snaps, not Ross Halfin, and so the chances of the trip degenerating into a gross-out seemed minimal.

We pulled up early for the sound check and breezed into the next door bar, a kind of cowboy joint called Zubies to shoot some pool while Louis, the band's slap-head US road manager, went to recce the venue. The locals were down to earth and friendly. Well why not? The band members Kate, Jane, June and Ramona were pretty, as was Virge; while me and their roadie Chris, a young skinhead from East Ham, were clearly no threat. We had a beer and a laugh with the resident bar-flies.

Then Louis stormed in spitting feathers. The club was trying to charge the band extra for the PA and the sound guy, and he wasn't having any of it. He had pulled the gig. The mood changed in a moment. The faces of the friendly locals clouded over. We weren't just two geezers with a gang of stunners in tow, we were a band. A freakin' asshole punk band.

The guys playing pool stopped and started to tap their cues across their palms menacingly. The odds weren't good. They were twelve or thirteen fully grown geezers. We were five girls, me, Chris, and a "fucking prick with ears". We headed for the door, the whole bar followed. Pool cues were being tapped harder, as hard as our hearts were beating. As we stepped out two cop cars pulled up in the parking lot. Hurrah, we thought. The cavalry.

Wrong. Glaring at us, the cops left their cars, pulled out their night sticks, crouched down and started to drum the ground. They began to chant: "Punk rockers go home!" The crowd joined in. "Punk rockers go home!" Huh? The girls looked Moddish, me and Chris had crops, and Louis was still a bald prick.

What we didn't know was that despite the two buildings being owned by the same guy, and them sharing a car-park, there was an on-going war between the Zubies regulars and the Cuckoo's Nest punters.

We headed for the tour bus and were relieved when it started first time. The nightmare didn't stop. We drove off; a cop car drove after us. They trailed us for an hour, all the way back to la-la land. We convinced ourselves we'd be pulled over and left for dead in a ditch. Those with us with any bottle promptly lost it, along with various pills and small wraps of whizz and Charlie. Legs were vigorously crossed, there was no way we'd be stopping for a roadside slash. All this for trying to play a gig. Imagine the fuss if we'd knocked them for the beer as well...

The Cuckoo's Nest was later targeted by a twelve man police team. The following January one of the punks tried to run down two cops in the parking lot. The city council revoked their live entertainment licence soon after. The Vandals immortalised the hostilities between the two clubs in a song called 'Urban Struggle.'

THE Modettes were four women – American guitarist Kate Korus, Swiss singer Ramona Carlier and two English musicians, bassist Jane Crockford and drummer June Miles-Kingston who later played with the Fun Boy Three. They looked Mod and played on Mod bills but they sounded pop-punk. 'White Mice' could have been a Penetration song. They did a cheery number about the Kray Twins, but their most memorable live staple was Edith Piaf's 'Milord' which Ramona song in French. Oh mon Dieu, elle était tellement fuckable, as I believe Jean-Paul Sartre once remarked.

THE MO

DETTES

THE JAM: EQUAL RIGHTS & JUSTICE

Hammersmith. November 29, 1980.

Dogma dictates that the Hammy Odeon is a cavernous tomb bereft of atmosphere and incompatible with the rowdy celebration of modern rock music. But although I can't abide seats as a rule I've always found that the right performers, the real stars, can overcome all the artificial barriers and transform the old darling into a party time spectacular.

Dury's done it. Bondie, last month the Skids, and last week it was the turn of Weller's Wizards to bring revelry and a real sense of intimacy to thousands. All the more impressive given that the set included virtually all of the new album.

THE MOD REVIVAL

A couple of snatched listenings haven't convinced yours truly that the new material has captured the grand heights of greatness that the Jam achieved during their immaculate 'When You're Young' to 'Going Underground' period, but that said on vinyl and live evidence there's no disputing that they've not lost any of the gritty honesty, passion, compassion and pop maturity which have become the band's trademarks.

The Jam are a postive force, lyrically and musically, all the more powerful because of their masterly blend of robust rhythms and singalong pop that turns legs to elastic and leaves mouths like gaping caverns bawling along despite owners inhibitions. Given a free rein I'd rabbit on about them for yonks but rather than bore you stupid I'll simply precis the proceedings, kicking off with 'Dream Time' from the business 'Setting Sons' album chased by the more light-hearted but ultra-catching 'Boys About Town' and the more reflective 'Monday'.

'Going Underground' hits the first real peak with its gutsy power-protest and it's almost equalled by the sparser realism of 'Pretty Green' with its rumbling bass line and spirited crowd 'Oi' punctuations. Sprinkled 'la-la-la-la-la's' sparkle up 'Man In The Corner Shop', a dry observation on the British class system that's trumped by the insistent 'Set The House Ablaze' with its punch anti-authoritarian message.

The rest of the set progressed through the spot-on character sketch of 'Private Hell', 'Liza Radley', 'Dreams Of Children' and a ferocious 'Modern World' peaking again with the masterful 'Little Boy Soldiers' before once more building up through the rocking 'But I'm Different Now', 'Start', the discoid 'Scrape Away' swipe at old man Rotton, to the final triumphant 'Strange Town', 'When You're Young' and the raucous demands for more.

Other commitments meant I had to beat a reluctant retreat duing the fiery fury of first encore 'Eton Rifles' and as I sped into the night it was hard not to chew over the Jam's multitude of strengths and reflect that their integrity, honesty, bitterness and impeccable morality wedded to that tight evolving musical piston strength makes them one of the most relevant and most enjoyable bands in Britain today.

And that ain't an opinion, that's a fact.

NEWS OF THE WORLD
GOSSIP AND LETTERS...

England's premier Mod outfit **The Chords** seem out to recreate the wild and wacky hotel smashing outrages of their earliest predecessors, it would seem.

Their recent UK tour included these horrific highlights. Doncaster: a radio unscrewed from a wall (Rock 'n' roll!) set off the hotel alarm, and thus summoning four fire appliances and the Old Bill to the scene, to find a reception full of grumpy sleep-deprived customers and angry Mums with screaming babes-in-arms...

Stevenage: saw an outbreak of graffiti and accidental breakages amounting to a bill for £186, including cleaning claims for twelve x Vomit stains and three x urine stains (the sick bastards were taking the piss, obviously). Guildford: clocked up a £120 bill after a TV set went for a swim in a hotel bath.

Manchester: saw the band encounter popular Cockney Comic Jim 'Nick Nick' Davidson; together they wildly mooned the DJ at a post-gig nightclub. Back at their hotel, the boys came across a room with its door ajar, with two drunken executives snoring their heads off inside it. Natch, in less time than it takes to say "Oily rag spam" the business types were plastered in toothpaste and shaving cream. Their screams awoke the entire establishment next morning.

Mr Pete Townshend was unavailable for comment.

THE MOD REVIVAL

The Purple Hearts have December gigs in and around London at Canning Town Bridgehouse, Islington Hope and Anchor, Feltham Football Club, and Fulham Greyhound. Throughout next year, the members of the band will spend much of the time pursuing separate careers, though they will link up from time to time for occasional Hearts gigs.

LONG TALL AND NOT HERE: Long Tall Shorty dropped out of the Chords tour lat week after some stick from Nothern skins. The day was saved at Manchester by local band the Fast Cars who provided a short set of new wave pop featuring some nice ideas but rather naive lyrics.

The Chords have sacked their singer Billy Hassett in a dramatic move at the end of their British tour.
Said the remaining members in a phone: "We got rid of him because of his lack of commitment in the band. We'd been having problems all through teh tour, but the gig at the Music Machine Camden last Friday was the final straw."

The Chords are keen to point out that the are still going strong and auditioning for a new vocalist this week. Anyone who is interested should telephone 01-499 8686 extension 45.

STOP STIRRING - THE MODS ARE ALL RIGHT

I was very annoyed by John Blake* last week. I am a Mod and proud of it. I am a Mod because I love the music and the clothes, not because I like fighting Rockers, damaging shops and injuring innocent holidaymakers. To describe the possibility of Mods versus Rockers battles as "a whole lot of excitement on a few South Coast beaches" is totally irresponsible. Unfortunately words like "fun" and "revenge" have been used by other papers and if much more like this is said the situation will worsen. I don't want to end up in hospital because I happen to like Motown, so please, when you write about Mods in future, just stick to the music and the clothes, after all that's what it's all about. **Tony Sydenham**.

*John Blake was at the time pop columnist for the Evening Standard

PROUD TO HAVE BEEN ONE OF THE FEW GIRLS
ON THE SCENE IN THE EARLY DAYS

Maxine Lordan

GOING UNDERGROUND
MODS & SODS

THE MOD REVIVAL OF 79 WAS A HOME FOR PEOPLE LIKE ME. A YOUTH CULT FOR THE ASPIRATIONAL WORKING CLASS, WHO LIKED MUSIC WITH ENERGY AND CLOTHING WITH STYLE. TEAR UPS, FOOTBALL, SCOOTERS, LIVE GIGS AND CLUBBING WITH MATES. SO GLAD I WAS A PART OF THIS AS BOTH A MOD AND A MUSICIAN, BECAUSE IT WILL NEVER HAPPEN AGAIN!

Derwent Jaconelli

MODS AND SODS

The Bridge House

The Bridge House in Canning Town, East London, was always my favourite venue. It was never glamorous, but it had a heart as big as the neighboring fly-over and it was as important in Britain's musical history as the Roxy was.

I knew it first as a pub rock venue. Bands like Remus Down Boulevard, Filthy McNaughty and Jackie Lynton's Happy Days were regulars. But guv'nor Terry Murphy was shrewd enough to run an open booking policy, which meant many major acts played early gigs here, from Alison Moyet to Iron Maiden via Bad Manners.

The small, atmospheric corner of London's East End was also to play midwife to some vitally exciting youth cults. The new Mod bands of 1979 incubated here, groups such as the Purple Hearts, Secret Affair, the Chords, Beggar, Squire and the Merton Parkas.

The Bridge was a favourite Glory Boys haunt – the other was the Barge Aground at Barking – and it always chock-a-block for Mod nights. Many of the 2-Tone bands appeared too. It was a heady time to be young and alive.

When I managed the Cockney Rejects, from near-by Custom

House, it seemed logical that they should play here too (their first gig was supporting the Little Roosters) and so the pub became the birth-place for the new exciting street-punk of the Oi bands too. The Rejects, Cock Sparrer, the Business...these groups, who went on to inspire today's monster bands like Green Day and Rancid, cut their teeth here. Many American punk rockers still make the pilgrimage to E16 to see the site of this temple of spiky dreams.

Canning Town was always a rough area, and many of the pubs were notorious for trouble, but not the Bridge. The Murphy family made sure of that. Bands and punters alike appreciated the good-time feel of the place. I loved it enough to have my 25th birthday party here. Cock Sparrer reformed for it, Terry's wife even baked me a cake, which much to her horror ended up in my face, but I enjoyed the evening far too much to remember much about it now.

In fact, the many years I spent here have merged into a series of indistinct but happy memories. Stand-out gigs include performances by Steve Marriott, Judge Dread, Iron Maiden and

Rory Gallagher. And for every one of them, the place was more packed than a Toyko tube train.

At one stage, when the Purple Hearts were on stage, the cellar needed emergency building work because the sheer weight of Billie Bunters above was putting a severe strain on the ceiling. Millions Like Us, indeed.

I saw Depeche Mode here, played with their synthesizers mounted on beer crates. And Terry Murphy allowed me to put on two Prisoners Rights benefit gigs which saw the Cockney Rejects at their brilliant, blistering best.

Back then, Terry's son Glen, who was to go on to find TV stardom as George Green in the ITV smash hit series London's Burning, was a humble barman. Another son, Darren, now sadly passed away, played bass in the legendary Wasted Youth, an early goth, post-punk outfit with echoes of Syd Barrett. They were better than I gave them credit for, but hey, you can't be right about everything.

Terry formed his own Bridge House record label – another first! – to bring out Wasted Youth's records and other seminal releases like the Mods Mayday compilation of 1979, although it should be said that accusations about a number of unauthorized pressings mar its memory for some of the featured bands.

I can never drive through Canning Town without looking over at where the venue used to stand and feeling a warm glow of nostalgia. Today's charts are full of manufactured muppets and karaoke warblers. The Bridge House stood for something better: real music, raw music. The sounds of the street.

Tony Class

Tony Class deserves a special mention for starting the first Mod club nights that featured DJs, not live bands.

His first three clubs, of the 63 venues he went on to use in London, were, The Hercules Tavern, Lambeth North (November 9th 1979, The Red Lion on Westminster Bridge Road, (January, 1980) and The Walmer Castle in Peckham (February, 1980.)

Tony recalls: "Being a Mod in the Sixtiess, it was soul-destroying to reach the age when I could legally ride a scooter, in 1967, only to see that the scene was petering out. When my younger brother, Robin, bought a scooter in '78, (Li150, 'English Rose') and was

hanging about in Hastings with The Teenbeats it brought the memories flooding back.

"As my brother and I were both DJs, I suggested we organise a Mod Night in the pub where we had a residency, The Hercules Tavern on Hercules Road. In truth, I just wanted to relive my youth.

"I was 28 when we started Mod Nights at The Hercs. It was so successful I decided there and then that this was where my future lay, through thick and thin, and that I would do everything in my power to keep the Mod scene alive for as long as I could.

"Through the Eighties and Nineties I organised and DJed at 63 London Mod Clubs and more than 150 Mod Rallies around the UK, booking numerous Mod bands along the way. My work was done."

Tony Class was at his height between 1981 and '83 packing out clubs 7 nights a week in London and the home counties; other younger Mod DJs such as the legendary Eddie Piller and Paul Hallam (aka 'The Stalin of Style') followed suit. London DJs Hallam and Richard 'Shirley' Early ran a club night named

Sneakers, while Tony ran Club Mod at the Bush Hotel until 1986 when the venue changed to an O'Neill's. Sadly Tony died in the Spring of 2014 but his legacy lives in in clubs and scooter rallies all over the world.

Squire

The problem with Squire is they were born too late. They sounded like a Merseybeat band. There was no post-punk punch in their pop. Songs like 'The Face Of Youth Today' sounded like the sound of youth yesterday, specifically the early Sixties, which may explain why they didn't make much impact.

A couple of them had been to school with Paul Weller who'd given them a Jam support slot but apart from a shared love of The Beatles and Tamla, that was all they had in common.

Squire hailed from Guildford in Surrey. Singer Tony Meynell saw Mod as a rebellion against punk. "Instead of being scruffy, it's a smart image," he said. "And we're certainly not looking for trouble, just the opposite."

The band, which also featured Steve Baker on guitar, Enzo on bass and Mike Ross on drums, were picked up in issue two of Maximum Speed. Their first single 'Get Ready To Go' on the Rok label was bog-standard power pop.

Squire were signed by I-Spy but failed to dent the charts.

The Fixations – The Sound Of Young London

The Fixations aren't one of the better known of the Mod Revival bands but they were bloody good live and widely respected on the Mod circuit.

They actually began life in a Scout hut in Islington, North London, in the summer of 1976, but didn't become The Fixations until 1978, picking the name because it "sounded Motown" – Mod was always going to be their destiny.

They were gigging by the November, earning themselves an early mention in Sounds.

The band consisted of Paul 'Pad' Cathcart (vocals and lead guitar), Paul Cattini (vox/rhythm guitar), Ken Gamby (drums), Noel Hughes (bass), and last recruit Richard Sharp (rhythm guitar, although he later switched to bass when Noel left).

Not only was Richard a great musician, he also managed a King's Cross off licence, making him a must-have recruit for any thirsty young combo.

Uniquely, the Fixations included no covers in their set but their own songs had attitude and promise and they played with supreme confidence.

They went down well live supporting the likes of the Chords, the Purple Hearts and the Teenbeats, and definitely had the talent and the songs to have followed their contemporaries into the charts. Unfortunately, their management dumbly turned down record company interest and even the tasty double A-sided single 'No Way Out'/'Catty Remarks' that they recorded for Carrere Records didn't see the light of day.

It was later released on the retro compilation, The Sound of Young London, on Detour Records.

Ken and Pad have since published a book about the band's experiences called, The Fixations Modest Recognition.

The Spiders

The Spiders began life as an all-girl punk band called Muvvers Pride. All four of them worked at BOY in the Kings Road, and played the usual spiky circuit including the Roxy, the Vortex etc.

When the Muvvers split, guitarist Dee Hurley and blonde stunner bassist Lynne Easton formed The Spiders with Rob Eagan on drums and Debbie Sanders on vocals. The South London foursome debuted at Vespas at the Global Village, Charing Cross. It was such a shambles that their original drummer walked off and audience member Rob stepped in to salvage what was left of the set.

The eight-legged combo rehearsed for months in a Beckenham garage for before they started gigging the Mod circuit, supporting variously the Merton Parkas, The Mods and the Bodysnatchers. Keyboardist Marcia Cobweb (actually Lobowfski) joined later.

The Spiders released a cover of the Tommy James & The Shondells' single 'Mony Mony', b/w 'Who's The Other One?' on Red Shadow Records.

Sadly Lynne, who once dated Adam Ant and who became a top pop make-up artist after the Spiders split, died in 2006.

Dolly Mixture

New wave trio Dolly Mixture were formed in 1978 by bassist and singer Debsey Wykes, guitarist/vocalist Rachel Bor, and drummer Hester Smith - three school friends who shared a love of The Shangri-Las and The Undertones - the Dollies supported Feargal and the lads on an early UK tour.

John Peel in Sounds was an early fan. But although they were popular on the Mod/Ska circuit there only real taste of chart success came when they sang backing vocals for the Captain Sensible's hits 'Wot' and 'Happy Talk'.

They disowned their own debut single, a cover of the Shirelles hit, 'Baby It's You' (Chrysalis, 1980) produced by Eric Faulkner of the Bay City Rollers. Their second single, 'Been Teen' was the first to be released on Paul Weller's Respond label. It was followed by 'Everything And More', also released on Respond. Both singles were produced by Captain Sensible and Paul Gray of The Damned.

The bands stopped gigging in 1984, and the Dollies mixed no more.

007

The band was formed at the height of the Modrevival in 1979 by drummer Steve Walters along with lead guitarist Tony Evans and vocalist Tony Ward.

A chance meeting between Tony Evans and me in a Bethnal Green pie and mash shop (the east end delicacy!) brought my brother Russell Wood into the fold on bass guitar and I invited myself in on rhythm guitar.   007 were now a classic 'twin guitar' band - twice the power and twice the volume!

Steve's powerhouse drumming pushed them through every song with the Evans' guitar filling the sonic sound scape with big chords and lead guitar lines. Russell was the driving bass player that the band had been screaming out for mainly because they needed a bass player and they needed a driver for the van!

Born at a time when the sound of the New Wave was still ringing throughout the land. The band's love of all things mod/60's fused with the prevailing contemporary music of the times and it would shape their basic look and sound. The sound was hard edged but still retained a pop sensibility (underneath all the volume!), evident in songs such as Can You See Me, Cover Girl and Nearly Man (all available at good a record shop near you - and possibly at a few bad one's too!).

The band look was a mix of classic cycling shirts, Fred Perry and Ben Sherman shirts and mohair suits. Never was the aphorism 'Clean living under difficult circumstances' more apt than when applied to us! The band seemed to thrive on tension and aggression but it wasn't all bad - this energy being channelled into the gigs for the most part. Some gigs exploded with such passion and intensity that we were as shocked and stunned as the audience and were left exhausted afterwards.

A gig in Brighton (surely the spiritual home of Mod?) reached its climax with all the guitars being smashed onto the stage. The peak of the crescendo arrived to the sound of splintering, screaming guitars and ear splitting feedback.

Eddie Steady Go

Simon McEwan, AKA Eddie Steady Go,was the Mod Revivals own John Cooper Clark. Managed by The Teenbeats and Long Tall Shorty manager (and Marquee DJ) Jerry 'Parka' Floyd he would normally come on stage before one of those acts and bravely,through much heckling,launch into the likes of "Mods do this","Social Climbers Christmas","Housewives choice" etc. Rumour was he was a chef who came from Bury.

Speedball

One of the earliest of the new Mod bands, Speedball hailed from Southend-on-Sea in Essex and joined the Purple Hearts in early forays into the London scene.

They started out as schoolboy punk band Idiot and lived up to their name when bassist Paul 'Blue' Dunne and guitarist Barrie Godwin, both 17, were nicked for stealing guitars from their local music store, Sound Sensation. Both did time in Borstal. It could have meant the end of the band, but singer songwriter Rob Paveley, then 19, and drummer Dave Dyke, then 17, put an advert in Melody Maker.

Waterloo Mod Guy Pratt, also 17, answered the call and Speedball carried on as a three piece gigging solidly around London and the South East under the management of fanzine writer Roger Allen. And Rob changed his surname to Beulo.

Speedball could have been the first Mod Revival band to release a single. They recorded two Paveley songs 'No Survivors' and 'Is Somebody There?' as a double A side 45 for No Pap Record but various sleeve mistakes (including calling the band Speedballs – d'oh!) meant the singles were withdrawn. They were finally released in the summer of 1979, and supported by the band's own 1000 Faces Tour.

They were said to be stunning live, with strong original numbers such as 'Sixties Girl' and 'Boys & Girls' as well as a cover of the Scouts song 'Ging Gang Gooly' which they'd first performed as Idiot. Their other covers were 'First Time' by The Boys and the Clodagh Rodgers hit 'Come Back & Shake Me.'

Their hardcore following were from local scooter club the Quadropheniacs (descended from the Sharks SC), and called themselves 'Quadropheniacs Faces'.

Speedball split in 1980 when Dave emigrated to Sweden, while Rob eventually emigrated to Australia. But his 'No Survivors' song was not prophetic because there was one survivor - Guy Pratt went on to become a world-famous session bass player working with the likes of Pink Floyd, Michal Jackson, Roxy Music, Van Morrison and Madonna.

*Footnote: Guy is the son of Mike Pratt who played Jeff Randall in TV's Randall & Hopkirk (Deceased).

The Two Tone Pinks

Formed in Salford In early 1979. Featuring Dave Moore on lead guitar, Graham Briggs rhythm guitar, Mark Harris bass, Pete Bates drums and Hydn Rydings on vocals.

The bands name was taken from an amphetamine popular with mods and northern soul dancers from the previous decade. Their first gig was in August 79' supporting The Selector in Hulme Manchester for Tony Wison. They split in December 1980 with one track on a compilation album "A Sudden Surge Of Sound" which also included ex X-Ray Spec - Laura Logic and The UK Subs.

The Onlookers

Although formed in 1979 The Onlookers reached the Mod public slightly later. They were a four-piece Mod band with psychedelic undertones and keyboards from Slough in Berkshire. They got their first Extraordinary Sensations coverage in 1981, and are chiefly remembered now for their 1982 three-track e.p. 'You & I' (Demon). 60s-influenced, their set included a cover of the Small Faces' 1967 song 'Green Circles'. The NME hated them for their psychedelic look (their review barely mentioned the music; so no change there...)

The Onlookers were Nick Stone (lead guitar & vocals), Mark Leach (bass), Peachy Dean (rhythm guitar and vocals), and Mark Bevis (drums).

THE MOD REVIVAL

Beggar

Formed in south Wales, Beggar relocated to London in time to
get on the bill of the now infamous Mods Mayday gig at the
Bridgehouse in Canning Town. Consisting of Nigel "Bryn"
Gregory, Jeff John, Mike Slocombe and Mark Williams in June
1979 they embarked on a tour of Scotland that was brought to
an abrupt end when, after a few too many whiskies they were
arrested after breaking into a gift shop. Back in London they
carried on gigging before setting of for a tour of the north, cut
short this time when guitarist Jeff Johns quit the band. The band
carried on until June 1980 with Oisin McCool filling in as Johns
replacement. Bryn Gregory resurfaced in The Co-Stars in the mid
80's. And again those fine chaps at Detour have recently issued an
albums worth of recordings!

The Directions

Formed in Shepherds Bush in December 1978 by brothers John
& Tony Burke along with bassist Martin Wilson, while drummer
Steve Martinez joined in April 1979, The Directions recorded one
of the most sought after singles of the period. After gigging on the
local circuit they were soon offered a slot at The Global Village
in Charring Cross alongside The Teenbeats and The Sta-Prest,
who both refused to play with the PA that was in place. By the
time a better PA had arrived the show was running late and it
looked like The Directions wouldn't get to play at all. Talking to
vocalist John Burke in 2005, he told me that when they went into
the studio to record a single, Three Bands Tonite was the latest
song his brother had written so they recorded that. A week later
it would have been something else. 2000 copies were pressed and
then 800 copies were ruined in a flood in their managers office.
The Directions soldiered on until 1981 before calling it a day,
though in 1983 they remerged minus John Burke as Big Sound
Authority and achieved a modicum of success with an expanded
line up.

TIME FOR ACTION

The Circles

Formed by Mick Walker, previously of the Interjectors, along with ex Neon Hearts drummer Keith Allen, Tony Lowells and Glen Tanter, The Circles were the prominent Mod band in the West Midlands and were soon signed to local label Graduate in September 1979. The single Opening Up was released in December before getting picked up and reissued the following March on Chrysalis. A second single, Angry Voices appeared before the band split, although in 1985, Circles, a recording from 1979 was released as a single. The band have since reformed on occasion and have recorded and album for Detour Records.

Department S

Department S had started life as Guns For Hire, a group of gig going friends who didn't actually exist as a band yet ended up recording who one single for Korova Records in 1980. Featuring Tony Lordon, Vaughan Toulose, John Hasler and Mike Herbage, the band ended up playing a couple of gigs before taking things a little more seriously with a name change and the addition of Stuart Mizon and Eddy Roxy, later replaced by Mark Taylor. 2 hit singles followed in 1981, Is Vic There and Going Left Right. Reformed in 2007 the band now includes ex-Back to Zero guitarist Sam Burnett along with Herbage, Taylor, Mizon and Roxy.

The Rage

The Rage deserve special mention for being the post '79 Mod supergroup. Following the demise of Long Tall Shorty in 1984, Derwent Jaconelli vacated the drum stool to further a career as a singer - taking LTS' ace guitarist Steve Moran with him. Recruiting a Purple Heart - Just Jeff - on bass, and a Chord Buddy Ascott on drums. The initial ambition was just a one off support slot at the Hearts' Christmas show at London's 100 Club. It went rather well - some understatement considering the topless dancers who got carried away and stormed the stage. Championed by Sounds' Garry Bushell The Rage quickly became flavour of the month on the post-revival Mod scene. A 6-song demo for Stiff

Records prompted further interest but the group declined the offer of a contract. Further tours followed and a demo for Polydor saw another offer to sign but again our reticence prevailed. There was a release of "Looking For You" under Diamond Records which was quickly withdrawn. Within a couple of years first Jeff then Buddy left and though The Rage limped on in various guises there would be no official release until 2018's compilation "All" on Detour Records. Buddy remembers "It was a blast while it lasted - especially our hopelessly anarchic mini tour of Italy - and I have mainly fond memories of our time together...and I still haven't worked with a better frontman than Derwent - a veritable force if nature."

THREE BANDS TONIGHT

THE BEST OF THE REST

MOD CULTURE FROM THE EARLY SIXTIES TO THIS DAY HAS NEVER DISAPPEARED - IT'S JUST NOT ALWAYS BEEN NEWSWORTHY. BUT THE MUSIC, THE FASHION AND THE IMAGE OF MOD REMAINS, ITS AN EVOLUTION. IT WILL ALWAYS BE A PART OF BRITISH CULTURE.

Dave Cairns

TIME FOR ACTION

The following pages feature photographs in order of
007 - courtesy Gary and Russell Woods mum,
Speedball - courtesy Julian Leusby,
Dolly Mixture - courtesy Julian Leusby,
Gary Lammin of Little Roosters - Jiri Smetana,
Back to Zero - courtesy Brian Kotz,
Long Tall Shorty - courtesy Roger Allen,
The Graduate - Steve Wright,
Squire - courtesy Alan 'Fred' Pipes,
The Fixations - courtesy Julian Leusby,
Eddie Steady Go - courtesy Julian Leusby,

This book would not have been possible without the help and photographs of Virginia Turbot, Paul Wright, Richard Adams and Paul Calver.

Virginia Turbett was a teenage punk who became one of Sounds' best-loved photographers. I first met her on a Right To Work march in 1978. She was a fan of the revolutionary socialist punk band Crisis, whose female following were known as 'the Effects of Crisis'.

She took great pictures so I encouraged her to become a pro. Virg accompanied me on many an adventure, including The Jam in Sheffield, Secret Affair in Southend and perhaps more glamorously the Modettes in Los Angeles.

She was professional, principled and fun to be around. Bands took to her easily and her pictures - some of which are included in this book - were always terrific. Virginia has lots more pictures where these came from and they can be purchased by contacting her on virginia@virginiaturbett.com **GB**

Paul Wright. Someone kept telling me about this band called The Chords, who they had seen play at the Wellington pub in Waterloo. I wanted to see what all the fuss was about so I went to one of their gigs and that was how I got into the Mod scene in 1979.

I took photographs of many of the Mod bands that I went to see at that time, often standing on the edge of the stage at the Marquee Club snapping away while try- ing to avoid the bouncers.

PW

Richard Adams was Chords Buddy Ascott best mate at school. He went on the road with the band initially as a drum roadie but was more suited to taking photos!

Paul Calver was a friend of Secret Affairs Dave Cairns. 'Ian and I met photographer Paul Calver at Loughton college back in 1978 and when we started gigging with Secret Affair back in January of 1979. he was at many of the early shows and forever taking pictures. He also ran a rehearsal room where we rehearsed and he provided a van and roadies too.

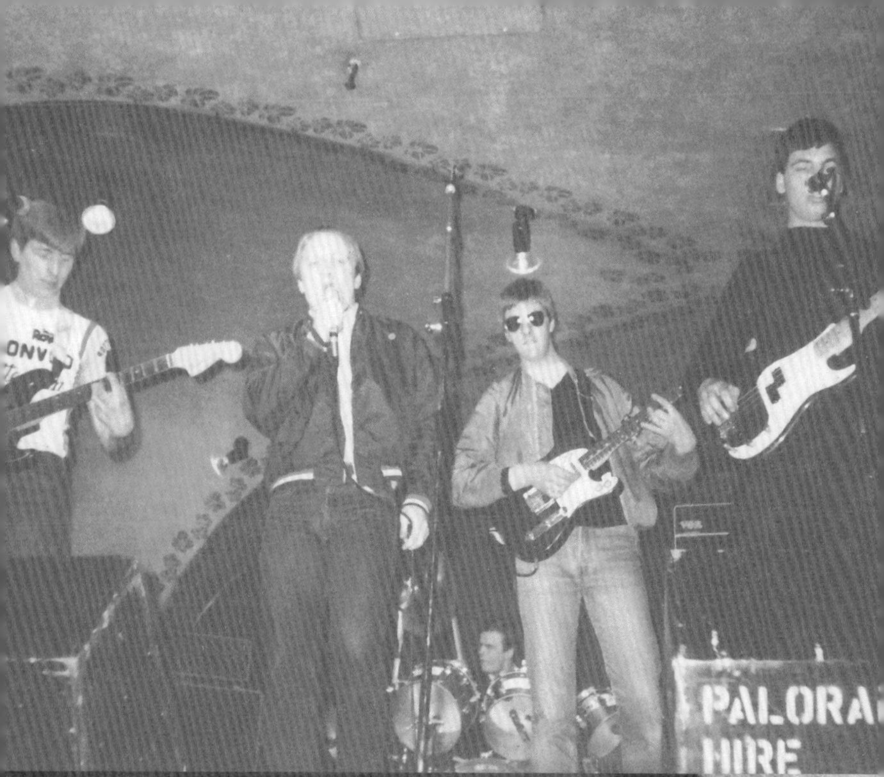
PALORA
HIRE

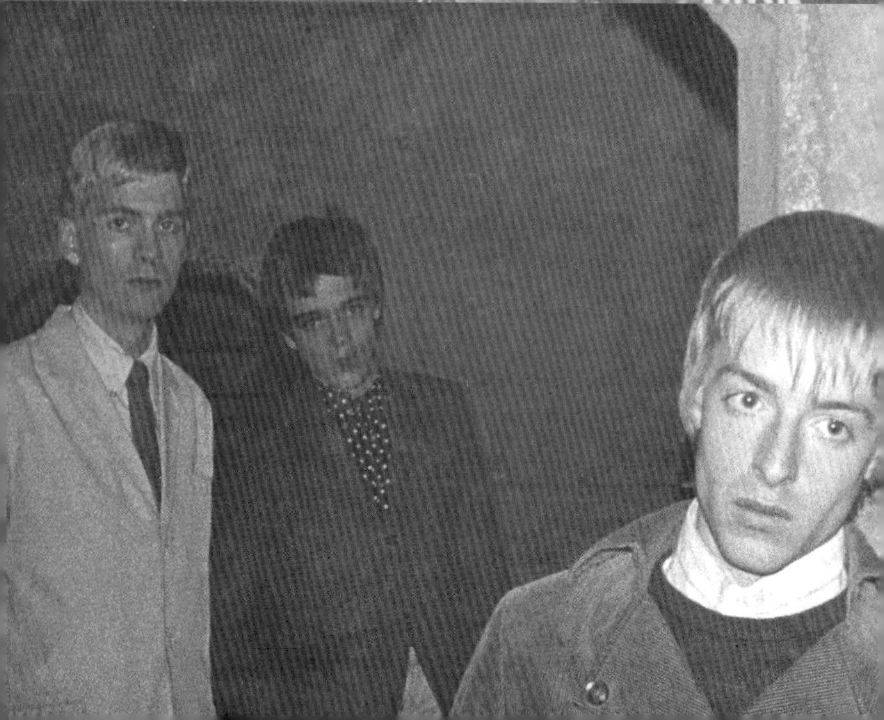

Stuart Parris

Keith Mono

Tony Perfect

Mark Reynolds

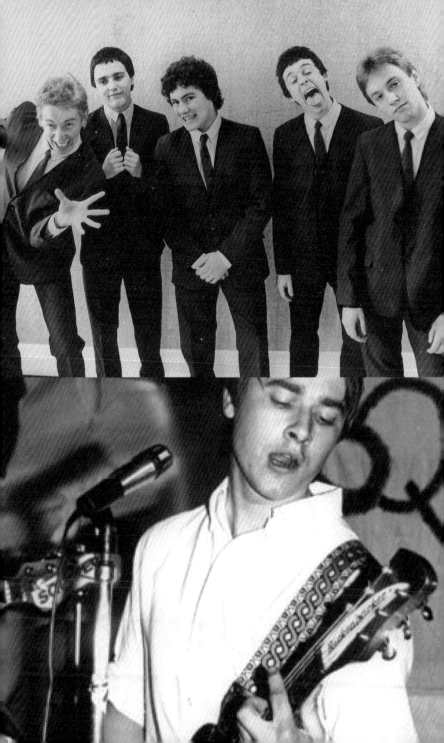

TOWN HALL
TORQUAY

WED 30TH JULY

Mod Stars of
Wheels Fame

MERTON
PARKAS

plus   TOP SUPPORTING GROU

ADVANCE TICKETS £2·00

WED 6TH AUG

HIT SINGLE
SLEEPWALK

ULTRAVOX

plus   TOP SUPPORTING GROU

ADVANCE TICKETS £2·50

ADVANCE TICKETS from
Flox Records, Fleet st. Torquay Tel. 22385
Castle Records, Higher Union st. Torquay Tel. 28106
Soundz, Hyde rd. Paignton Tel. 556893

DOORS OPEN 7·30pm   Licens

No Age or Dress Restrictions

NOW IT'S GONE

GONE

THE EPILOGUE

IF ANYTHING IT WAS A
MOVEMENT AND MORE TO
DO WITH THE PEOPLE THAN
THE BANDS. A REVIVAL OF
THE FASHION AND THE
CULTURE. I THINK IT WAS A
BIT MORE PEOPLE POWERED
THAN BAND POWERED

Ian Page - Secret Affair

MOD: THE EPILOGUE

S O that was the Mod Revival. It may not have set the charts alight, but it was never what its detractors accused it of being. It wasn't fake, it wasn't thick, and it wasn't worthless. On the contrary, late 70s Mod was a genuine phenomenon brought to life on the streets, rather than in pop industry boardrooms, by kids who had become disillusioned by punk but who kept its love of energy, sulphate, d-i-y ethics and three minute pop songs alive.

Songs like 'Frustration', 'Millions Like Us', 'Maybe Tomorrow', 'My World' and 'Time For Action' still have a resonance today.

The Mod Revival hung on here and there until 1983, by which time all the leading bands had called it a day. But as a growing movement New Mod never survived into its second summer. Grassroots fears of the scene being diluted after Quadrophenia seemed to become reality as posers flooded into West End clubs like Vespa's where the likes of Steve Strange could be found sowing the seeds of the New Romantics, and Billy Idol started playing 'Mod' sets.

To add to a growing sense of disillusionment, a dire *Daily Mirror* piece published on August 23, 1979 ludicrously described The Who as the 'vanguard of the new revival'. The *Mirror* revealed that Townshend's crew had teamed up with a Covent Garden boutique (Suuchi's of Wellington Street WC2) to turn out purple suede parkas (very street, and a snip at a mere £125 a pop – about £550 in today's money).

In September, top London models could be seen prancing around the Lyceum stage in over-priced parkas and zoot-suits.

Of the class of '79, Secret Affair achieved the most and lasted the longest. 'Time For Action' – a Top 20 smash released on their own I-Spy label through Arista – peaked at 13 in the chart and sold an extremely credible 198,000 copies.

I-Spy's subsequent releases did less well. They included two singles from Squire – 'Walking Down The Kings Road' and 'The Face Of Youth Today' which although critically acclaimed didn't bother the charts too much.

There was also a fresh pressing of the *Mods Mayday* compilation album and the single 'Rudi Got Married' by the late, great Ska legend Laurel Aitken (real name Lorenzo) from Cuba via Leicester, which got as far as Number 60 (the follow-up, 'Big Fat Man' sadly flopped).

The Chords and the Purple Hearts followed the Affair's success with 'Now It's Gone' (Polydor) and 'Millions Like Us' (Fiction), which peaked at 63 and 57 respectively. (Billy H from the Chords bitchily remarked: "Millions Like Us? Dozens like us more like, judging by the chart position." Saucer of milk to Deptford please.)

The Jam provided the single of the late summer of '79 with 'When You're Young', which caught the spirit of young Mod, and the futility of life at the bottom of the scrapheap, better than anyone since Townshend.

August Bank Holiday was probably the last time all the disparate wings of the original 'new Mods' ran amok down Southend way (see Notes From A Teenage Rampage). The uneasy alliance between Mods and skinheads on that day was to be short-lived and Mod v. Skin battles were to become a sad and ironic part of street-life thereafter. This antipathy was made far worse by Scottish punk band the Exploited whose 1980 song 'Fuck A Mod', (the b-side of their debut single 'Army Life') was a tirade of mindless violence to the tune of 'Jingle Bells' which stoked up shocking levels of tension and hostility.

To singer Wattie Buchan, 'Mod' was a betrayal of the punk revolution; to ex-punks down South, his band was a Johnny Come Lately caricature of what punk actually was.

Cynicism and disillusionment were setting in at the roots, but there were still seriously good records being released, not least the Affair's *Glory Boys*, album (reviewed elsewhere in this volume). Yet Mod as a whole was never to recover from the death-wish that appeared to grip young Mod dudes on the brink of what should have been the scene's big breath-through. It was like a collective speed come-down.

Artistically as well, Mod was over-taken by the 2-Tone revolution that it had nurtured at its bosom. The bands had started on the Mod circuit and an elite group of Mods picked up on 2-Tone at the expense of the Mod bands, adopting the rude boy look. "It was strange," Simon Stebbing recalled much later in *Mojo*. "We were on the up-and-up in 1979 and had the Beat, Madness and Dexy's Midnight Runners supporting us. Within weeks these bands had leapfrogged over us and were scoring Top Ten hits while we were down at the lower end of the chart."

Dexys were the biggest soul-influenced modern pop band to break with two Number One singles and two Top Ten albums between 1980 and 1982.

Meanwhile Paul Weller, who'd always kept his distance, led the Jam away from the imagery and pop appeal of *All Mod Cons* in favour of the harder, less obviously sixties influenced and more politicised sound, which preceded him disowning guitar-orientated rock to embrace stylised white soul in 1983.

One by one, the new Mod bands floundered, although Secret Affair held out longer than most and attracted a new younger pop audience. Their second album *Behind Closed Doors* contained the wonderful 'My World' – a Top 20 hit – and boasted a less uniform sound, with big brash string and sax arrangements. But overall it lacked the vision and focus of Glory Boys. Most of the songs were written either by Dave Cairns or Ian Page separately. Page lacked Dave's grasp of melody and arrangement; while Dave's lyrics seemed a little too focused on a movement that was already eroding from the base up.

Seb Shelton then quit the band to join Dexys. They replaced him with Advertising's drummer Paul Bultitude and tried to crack the states. In 1981, Secret Affair released 'Do You Know', their fifth and least successful single (it conked out at 57). The sixth, 'Lost In The Night' flopped, as did the next album, *Business As Usual*. The boys split ingloriously in '82.

Neither the Purple Hearts nor the Chords proved capable of equalling the Affair's chart achievements, even though the Chords' Top 40 cracker 'Maybe Tomorrow' was moderately magnificent.

It should have done better. They did *Top Of The Pops*, and one more appearance would have pushed it Top 20. But their vital return booking was scuppered by a technicians' strike. Billy H explained: "The strike meant we couldn't go on and that was the same week that *Sounds* and the *NME* went on strike." It was their best chance of making it big, and it was snatched away from them.

THE MOD REVIVAL

The Chords eventually ran out of time at Polydor and split up; while the Purple Hearts went on to dabble with late-Small-Faces-style psychedelia for a while before breaking up themselves, only to regularly reform for 'one-off' gigs. Both their albums smacked of too-much-too-soon, under-production and under-finance, although their potential was never in doubt. The Hearts' second single 'Frustration' frustratingly peaked at 92. The follow-up, 'Jimmy' from their debut album Beat That, did better, reaching Number 60. It was their last (minor) hit and the band split in November 82 after their US tour failed to take off.

Back in 1980, as the charts exploded with 2-Tone acts, Mod was out-done by other soul-based live bands who either revived sixties soul better than them (the Q-Tips) or renewed it more successfully (Dexy's).

By the time the Biz and the teeny-boppers had lost interest in Secret Affair, there weren't many Mods left. The early eighties were certainly deadly dull by '79 standards and one by one the bands split up disillusioned, the bandwagon jumpers among them finding new wagons to leap on to. Billy Hassett 'did a Roots' and went 'home' to Ireland. Apart from small dedicated local scenes, mostly in the Home Counties, the only place to really find Mods was at Jam gigs. Then in 1983, Weller courageously/frustratingly broke up the band to launch his new project the Style Council with former Merton Parka Mick' Mr. Piano' Talbot.

Ironically, as the Jam became toast, an exciting 'new mod'-influenced band emerged – The Truth. Former in 1982 by former pub rocker Dennis Greaves (of 9 Below Zero fame), The Truth for Dennis just meant widening his influences from New Orleans to include the Detroit sound of Motown too. I first became aware of the band in early '83 when I came across a mob of Truth fans outside the Marquee who really looked the business. A million miles from the Parka-clad teenies who'd diluted mod and the glue-sniffing face-tattooed scruffs who'd polluted skinhead, these kids were wearing button-downs and Fred Perrys, polished brogues, neatly pressed Tonik trousers and socks whiter than your granddad's shaving foam. The thing is, they obviously cared about their appearance and, as it turned out, The Truth were good enough to do "the kids" justice. Bloated on gutsy black stompers, with an obvious debt to mid-period Jam, The Truth's live set was a raging inferno of populist punch-the-air soul, strong on sing-songs, high on energy and embellished by a handsome Hammond organ.

They started gigging in October '82. By January '83 WEA had beaten Stiff in a two-horse race to get their autographs on recording contracts.

The first vinyl fruit of the pairing was the single 'Confusion Hits Us Every Time', a fine thing indeed. However, the Jam split led WEA to think The Truth could take over the Working Wonder's crowd overnight. 'Confusion' was hyped like crazy but didn't make the Top 10. Thereafter the label pressurised the band into making ever more wimpy and lightweight singles which did nothing for their street-cred. Eighteen months later and they'd parted company. Their IRS released live mini-album *Five Live* gives a taste of how good they were in concert.

As a side bar, it's worth pointing out that two of the assumed-to-be significant bands of the mid-eighties began as mod groups, namely Seventeen who became the Alarm and Graduate which mutated into Tears For Fears; the first changing their image but not their sound, the latter totally shaking off their mod roots. Seventeen formed in Rhyl, North Wales, in 1978. They had a pop-mod sound, released an indie single called 'Don't Let Go', and were kicked off a Dexy's tour support slot after just one show. At one stage the band, led by singer Mike Peters, came to the offices of *Sounds* in Covent Garden and attempted to kidnap me to drum up rock press coverage. I was with Hoxton Tom at the time who suggested pleasantly but firmly that the four of them fucked right off, which was enough to kill the abduction plan stone dead. We invited them round the White Lion for a few beers instead.

In '81, they changed their name to Alarm Alarm, which they swiftly shortened to The Alarm. They moved to London, released their debut single 'Unsafe Building' and developed unsettling mullets. IRS signed them in '82 and they supported U2 on tour in the US. The U2 influence was easy to detect on their 1983 album *Declaration* and the superb anthem '68 Guns' went Top 20.

By 1984 the legacy of 'Quad-Mods', teeny-mods and all the other dumb mutations had long gone and only the truly dedicated were left. On the way a lot of people had fallen by the wayside. Ian Page had resurfaced on CBS with a flop project called Bop. Chris Pope, Buddy Ascott and Grant Fleming could now be found doing the rounds in a Big Country style guitar band called Tin Soldiers and the three baboons from Maximum Speed had disappeared off the face of the earth. Most of the Glory Boys now dressed Casual and their contact with the music biz seemed confined to ticket forging, ticket touting, selling snide merchandising and other dubious activities. Some ended up in a Swiss slammer for shop-lifting pricey label-name clobber. The advantage the surviving Mods and the new recruits had was the ability to learn from past mistakes. What they were doing was fairly unparalleled in youth cult history – they were consciously attempting to safe-guard their ideals and organise their activities. In '84, serious Mods weren't content with merely going to gigs. They'd organised themselves into a scattered network of dedicated modernist societies working almost like regional councils to cultivate the Mod cause and protect it, for example, from the sort of shallow press overkill that boiled the '79 Renewal down to a cheap throw-away fad. There was the Fellowship Of Style in Oxfordshire, the Inner Circle in Guernsey, the 24th Hour Mod Society in Leeds, the Emerald Society in Eire and most influential of the lot, the Phoenix Society in London. The faces behind the Phoenix Society were bods like rhythm and soul DJ Tony Class, dashing Dagenham activist Eddie Piller, editor of the best contemporary mod' zine Extraordinary Sensations and later to start the Acid Jazz label, and the American-accented but London-born gay Mod Mark Johnson, the 31 year old brains behind *The Phoenix List*, a weekly news sheet of mod events, developments and debate.

In November '84, the Phoenix Society took the unprecedented step of organising a Nation Mod Conference – they hoped the first of many – in the Boston Club in Tufnell Park. The day started with a chaotic, cop-disrupted, scooter run to Buck House with 500 scootering participants. And in the afternoon 300 Mods from all over the country gathered for the Conference where the unwanted attendance by a bunch of sartorially inelegant scooter boys full of beer and abuse served only to emphasise how great the divide had become between them and the Mods – which was precisely why that afternoon saw 1985s Mod runs decided separately from the scooter clubs' runs, why Mod dos banned what they saw as scruffy scooter boys and why many of the speakers could be heard condemning 'scooter thugs'.

The afternoon also heard a message of support from Ronnie Lane and a well-received diatribe from Irish Jack, the legendary Goldhawk Road Mod turned Guru who spoke with poetic licence of "floating in a honey-comb of Mod purity". With the audience eating out of his hands, Jack concluded: "Peter Meaden would have been proud of you. Jimmy Cooper would never have believed it." And then Mark Johnson defiantly filled in the facts about new Mod's history.

In the evening, the Mod DJs took over and around 500 more turned up, including Mods, suede-heads and stylists from all over London and the Home Counties; 800 faces testifying to the enduring lure of mod ideals. Live on-stage were Fast Eddie, who specialised in reasonable, albeit uninspired, covers. My one over-whelming memory from the night was Irish Jack coming over all misty as Prince Buster's 'Madness' echoed from the downstairs PA. "I haven't heard this for years," he said, grinning like a pill-head who's found the back door to his local chemists open after hours.

I don't think he stopped smiling till the music stopped at 2am the next morning.

Of course, it was all wish fulfilment. By the fag-end of 1986, this new New Mod affair had fizzled out.

London DJs Paul Hallam (aka 'the Stalin of Style') and Richard 'Shirley' Early kept the scene alive at a local level. Their Shepherd's Bush club nights were packed with well-tailored enthusiasts grooving to pure soul and rare R&B sounds. Tony Class, who sadly died in 2014, ran the popular Club Mod at the Bush Hotel until 1986 when the venue changed to an O'Neill's. Hallam moved his Sneakers Club to the Hammersmith Clarendon and the 79 Club, which added the best 1979 songs to the mix, to Oxford Street, but lost interest in June 87 due to the lure of the Beastie Boys. No stand-out bands emerged after The Prisoners and Making Time.

Eddie Piller and a few of the other faces grooved stylishly over to the jazz scene; other Mods followed their sixties predecessors by moving on into psychedelia. Those who remained went even further underground, picking up on the white psyche/R&B sound of the UK' 67–'69. This they called freakbeat. Others drifted off into northern soul. The scene was not heard of again until the Acid Jazz inspired, Mod-influenced club scene of the early Nineties which was soon over-whelmed by Britpop – and that was even more of a Mod baby.

On one hand, Britpop was a welcome reaction against the grimness of grunge. On the other, it was a throwback that underlined the mounting suspicion that modern rock would spend more time looking back at the past than carving out a fresh future. Britpop broke through in '94, although the term was first used by John Robb in Sounds in the late Eighties. The bands had catchy tunes, played loud with no thrills and no real point of view.

But at least pop was up-beat and exciting again. The new British bands-with-attitude ranged from the lairy Manchester herberts Oasis to the arty Blur, via Suede, Pulp, Ocean Colour Scene, Elastica, Supergrass and The Verve. Their heroes included the Kinks, the Who, Weller and the Small Faces. Their debt to Mod, along with glam and punk and post-punk Manchester, is hard to miss. Blur's video for their hit single 'Parklife' memorably used actor Phil Daniels of *Quadrophenia* fame, and there's no escaping the echoes of the Small Faces and the Kinks in the song's larky Music Hall feel.

THE MOD REVIVAL

Britpop led to a massive revival of interest in Mod, sixties beat groups and classic soul and R'n'B. Mod events team, the New Untouchables or NUTs – set up by Rob Bailey and Jason Ringgold in 1997 – capitalised on it with newsletters and club nights, national and international weekenders, scooter runs, clothes and record markets and the relatively new phenomenon of the internet.

From 1997 on, London clubs nights like Purple Pussycat, Hipsters and the Mousetrap inspired a new generation of Mods and sixties enthusiasts. New bands and DJs were and are actively encouraged. In 2004, over 4,000 attended their London event, held at the Rocket, celebrating 'Forty Years of Mod' – "Not from its birth," explains Rob, "but from a pinnacle year in its history". NUTs events were and remain good-humoured – 500 attended Bailey's super-Mod do at Christmas 2008 without a single punch being thrown.

Britpop's own influence can be seen clearly in today's third generation bands such as the Kaiser Chiefs, the Dirty Pretty Things and the Arctic Monkeys.

Abroad, the 1979 Mod renewal sparked copycat scene in the US in the Eighties, which thrived in Southern California, with bands such as the Untouchables. The 2-Tone bands proved to be more influential on the LA and Orange County scenes.

Just like the old punks, most of the 1979 school of Mod bands are still going to this day, finding enthusiastic audiences the world over.

Back home, 1996 saw the first serious Mod revival revival...when Paul Hallam and Dave Edwards put on a Chords come-back gig at London's 100 Club on August 29. The response was phenomenal with 450 punters cramming into a venue designed to hold a maximum of 290 before they had air-conditioning installed...many of them squeezing middle-aged guts into badly-fitting Ben Shermans and Fred Perrys. There were touts outside flogging tickets at twice their price.

Both Chris and Buddy describe it as the best gig that they ever played – and that was with Grant Fleming replacing Martin Morris on bass as well. Bar taking records were shattered and the idea of bands reforming and the Mod Revival being celebrated was sewn in a lot of minds.

Says Buddy: "There was a lot of interest in this gig – we told it could have sold out four times over…when I got back to The 100 Club for the show, the place was heaving. I had never seen it this packed – maybe they had sold it over four times! There were a lot of old faces in – Goffa, Guv, Damian, Clive, Dennis, Jude and Claire, Marcus, Jim. Marnie, Nikki, Mick...the atmosphere down there was electric. We got changed in the club's subterranean office. The crowd parted like the Red Sea, and we walked down a tunnel of ecstatic fans and loving friends, all cheering, clapping, pushing us on…thought I was gonna sob…one of the most emotional moments of my life – a vindication of The Chords, of our integrity…I couldn't contain my beams of delight as we launched into 'Something's Missing' far too fast to a moshing frenzy down front. After two numbers I was totally knackered, and after three I had to sit up straight just to try to breathe. It was like being in a microwave. No oxygen, no respite from the heat, taking deep breaths just filled me with more intense warmth…during 'So Far Away' my eyes were rolling back in my head and I prayed I'd faint to end the torture. Excruciating. It was a mercifully short set, and I think we must've slowed down a wee bit before the encores…before which I collapsed at the side of the stage. Overwhelming in every way – physically, musically, spiritually – when I die I wanna go out like this… I think we all felt so loved, so appreciated…is this why I picked up drum sticks in the first place? My feelings told me it must be the case…

"Backstage the plaudits rolled in as the beers arrived…jubilant scenes, a cavalcade of compliments passing the open door – "Different class!", "Best gig in 10 years!", "Best I've ever seen you play!" The crowd carried the band tonight, we weren't so good, but they were! Drinks with all continued until the bastards closed the bar at 1 am, and it was time to think about gig in Nottingham tomorrow and get home… an astonishing triumph? How ever did we pull that off?"

Unfortunately, the success of the show wasn't duplicated. The Chords went off on a short six-date UK tour and found themselves playing to two Mods and their dogs in empty clubs. On the plus side, the band re-recorded their anthem 'The British Way Of Life' with Chris Pope on vocals, Tony Barber from the Buzzcocks on bass and the Who's brass section.

The next retro gig was the Mods Mayday All-Dayer at the Forum three years later which saw most of the class of '79 back on stage, including The Chords, the Purple Hearts, the Killermeters and Secret Affair (sort of – Dave Cairns and Ian Page weren't talking at the time, so Ian did it as Ian Page & The Affair). Also on the bill were Rosko, Squire, Small World and The Circles.

Page refused to be on the live compilation album recorded on the night that came out on the Detour label.

Tony Perfect's Long Tall Shorty reformed in 2002 and played their first gigs at Terry Rawlings's gallery in Waterloo initially attracted forty to fifty old faces. At this time there was no Revival scene, no other bands playing and nowhere to go. Tony built up over venues and went on to run the Piccadilly Blue Club which gave veterans somewhere to congregate once a month. John Woodward believes that Perfect doing this made subsequent reformations easier. It certainly gave the bands somewhere regular to play.

Self-styled "giffer punks" Shorty went on to play most of Western Europe. Their recent albums, Kick Out The Shams and The Sounds Of Giffer City, are more redolent of the Stooges and the Dolls than the Teenbeats (in 2009/10 the trio also made up three quarters of the Gonads, described by experts close to this book as the greatest punk band who never made it).

As I wrote the original epilogue, in the summer of 2012, The Chords were just back from a successful tour of Australia and Japan. While Pope, the new band formed by Chris Pope and Buddy Ascott, recently recorded their third album of critically acclaimed quality modern pop.

The Purple Hearts returned, gigged a bit, packed it in for a while and came back again playing Islington Assembly Hall on September 15, 2012 with tickets selling at £15 a pop.

Secret Affair reformed for three gigs in 2002, including the Shepherd's Bush Empire, returning again in June 2003 at The Scala to promote a *Time For Action* CD anthology of hits and rarities. The London Scala show was filmed and released on DVD as *Live At The Scala* later that year.

Due to the upsurge in online fanbases and guestbooks a new page called modrevival.net began to generate a community of Mods and fans from around the world long and Secret Affair, with the help of long term fan Tracey Wilmot set up their first website Secretaffair.info which re-ignited the band's fan base. In 2011 they re-recorded 'Time For Action' for the Save The Children campaign and Dave Cairns appeared on TV's Never Mind The Buzzcocks.

Back then it looked like their fourth album Soho Dreams would never materialise. Page and Cairns, whose Itchy & Scratchy style relationship was still best described as 'fractious', had been collaborating on it for six years. But writing this 2019 update, I can report that it was eventually released in 2012 on limited edition red vinyl on their iconic I-SPY label supported by a 13-date UK tour. The album was splendid, a real labour of love. It came with a gatefold sleeve and a 12-page booklet and showcased the entire range of Page and Cairns' unique vision.

They also released a single from the album, *All The Rage*, digitally and on video.

The band continued to tour regularly, with a 35th anniversary tour in 2014. That year also saw all four of their albums released in a deluxe anniversary box set entitled *Secret Affair Est 1979*.

In September 2016 the band appeared on Vintage TV performing new tracks as well as their classic song My World In October they released their first single since 1982's 'Lost In The Night', a cover of Frank Wilson's Northern Soul classic 'Do I Love You (Indeed I Do)' b/w 'Crumble Gunn'. It was produced by Ian Page and available only on limited edition vinyl via I-Spy as a collectable vinyl exclusive – "a gift to the fans," said Dave Cairns. Like Soho Dreams, the single was sold mostly on the road.

This year they celebrated their 40th anniversary with a 14-date 'Glory Boys' Spring tour including a sold-out Mods Mayday event show at Islington Assembly Hall in North London also featuring Squire, The Lambrettas, The Chords UK, the Truth, the Circles and the Vapors. Secret Affair continue to successfully play twenty gigs a year and already have plans in place for a 2020 tour – you can find the details on the band's Facebook, Twitter and Instagram accounts.

The Chords split up again after Japan, but Chris Pope revived the band as the Chords UK without Buddy. The Chords UK have released two solid, pledge-funded albums 2016s *Take On Life* and 2018s *Nowhereland*. As I write, Chris is just about to release a British Way Of Life EP, with the title track and Now It's Gone both gloriously re-recorded. A British Way Of Life Chords UK tour is lined up for October/November this year supported by Department S, including the 100 Club in November. Chris released a new Pope album in 2014, Peace Of Mind, and remains a terrific songwriter. He tells me he's releasing a compilation album of the best Pope and Chords UK material in 2020. You can find details on The Chords UK Facebook page.

Of course the biggest success of the Seventies was the Modfather himself, Paul Weller. Weller defined two eras, first with the Jam and then the Style Council, continuing to produce influential solo albums throughout the Nineties. The acoustic, and almost folky, True Meanings, out last year, was his fourteenth.

Weller has firmly shut the door on his past, saying: "I would never reform The Jam. It's against everything I believe in."

But this didn't stop Rick Buckler and Bruce Foxton from launching From The Jam, as a kind of superior tribute band to themselves. In '86 Rick had formed Time UK with Danny Kustow from the Tom Robinson Band, while Bruce formed Sharp. Neither set the charts alight. Bruce then played bass with Stiff Little Fingers for the best part of 15 years.

THE MOD REVIVAL

In 2006, Rick came out of retirement to form the Gift with singer Russell Hastings and guitarist Dave Moore. That year Bruce joined them on stage for a smattering of gigs. In 2007, thirty years after The Jam were signed, the two launched From The Jam. Weller called the project "sad" but it proved popular with punters all over the world. Too popular? Cynics claim that Weller deliberately befriended Foxton again in 2009, after decades of mutual loathing, to derail the project. Bruce played on two tracks on Weller's 2010 *Wake Up The Nation* album and in May that year they appeared on stage together for the first time since 1982. Understandably perhaps, Rick quit From The Jam and launched a new band called The If, with Tony Perfect on guitar, which packed it in just before Time For Action was first published.

Bruce has carried on as From The Jam (shouldn't that be From From The Jam?) without him. In 2012 he released his solo album *Back In The Room* (the first since 1984s *Touch Sensitive*). It was recorded at Weller's studio with Paul guesting on a couple of tracks. A third solo album, *Smash The Clock*, followed in 2016 and reached 31 in the album charts.

Back in the day, many of the late seventies revival Mods – and Skins – got involved in the scooterist scene bequeathing the Scooter Boy subculture, which flourishes to this day with club nights and rallies where you are just as likely to see Bad Manners or the Cockney Rejects as an old Mod band.

Today, hundreds of small bands and tens of thousands of would-be Mods and scooter boys all around the world identify with Mod and use its symbols; although the gulf between them, their attitude to clothes, life and culture, and those of the free-thinking Mod pioneers featured in 1962s Town magazine is wide enough to park a thousand Vespas sideways.

But the simple truth is that, once again, a street movement denounced as "hype" by the snooty UK rock press in 1979 has gone on to pass the test of time.

Garry Bushell June 23, 2019

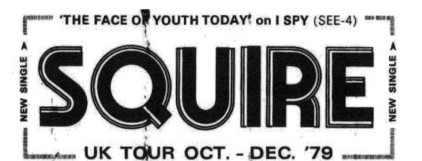

'THE FACE OF YOUTH TODAY' on I SPY (SEE-4)

NEW SINGLE

SQUIRE

NEW SINGLE

UK TOUR OCT. - DEC. '79

Gandiegar Promotions Presents At
NOTRE DAME HALL
6 Leicester Square, WC 2

Saturday November 10th   7.30pm - 11pm

BACK TO ZERO
THE MODS
SPEEDBALL   LES ELITE
EDDIE STEADY GO

Monday November 12th   7.30pm - 11pm

THE QUADS
DOLLY MIXTURES
+ Support

Both dates £1.75 each. Tickets on sale now from the Notre Dame by
post or to personal callers, or available on the night.

GLOBAL VILLAGE
Villiers Street, Charing Cross

Terry Draper for Engin-Ear Productions Ltd presents

All Night   **ANGEL WITC**
Friday August 10th   **URCHI**
    IRON MAIDE
+ D.J. Joe Lung

Doors Open 9 pm. Licensed Bar till 3 am
Hot Food and Soft Drinks throughout

Saturday August 11th   **ESSENTIAL LO**
    MONOCHROME S
    prag V
+ D.J.

Doors Open 9 pm. Licensed Bar till 3 am

Monday August 13th
THE MODS
+ The Lambrettas
+ 6 More Prophets
+ The Spiders + D.J. Jerry Floyd
Doors Open 8.30 pm, First Band on Stage 9 pm, Open till 3 am

All bookings via W H Smiths & Ronnie Scott Directions 01 439 7793

STRAIGHT MUSIC PRESENTS

PURPLE HEARTS
THE TEENBEATS
SQUIRE

ELECTRIC BALLROOM
184 CAMDEN HIGH ST NW1 NEAREST TUBE CAMDEN TOWN

SATURDAY 20th OCTOBER at 7.30

DARRYL HARTLAND
RAINBOW ALL DAYER
232 SEVEN SISTERS ROAD, FINSBURY PARK   Nearest Tube: FINSBURY PARK

SATURDAY AUGUST 1st — 12 to 12 Midnight

LAMBRETTAS

HIDDEN CHARMS — DOLLY MIXTURES
LONG TALL SHORTY — QUESTION
REACTION — RETREADS — MODS

D.J.'s NEILL SIMONE, TONY CLASS, JERRY FLOYD, 81, KEITH HURELY, F. DAVE BRO
FANCY dress VALUGATER & SPECIAL CUVETTE & Roaring Competition & Souvenir Compet

John, dates from RAINBOW or Darryl Hartland Mod Club

WHALES ARE
DISAPPEARING.

ONE IS KILLED EVERY 20 MINUTES.
PLEASE HELP NOW.

To stop the whales disappearing altogether, we need
money urgently.
Please be a friend to the whales and give generously
SAVE THE WHALE
Please make cheques payable to Friends of the Earth
FRIENDS OF THE EARTH.
9 Poland St. London W1V 3DG.

WHISKY A' GOGO
(35 Wardour St W1)
Presents Londons Only Regular

MOD DISCO +
(D.J. Jerry Floyd)

LONG TALL SHORTY
(On Stage 10.30)

THURSDAY 14TH FEB
Half Price Drinks Before 10.30. Open 9-3am.
Adm. 2.00 or 2.50 With 1st Drink Free.

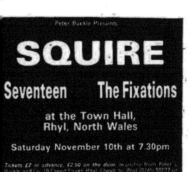

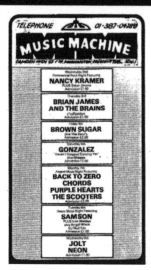

by SUE BUCKLEY

ACROSS
1. Distance for the Chords (2.3.4)
5. A depressed Café (3)
7. They've a nine month disco (5.6)
8. Traffic for passionate Rumour (9)
11. Cunning funk band boss (3)
12. Monks in this Beatles' road? (5)
14. Young Rascals classic pastime? (7)
15. Where Iron Maiden find Dracula (12)
17. Soul brothers who went to Atlantis (5)
19. Miller flying like Leadon? (5)
21. Peter played these out of bounds (5)
22. Boss Ant (4)

DOWN
1. Parker in amazement (12)
2. Mist on Tyne (3)
3. Crass' lock-up? (7.6)
4. Which High Numbers? (3)
5. They passed in night for Nelson (Bill and Lord) (5)
6. She didn't know what to do with herself (5)
9. XTC's pal (5)
10. He flew endlessley (3.5)
13. What AC/DC were doing about the bush (7)
16. Poly's adolescents are free of this one (4)
18. Rick no longer in the affirmative (3)
20. He's on Bob's side (3)

LAST WEEK'S ANSWERS
ACROSS: 1. Surf's Up 4. Horslips 7. On Through The Night 11. The Enid 13. Allan 15. Berry Gordy 17. Isley 20. Freda 21. Shoot Out The Lights 24. Flares And Slippers 30. Springsteen 32. Hi 33. Wheel 34. Promises.
DOWN: 1. Sports Car 2. Rotten 3. Strange Little Girl 4. Ha Ha 5. Lindsay 6. Page 8. Under 9. Hendrix 10. Teenbeats 12. Iggy 14. Love 16. Toto 19. Lou 20. Fripp 21. Soft 22. Ted 23. Heep 25. Apple 26. Angel 27. Sheep 28. Iran 29. Slits 31. E.M.I.

MODS 79

DANGER!! THE JAM

GLORY BOYS

TONi FOX + FRIENDS

R'N'B

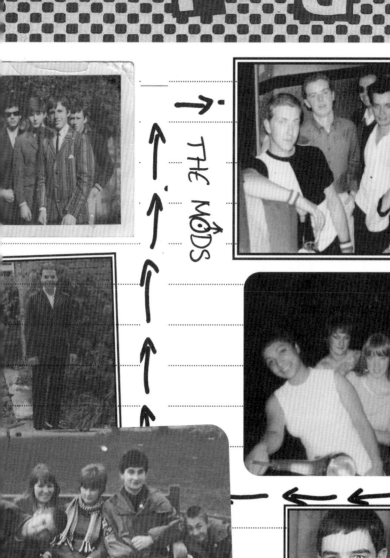

THE MODS

PURPLE

WHO
THE F**K
IS
DAVID WATTS

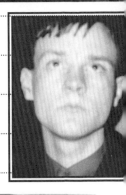

CALIFORNIA DREAMIN'

GOING UNDERGROUND

BUSH + CASTLE

BREWSTER

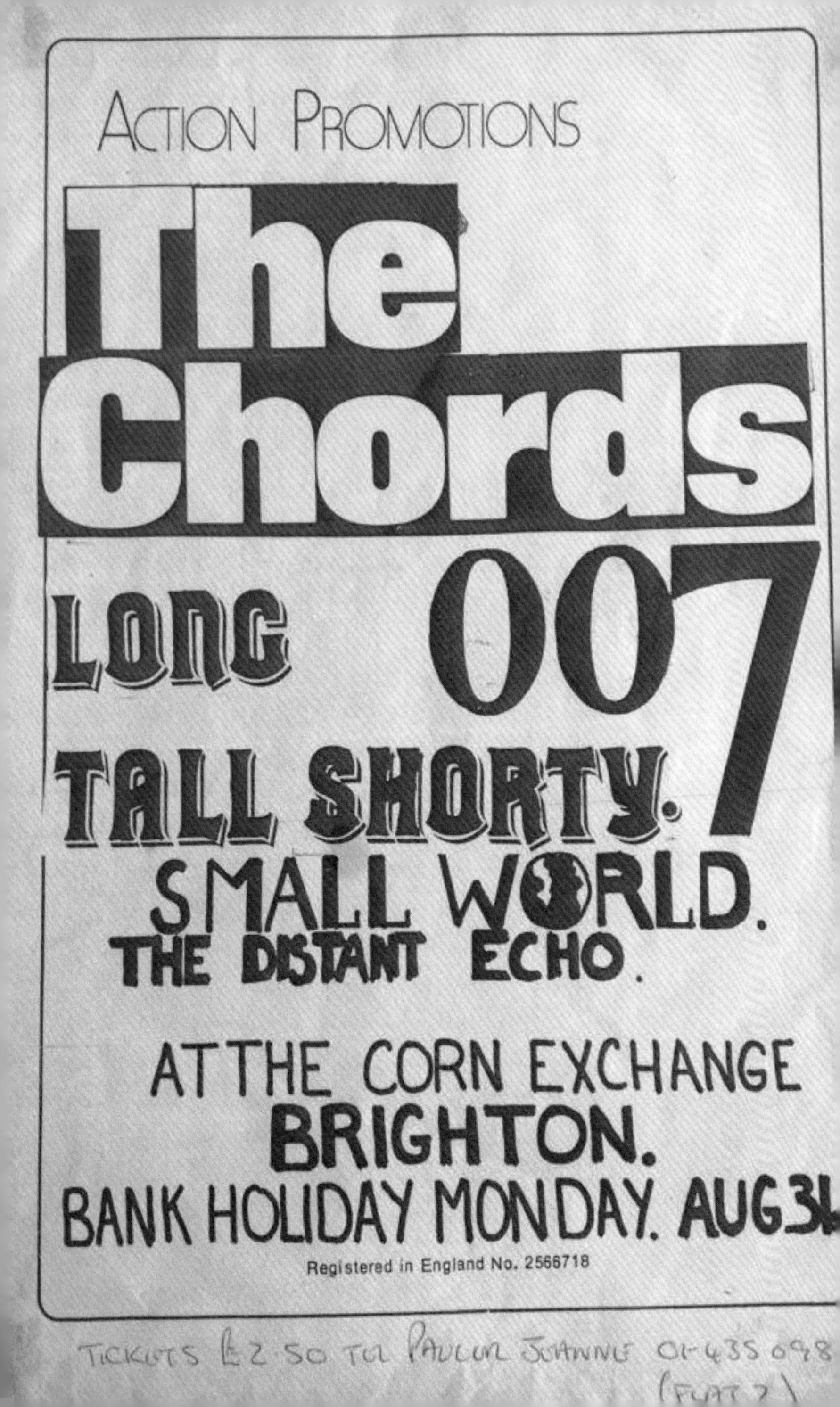

ACTION PROMOTIONS

The Chords

LONG 007

TALL SHORTY. 7

SMALL WORLD.

THE DISTANT ECHO.

AT THE CORN EXCHANGE
BRIGHTON.
BANK HOLIDAY MONDAY. AUG 31

Registered in England No. 2566718

TICKETS £2·50 TEL PAUL OR JOANNE 01-435 098
(FLAT 7)

ABOUT THE AUTHOR

Garry Bushell was born and raised in South East London. He started his career on the rock weekly Sounds, interviewing everyone from the Clash and the Steel Pulse to Blondie, U2, the Specials and Iron Maiden. The son of a fireman and a bank secretary, he is best known for his award winning Bushell On The Box TV column. Garry managed punk bands the Cockney Rejects, The Blood and Maninblack; his own group the Gonads have been going for 42years without any noticeable success, and his Rancid Sounds punk and Ska show appears regularly on 2nd City Radio. He has five children and four grandchildren, and lives in Kent.

TIME FOR ACTION

THE AUTHOR would like to thank Tracey Wilmot, Terry Rawlings, Tony Morrison, Tom McCourt, Bert Scott and Buddy Ascott, Dave Cairns, Gary Sparks, Jim Doak, Grant Fleming, Paul Hallam (the Stalin Of Style), Wattsie Watts, Chris Pope, Eddie Piller and everyone who was there for the ride.

The Publisher and The Stalin of Style would like to thank: Roger Allen, Dave Edwards, Paul Wright, Virginia Turbett, Tony & Maxine Lordan, Tracie Wilmott & Toni Fox without whose help and guidance this book would have been a lot less jolly.

Plus: Paul Calver, Jim Watson, Richard Adams, Simon Stebbings, Andrea Locking, Karen Voss, Belinda Stokes, Drew, Bob Morris, Mick Wheeler, Julian Leusby, Brian Kotz, Dagenham Dax, Clelia in Milan, Billy Hassett, Martin Mason, Richard Early, Ian Brydon, Lee Huggie Norbal, Dizzy Holmes at Detour, Gary and Russel Wood, James Travis, Stuart Swift, Wids for driving (while we drove him mad), Lol, Tesco Eddie and the Fleece - FK Teplice ultras, Derwent Jaconelli, Ian Page, Antony Meynell, Mr Spizz Energi, Simone Murmann, Sandra Brunner, Steve Allison, Gina and Carl, Peter Jachimiak, Simon Margrie for keeping those mods in line in Australia, Eddie Hadlow, Simon Sternschuss, Cass P, Brian McDonough, Pete Wynne, Ronnie (the Mod Plumber) Diamond, Emilie West, Yumi Takahashi, Malcolm Knox, Jim Watson, Dei Treanor, Bob Piper, Donna Boardman, Darren Russell, Paul Hurst, Amanda Austin, Maddy & Bob, Lucia Hall, Tony Rice, Paul McEvoy, Gary Crowley, Jens Bredahl, Dom Whellams, Gary Loveridge, Rodger Grant, Rob Poyton, Siobhan Ellis, Jane Garry, Callum and Jodie, Brian Conyers, Barry Cain for inspiration, Nick Allen, Tony Clark, Amanda Hickey, Andy Hilson, Steve Wright (not that one), Warren Bright, Kevin Jay, Dave Galea, Tony Morris, Dom Morgan, Laurence Cain, John Brewster (for setting the pace), Ana Hallam for marker pen stuff, Des Mannay, Michael Stoner, Mike J, Richard Sandow, Steve Gray (KM Mod), Timothy Man, Lenny George, Karena Marcum, Aaron Jones, Kevin Duffy, Jane Williams, Tetley, Ed Silvester, Ste Holding, David Marlborough, Paul Phillips, Mappy and Mrs H for once again again putting up with paper all over the dining room table and countless other people we've forgotten.

Remembering Tony Class, Ilan Ostrove and Simon Bullock.

OTHER TITLES BY GARRY BUSHELL
'79 Ska Revival: Dance Craze
Sounds Of Glory Volumes 1 & 2
Cockney Reject (with Jeff Turner)
Running Free
Hoolies
The Face
Two-Faced
Face Down
All Or Nothing
Hell Bent
Bushell On The Rampage
1,001 Reasons Why EastEnders Is Pony
I Had A Good Eight Inches Last Night
The World According To Garry Bushell

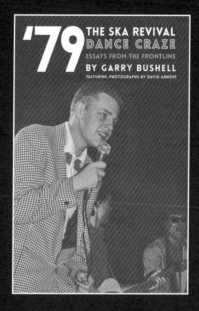

SECRET AFFAIR

THE CHORDS

MODS AT BRIDGE HOUSE

PURPLE HEARTS

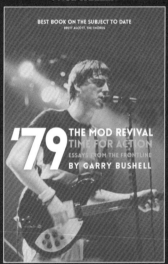

POCKET GUIDE TO
SKA
MICK O' SHEA

POCKET GUIDE TO
MOD
PAUL 'SMILER' ANDERSON

THE POCKET GUIDES

FROM THE PUBLISHERS OF THE
DEAD STRAIGHT MUSIC GUIDES